D0767917

Dispatches from a Coup in Progress
Volume Two

Year of Lead

Edited by Brian Mier

Cover illustration by Adriana Galuppo

Contents

1

Acknowledgments

This book represents the second in our series, *Dispatches from a Coup in Progress* and many of the questions raised in this book were the result of ongoing dialogue with *Brasil Wire* contributors and key allies. For the new knowledge generated through this dialogue I would like to thank Bryan Pitts, Rafael Ioris, Michael Fox, Sean Mitchell and Aline Piva.

Many of the chapters in this book first appeared as articles in Brasil Wire. Some originally ran in Portuguese in Brazilian independent media vehicles. I would like to thank Silvio Caccia Bava from *LeMonde Diplomatique Brasil*, and Fernando Morais and Lydia Aboud Lopes from *Nocaute* for allowing us to translate and reprint some excellent articles.

I would like to thank Leonardo Attuch, Gisele Federicce and the staff of *Brasil 247*, for having me on their show as a frequent guest in 2018 and, especially, enabling me to interview Sarah Cleveland on one of their programs, the results of which appear in this book.

I would also like to thank Michael Brooks, for providing constant coverage of the travesty of justice committed against Luiz Inácio Lula da Silva in 2018, for having me on as a guest on his radio show and for writing the introduction to this book.

During the month before the disastrous 2018 presidential elections, *New Socialist* hired me to commission and translate three articles on Brazilian political conjuncture, which also appear in this book. I would like to thank New Socialist, and Ellen O'Rourke for enabling us to run these articles on Brasil Wire and in this book.

I would like to thank Daniel Hunt for his constant feedback and support during my 4 years at *Brasil Wire* and during the preparation of this book. I would also like to thank Sharon Mier for her editing support.

Finally, I would like to thank the following group of *Brasil Wire* readers for providing financial support so that this book project could get off the ground. It would have been very difficult to pull it off without them: Alexander Jeri, Chuck Mertz, Tamara Smith, Sean Mitchell, Matt Schultz, Fredrick Lonberg-Holm, Jon Evans, Robson Coccaro and Fabio Pappalardo.

About the Contributors

Celso Amorim is a Brazilian diplomat who served as Minister of Foreign Relations for Presidents Itamar Franco and Luiz Inácio Lula da Silva. He also served as Minister of Defence under President Dilma Rousseff.

Marcos Arruda is a Brazilian Economist affiliated with the PACS Institute in Rio de Janeiro, and the Transnational Institute in Amsterdam. During the Military Dictatorship, he was imprisoned, tortured and exiled from Brazil.

Michael Brooks is the host of the Michael Brooks Show, co-host of the Majority Report and a contributor on the Count The Dings network. A writer and pundit, he has written for Jacobin, Al Monitor, Al Jazeera, the Washington Post, among others.

Sarah Cleveland is a law professor at Colombia University and Vice President of the United Nations Human Rights Committee.

Guilherme Soares Dias is a journalist who has written for Brazilian newspapers such Valor Economico and Estado de São Paulo. He is a member of the São Paulo Commission of Journalists for Racial Equality, and is a founding editor of the digital magazine Calle 2.

Ricardo Duwe is a historian who is currently finishing his Doctorate at Universidade Federal de Santa Catarina.

Alfredo Saad Filho is a Professor of Political Economy at University of London's School of Oriental and African Studies (SOAS) and Head of its Doctoral School.

Juliana Gonçalves is a journalist and human rights activist. She is a member of the São Paulo Black Woman's March, and the São Paulo Journalists for Racial Equality Commission, which is a consultative body of the Journalists Union. She is a frequent contributor to Brazilian progressive newspapers and magazines, such as Carta Capital and Brasil de Fato.

Rejane Carolina Hoeveler is a doctoral student in history at the Universidade Federal Fluminense, a prolific author and an activist within the PSOL party.

Gleisi Hoffmann is Congresswoman and National President of the Partido dos Trabalhadores (Workers Party/PT). Beginning her career as a student activist she is also the former national President of União Brasileira dos Estudantes Secundaristas (UBES/Brazilian High School Students Union).

Daniel Hunt is a founding editor of Brasil Wire, writer, researcher and film maker based in São Paulo.

Valeska Martins is a lawyer, a member of the Instituto dos Advogados de São Paulo Human Rights Commission (São Paulo Lawyers Institute/IASP) and a member of former President Luiz Inácio Lula da Silva's defense team.

Brian Mier is a geographer and sociologist and co-editor of Brasil Wire. Currently working as Brazil correspondent for TeleSur English's news show From the South, he has lived in Brazil for 24 years.

Sean T. Mitchell is associate professor of Anthropology at Rutgers University, Newark. He has carried out many years of research in Brazil and is the author of Constellations of Inequality: Space, Race, and Utopia in Brazil (University of Chicago Press).

Gaía Passarelli is a writer, journalist and television presenter from São Paulo.

Bryan Pitts is associate director of the Center for Latin American and Caribbean Studies at Indiana University. He is completing a book on the overlooked role of civilian politicians in the demise of Brazil's 1964-85 military dictatorship.

Aline Piva is a Brazilian writer and pundit who was the founder and director of the Brazil Research Unit at the Council on Hemispheric Affairs (COHA) and currently teaches international law at Universidade Bolivariana da Venezuela, in Caracas. She is a frequent contributor to the Brazilian blog Nocaute.

Larissa Jacheta Riberti is a history professor at Universidade Federal do Rio Grande do Norte and a writer for the truckers' publication, Chico Bento.

Joana Salém Vasconcelos is a doctoral student in economic history at Universidade de São Paulo and author of História agrária da revolução cubana: dilemas do socialismo na periferia (ed. Alameda, 2016).

Luciana Waclawovsky is a journalist who covered Brazilian Congress for the Central Única dos Trabalhadores labor union confederation (Workers Union Central/CUT), from 2016-2018. She is currently working on a masters degree in Human Rights at Universidade Federal de Paraiba.

Marcelo Zero is a sociologist, international relations specialist and technical adviser to the Partido dos Trabalhadores (Workers Party/PT) in the Brazilian Senate.

Introduction

By Michael Brooks

Over the past year I've covered Brazil, the Workers Party, the rise of Jair Bolsonaro and the political imprisonment of Luiz Inácio Lula da Silva extensively. I've done this for several reasons. First, Brazil, like any other place in the World, matters in and of itself. It has many great activists, voices on the left, powerful examples of leadership and organizing that are almost never given any attention in any form of English language press, let alone the constant failures of prestige outlets like the New York Times, Washington Post and Guardian to even report the story emanating out of Brazil over the last several years properly and objectively, in particular, the judicial coup that removed Dilma Rousseff from power in 2016 and the lawfare against and imprisonment of Lula da Silva without any material evidence. Lula is an iconic and presidential historical figure whose barring from the 2018 race made Jair Bolsonaro's fascist ascendency an almost certainty in retrospect.

I also find Brazil to be a powerful case study on how far right wing politics works in today's World and the misuse of corruption politics as a doorway for the fascist far right to take power. Even in the United States Trump's "drain the swamp" message, which favored vague and generalized complaints about corruption instead of a system-wide critique of capitalism, is easily harnessed by far right figures to delegitimize left wing activists, unions and left political leadership. This was taken to an extreme in Brazil, where the sprawling Lava

Jato investigation, which of course identified some stories of significant corruption in what is a highly corrupted political system, was weaponized by the future fascist Justice Minister Sérgio Moro in an effort to destroy the Workers Party and imprison and silence Lula da Silva.

Lula is also a major part of the story for me as anybody who follows my show knows. First, because Lula has an incredible record. At a time when George W. Bush was President and the Pink Tide was ascendent, Lula stood as a giant in international relations, respected across the globe and, most significantly, raised 40 million Brazilians out of poverty, eliminated hunger and struck an independent course in Brazilian foreign policy. This is a world unlike today where on the negative we have to deal with rising global fascism, from Trump to Bolsonaro or Narendra Modi but on the other hand there's a great counter-backlash of inspiring social democratic leaders like Bernie Sanders, the Democratic front runner. Lula governed with support in Latin America from the Pink Tide, but besides that, in a global landscape dominated by neoliberals and the far right, Lula still managed to be universally respected and achieve extraordinary things. The treatment of him is a travesty and his political imprisonment should concern everybody who cares about justice, human dignity, democracy, and also just the relentless persecution and abuse of a good person or any person for that matter. So understanding the tactics of lawfare, the misuse of corruption as a tool to elevate far right politics and the ways in which the extremes of Brazil's situation reflect and parallel our global predicament is essential.

Brasil Wire is the essential resource in following this story and the work that they do as a small independent website is unparallelled in almost any reporting coming out of the country into the English language press. First, because the writing, analysis, historical assessments and political understanding is always sophisticated, top notch, incredibly smart and reflects a leftist but also grounded and bottom up view of politics. Also, Brasil Wire gives voice to actual Brazilian activists, leftist intellectuals and politicians who are almost never given any sort of forum in the English language press. The Workers Party and the Landless Workers Movement and other great political parties and social movements in Brazil, are not only important to understand the Brazilian crisis, but like all other aspects of the Brazilian story, have many things to teach everybody working towards a more just post-imperial, post-capitalist politics anywhere in the World. Brasil Wire forwards these stories and these voices. Thirdly they get all the major stories right. If you were reading Brasil Wire you knew the truth about how the case against Lula was working. You would not be surprised to see that Judge Sergio Moro is no caped crusader but instead a deeply right wing, deeply vindictive and almost certainly corrupted individual who would go on to serve in this extreme far right, human rights violating, democracy canceling government. You also would know that Jair Bolsonaro would prove to be, in addition to being US and corporate subservient and incredibly dangerous, a buffoon and jackass who would do things like tweet out a gonzo pornography video from an official presidential account. If you were reading Brasil Wire you would have the right voices in your mind, the right understanding, and a sense of what was happening from the ground up – the only ways to build real and actual solidarity. This is why I am proud to write the forward to this book, proud to continue to work with the whole Brasil Wire team, and suggest not only that everybody purchase this but spread it far and wide. I wish to honor the memory of Marielle Franco and, of course, Lula Livre!

Preface

The need for Solidarity with Brazil

Speech delivered at UK Parliament, 20/11/2018

By Daniel Hunt

Acclaimed writer and director Jean Claude Bernardet said of Brazil in 2017: "We are watching the systematic dismantling of an emerging power".

Brazil has been under a cloud of propaganda for some years now. Having experienced the gap between what we were seeing on the ground and what was being reported outside, in 2014 a group of us created a media platform to provide a channel in English for Brazil discourse that was excluded from corporate narratives on the country.

Most of all, we did it out of concern for what was coming. It was already evident that something was wrong.

Right now, Brazil's situation needs to be understood not as a series of individual newsworthy events but a continual escalation of a process – a slow motion coup.

I moved to Brazil when it was still very much the country of the future. At the handover ceremony that closed the 2012 Olympics in London, its GDP had just overtaken the UK's for the first time in history.

What has happened since has been catastrophic.

2013 Revelations of US espionage against Dilma Rousseff's Government and Brazil's energy sector dovetailed with street protests which were turned against the Federal Government with the assistance of a hostile media.

2014 Aecio Neves' refusal to concede electoral defeat and the beginning of a politically partisan, US/Brazil Anti-Corruption Operation called Lava Jato, or Carwash.

2015 Economic sabotage, both via congress and judiciary, and telegenic synthesised protest movements, bankrolled by defeated opposition, coalition partners, oligarchs, foreign hedge funds and libertarian foundations.

2016 The illegitimate removal of Dilma Rousseff from office and violent repression of all resistance to it.

2017 Extreme, accelerated Neoliberal reforms that the Brazilian electorate had rejected four times at the ballot box, including a 20 year constitutionally enforced freeze on investment in public education and health.

2018 Operation Carwash's politically motivated jailing of leading candidate Lula enabled a Neofascist victory and overt return of the Military to Government for the first time since 1985.

The fine detail of the process that got us here has been scandalous, and difficult for outsiders to grasp, not least because sectors of the English language media were actually eroding international solidarity for Brazil's progressive forces at the very moment they needed it the most. They ran, uncritically, with lawfare's own narratives which made the Workers Party, and the left as a whole, synonymous with ancient corruption schemes woven through the entire political system.

During the coup of 2016, a Guardian/Observer editorial

all but calling for Dilma to resign was followed by a headline "Michel Temer: The Man Who Could Fix Brazil". One of their writers contacted us privately to explain that neither he nor the then Latin America editor had any idea who was writing this material.

We have found that much of the commentary on Brazil in English is influenced by and connected to lobbies and think tanks such as Council of the Americas and Atlantic Council – organisations which warrant special scrutiny.

But even the Economist has now recognised the political motivation behind the Operation Carwash it once championed. Had this media epiphany come a few years earlier, lives may have been saved.

Rupert Murdoch's Wall Street Journal went beyond normalisation and came out in shameless support of Bolsonaro, as they did Chile's Augusto Pinochet decades earlier, no doubt excited by the living link between the two Neofascists, Chicago boy finance minister Paulo Guedes, and the firesale privatisations he will enact.

During the election some of Bolsonaro's team wore shirts bearing not the face of their candidate, but of Margaret Thatcher. Chief Secretary to the UK Treasury Elizabeth Truss recently visited Brazil's Millenium Institute – the libertarian think tank founded by Paulo Guedes in 2005, and whose alumni came to dominate economic and political debate in Brazil's media since. Part of the Atlas Network, and affiliated to the Adam Smith Institute, Millienium is seen as a successor organisation to IBAD and IPES, the foreign funded NGOs which disseminated anti-government propaganda in the lead up to the 1964

Military Coup.

Democracy and Authoritarianism

With refusal of televised debate, massive voter suppression, systematic, automated disinformation and illegal campaign funding, there was a maze of irregularities in an election that was neither free nor fair.

Most importantly, it needs to be plainly understood that Bolsonaro was placed in a winning position only through the last minute removal of the leading candidate, political prisoner Lula da Silva, who was jailed for 12 years on a nonsensical charge by Bolsonaro's own Justice Minister to be, in a joint operation in collaboration with the US Department of Justice.
Even this alone should be an international outrage.

And it gets worse, the chief of the armed forces General Villas Boas has admitted that he intentionally threatened the Supreme Court so that they would not release Lula. The court voted to deny him habeas corpus by a single vote, of a visibly frightened Rosa Weber, who explained that she was voting against her own opinion. This was a decision that changed the course of Brazilian history.

57 million voted, knowingly or not, for a synthesis of fascism, religious charlatanism and neoliberalism. 90 million didn't vote for him, and no amount of votes is a mandate for the horrors he has advocated throughout his spartan political career.

Pinochet didn't kill enough, and 30,000 need to be killed for Brazil to function, he once insisted. Where there is indigenous land, there are riches beneath it, he boasted. To raise these subjects now, educators face censure, the criminalisation of their profession, of critical thought, a terrifying modern McCarthyism.

But it is vitally important that our attention is not focussed solely on Jair Bolsonaro himself.

Sovereignty and Empire

It is not to minimise Brazil's internal politics and age old class struggles when we talk of foreign interference – after all it has been thus in the region for 500 years; the struggle between the Senzala and Casa Grande, the battle between two competing visions of government, that of sovereign development, and that of submission to foreign capital by what Eduardo Galeano called "the commission agent bourgeoisie".

We of course shouldn't forget that British industrialisation was paid for in no small part by exploitation of Brazil. Until recently many of us believed that South America had finally broken from its colonial chains. We were wrong.

We could talk for hours about the sociological backdrop to this political moment, but that would have to include the decisive role of evangelical religion implanted from outside, and the undeclared war on corruption in Latin America, launched from the United States under the Bush administration, and expanded under his successors. At the peak of the so called Pink Tide, in 2009, then incoming Secretary of State Clinton, addressed the Council of the Americas and insisted that "the ballot box is not enough" in Latin America. Clinton talked instead of the need to work throughout the hemisphere to develop "strong, independent judiciaries", just as lawfare strategies and networks of collaboration were being developed.

Brazil's convulsions are not simply local troubles. Brazil's democratic descent did not occur in a geopolitical vacuum.

There is now what former foreign minister Celso Amorim described as a wholesale war on Brazilian sovereignty, with not only the sell off of its massive reserves of Oil, minerals, water, and strategic companies such as Embraer and Eletrobras, but also the arrival of US Military bases on Brazilian soil for the first time since the 1940s. This is a war on the Brazil which stands up to exploitative free trade agreements, the Brazil that breaks patents in the public interest, the Brazil that broke free of the IMF and World Bank, the Brazil that displeased capital by seeking to invest the proceeds from its own natural resources into public education, health, and national development.

In 2016 the British chamber of commerce excitedly described Norwegian Statoil's snatch of the massive Carcará oilfield as a "Viking conquest" – sealed while Rousseff was suspended from office, and powerless to intervene.

I'm sure everyone here would like assurances that our own foreign and commonwealth office will not abet a Neofascist Brazilian Government in any way, as it did during the 64-85 Military Dictatorship. During that time, under Edward Heath, the then UK Ambassador gave his enthusiastic support for the bloody rule of Emilio Medici, predicting that what he called a "benevolent dictatorship" would continue for "many years to come". To that government we exported our own torture techniques, trialled in Northern Ireland, which the Brazilian secret police christened "the English method" – terrors that 50 years later are celebrated by Bolsonaro and his supporters. Meanwhile, Brazil's 2016 putschists referred to Inquisitor Moro's interrogations in pursuit of Lula as "the Tower of London".

We need to watch the relationship between the UK and Brazilian governments very closely. No matter how good it may be for business, we cannot tolerate someone who threatens the criminalisation, expulsion, imprisonment, or worse, of social movements and political opponents alike, humoured, nurtured or protected, as "our bastard".

I was asked in early 2015 by UK diplomats what I thought about the idea of them meeting with Jair Bolsonaro. At that point he was not a realistic contender for the Presidency and I explained in very frank terms why such a meeting would be unacceptable.
I doubt that my advice was heeded.

Brazil is the most resource rich nation on Earth, and as so often in history, human suffering is a detail that governments in the global north are prepared to condone in exchange for access. And too often we make an artificial distinction between state and corporate power.
As will become even clearer in the months and years ahead, what is being done to Brazil is a neo-colonial project, conducted in darkness, and hiding in plain sight.

If this can be done to a country the size of Brazil it can be done anywhere.

Solidarity and Resistance

We don't want to study and understand the mechanics of what is being done to Brazil and the region now in 40 years time, we don't have that luxury. We need everyone to know how this works now so that it can be resisted by those who believe in independence, in universal human rights, egalitarian principles, popular participation, social emancipation, and protection of the natural environment – it needs to be understood now so it can be resisted, fought, and ultimately defeated.

From outside we can pressure our own governments, boycott the companies and organisations, and disrupt the networks which have enabled this calamity to happen.
These pigs, and their project of societal, economic, environmental and cultural vandalism, will fail.

The Brazil of its peoples unique struggles and endeavours, of its science, of its arts and letters, is also the Brazil that makes eyes light up all around the world. This Brazil is why we fight. The Brazil of Dandara, of Zumbi dos Palmares, the Brazil of Portinari, the Brazil of Pagu, the Brazil of Paulo Freire, the Brazil of Clarice Lispector, the Brazil of Marighella, the Brazil of Raoni, the Brazil of Chico Mendes, the Brazil of Santos Dumont, the Brazil of Darcy Ribeiro, the Brazil of Lina bo Bardi, of Niemeyer, the Brazil of Marta Viera da Silva, the Brazil of Doctor Socrates Brasileiro, the Brazil of Glauber Rocha, the Brazil of Elza Soares, of Chico Buarque, of Maria Bethânia, of Renato Russo, the Brazil of Moa do Katende, of Tupã, of Íemanja.... the Brazil of Marielle Franco.

For the Brazil we love to win, an extraordinary movement of international solidarity needs to be constructed. It is our duty to build it.

Editor's notes

<u>Year of Lead</u> is the second book in *Brasil Wire's* Dispatches from a coup in progress series. It's title represents the reworking of a Brazilian phrase that was coined to describe life under Military rule (1964-1985), "the years of lead". I chose this title because it was the best metaphor I could think of to describe the year 2018. This was the year that started off reeling from ultra-neoliberal reforms enacted by Michel Temer's coup government which plunged millions into extreme poverty, butchered the public health and education systems, transformed Brazil into a 'right to work' nation, bankrupted the unions, and delivered 75% of the nation's Petroleum reserves into the hands of Northern corporations. These processes were explained by Brazilian social movement and union members and organic intellectuals through the interviews presented in the first book of our series, <u>Voices of the Brazilian Left</u>. Although 2018 did not look very promising, as one could imagine, there was still hope that Luiz Inácio Lula da Silva would be able to rally the working class in order to take back the presidency and undo all of Temer's structural adjustments. This, unfortunately, did not come to pass.

In 2012, I walked into the office of State Congressman Marcelo Freixo in Rio de Janeiro to ask for help with a research project I was working on regarding changes in municipal law related to the World Cup and Olympics. I didn't expect to get much help, but I was greeted by a friendly woman who immediately made me feel welcome. As I waited to speak with Freixo, she and I made small talk. She was from Maré, a favela that I had worked in periodically over the course of several years in two different NGOs. We had a few friends in common, it turned out. I was completely charmed. Freixo eventually came in, spoke with me and helped me out. I had made a dumb mistake – asking for help on municipal issues in a state lawmaker's office – but neither of them made me feel dumb. They put me in touch with a colleague in the municipal legislature and I left thinking very highly of Freixo and his political party, the PSOL.

I moved to São Paulo in 2015 and lost touch with what was going on in Rio . Then, in March, 2018, I read some terrible news. A PSOL city councilwoman had just been assassinated in Rio with her driver. I clicked on a link and saw the photo and a horrible chill ran up my spine. It was Marielle Franco, Freixo's former chief of staff who had been so nice to me that day. This book is dedicated to her memory.

A few weeks later, Lula was ordered to turn himself in to the Federal Police. A sadistic and partisan judge, working in tandem with the US Department of Justice, had been allowed to rule on his own investigation with no jury. He sentenced Lula to nine years in prison without presenting any material evidence, in exchange for a cabinet position in the future government of right wing extremist Jair Bolsonaro. Nine was not a random choice of sentence length, but a reference to the nickname Moro's investigation team made for Lula. "9", referred to the fact that the former President had lost a finger in an industrial accident while working in a factory as a teenager, and Moro and his neo-fascist US proxy agents in the *Lava Jato* investigation certainly had a chuckle together over the length of Lula's sentence.

On the morning Lula was ordered to turn himself in, I was sitting at my computer, totally depressed about the country I love and have lived in for 24 years. That was it. In that moment, I turned my computer off and said, "fuck it. I'm going out there." Two and a half hours, three trains and a bus later, I walked up the street to the ABC Metallurgical Workers Union in São Bernardo de Campo, an industrial suburb of São Paulo that was the birthplace of the PT party. Lula was holed up here, at his former trade union headquarters, surrounded by friends and supporters. Out on the street a crowd was gathering. I ran into friends from the CMP and UNMP social movements and together we started drinking. Like most of the crowd, we were drinking to get our courage up for whatever was going to happen next. I had been in a protest in Brasilia the year before when martial law was declared and some police officers mixed live bullets in with their rubber bullets. These memories were with me as rumors spread via the local media that Governor Alckmin had ordered his "leg breaker" riot police to the scene. I wondered if I would be going home that night. The crowd swelled and formed a human chain around the union headquarters. The 7pm deadline came and went and nobody showed up to arrest Lula. A wave of euphoria passed over us but sadly it was momentary. The next day, worried about the safety of the union and social movement members who were willing to die protecting him, Lula turned himself in. He has been held in solitary confinement ever since and barred from speaking to journalists, in clear violation of the Mandela Rules.

With Lula taken out of the race, the stage was set for the return of client fascism to Brazil. The year ended with a new government being formed by a former military dictatorship official, with 23 military officers in his cabinet, promising to "purge" the nation of its leftists, gays and indigenous people.

The following book provides analysis of these events. The chapters included represent the best of *Brasil Wire's* 80 articles on Lula's imprisonment and the 2018 elections – more than any other publication in the English language. *Brasil Wire* editors wrote some of these chapters, but most were written by Brazilian's who know a lot more about this conjuncture than the score of grinning, low-paid corporate public relation shills who try to pass themselves off as foreign correspondents these days. Do not think their coverage of these events in Brazil was any more honest than the coverage of the oil coup in Venezuela or the lead up to the wars in Libya or Iraq.

This book aims to contribute to the growing body of knowledge on how democracy was dismantled in one of the world's largest countries and who must be to blame for this disaster.

In the words of Mozambique's Samora Machel, "The struggle continues."

Year of Lead

Part one

Sovereignty

U.S. Department of Justice and Operation Car Wash: Facts and Questions

By Brian Mier

It is no secret that American corporations have immensely benefited from Operation Car Wash (*Lava Jato*), the international corruption investigation that was initiated in partnership with the US Department of Justice, the SEC, the local Public Prosecutors Office in Curitiba, Paraná, and the Brazilian Federal Police.i American petroleum corporations such as ExxonMobil and Chevron are benefiting from Michel Temer's government systematic dismantling and privatization, at below market rates, of Petrobras and its massive offshore oil reserves. They are also benefiting from Brazilian law, MP 795, which will give $300 billion in tax abatement to foreign companies extracting Brazilian petroleum.ii,iii Boeing is now acquiring EMBRAER (also a target of Operation Car Wash as well as being the world's third largest manufacturer of jets), for the below-market rate of $3.8 billion.iv Operation Car Wash was also used to commit character assassination against President Dilma Rousseff, who was publicly associated with the scandal in both the Brazilian and international media for years. This helped pave the way for the 2016 coup which put Michel Temer in office. It was only after the coup, that news came out informing the public that Operation Car Wash investigators were not going to charge Rousseff with anything.v

It is also no secret that the US Government has been working to roll back the so called "pink tide" of center left and left governments in Latin America which flourished in the 2000s. As Mark Weisbrot from CEPR points out in a recent interview, Hilary Clinton admitted to supporting the coup government in Honduras in 2009, in her own autobiography.vi Operation Car Wash has been transformed into a multi-country operation that has now resulted in corruption charges – many of them as frivolous as those against Luiz Inacio Lula da Silva – against eight current or former Latin American leaders.vii

The US government was involved in at least 41 coups in Latin America during the 100 year period ending in 1994.viii In the case of many of them, such as the 1964 Coup in Brazil, the information about US involvement took decades to come out.ix After careful analysis conducted over the past three years at *Brasil Wire,* we already know enough, however, to show that there is a relationship between the US Department of Justice and Brazilian regime change through Operation Car Wash. Brasil Wire is confident that, as time passes, more and more information will be revealed indicating how the US contributed to an illegitimate regime change which has thrown millions below the extreme poverty line of USD

$1.90/day, caused increases in infant mortality and deaths during childbirth, and transformed Brazil into a union busting, right to work country.x,xi,xii,xiii

The following time-line is meant to further public understanding on the relationship between the US Department of Justice, the 2016 Coup and the political imprisonment of Luiz Inacio Lula da Silva. Glenn Greenwald of the Intercept points out, that Lula's imprisonment was obviously done to prevent him from running for the presidency this year, in a situation in which he is still the front runner despite being held in solitary confinement and illegally prevented from giving interviews for the past four months.xiv,xv This time-line represents a mixture of factual information with questions and informed speculation that is based on years of research. For the sake of clarity, the speculation and questions are in italics.

2008 – US Senator Ted Stevens, of Alaska, loses his reelection bid after being accused of receiving illegal reforms on a vacation home. Later, after a special prosecutor is assigned to investigate prosecutorial misconduct, the charges are reversed and two Department Of Justice officials are accused of criminal negligence.xvi Problems with the prosecution include: relying almost entirely on plea bargain testimony from a single, unreliable witness; exaggerating about the value of the reforms; leaking misinformation to the media; and violating Brady rules (destroying, hiding or refusing to admit evidence beneficial to the defense).

Could this case have been used by the DOJ as a blueprint for the remarkably similar, frivolous investigation against Lula?

October 4-9 2009 – According to a leaked State Department cable, The US Department of Justice holds a training event with Brazilian public prosecutors in Rio de Janeiro, called "Project Bridges".xvii The focus of the seminar is to develop joint strategies to combat financial crimes. Judge Sergio Moro is a keynote speaker. During the event, United States and Brazilian law enforcement officials discuss the possibility of initiating a joint corruption investigation, possibly headquartered in Curitiba.

All the actors are here. Could this have marked the real beginning of Operation Car Wash?

August 2, 2013 – In an act designed to strengthen the fight against corruption in Brazil, President Dilma Rousseff sanctions Law 12.850, which, for the first time in Brazilian history, enables plea bargain testimonies to be used as evidence in criminal proceedings. For the first time ever, Brazilian public prosecutors begin working with plea bargain testimonies.

Before this date, Brazilian public prosecutors had no experience building cases based on plea bargains. As the new law is ratified, public prosecutors engage in actions that have tactical similarities with Department of Justice investigations in the US – for example arresting executives and threatening them with disproportionately long prison sentences until they agree to testify against their target.

Did the DOJ provide Operation Car Wash prosecutors with training on how to work with plea bargains?

September 9 2013 – Edward Snowden reveals that the US National Security Agency has been spying on Petrobras Petroleum Company.xviii

Did the NSA share this illegally obtained information with the Operation Car Wash investigators in the US Department of Justice?

March 17, 2014 – The Brazilian Public Prosecutor's Office announces a new anti-corruption investigation called "Operation Car Wash". It is a joint operation between the US Department of Justice, FBI, SEC, a local Brazilian public prosecutor's office in Curitiba and the Brazilian Federal Police.xix Using the Foreign Corrupt Powers Act as justification, the US DOJ-led team announces that it is targeting Petrobras Petroleum Company and several of Brazil's largest companies, such as Odebrecht and Embraer. The team begins a series of leaks to the media seeking to associate Dilma Rousseff's name with corruption in Petrobras. During the next four years, top DOJ officials make repeated visits to Curitiba.

2015 – Operation Car Wash prosecutor Sergio Moro does not merely arrest construction industry directors responsible for bribing politicians and order the companies to pay fines. In an unusual move, instead of treating them as too big to fail, he forces the nation's five biggest construction companies to paralyze their projects, causing 500,000 direct job losses.[xx],[xxi] Economists cited by the BBC estimate that Operation Car Wash caused a 2.5 percent drop in Brazil's GDP in 2015, and the country is still reeling from the effects of the operation, with some economists estimating that the investigation tripled the dimensions of the Brazilian recession.[xxii] As the economy nosedives, moves are made to impeach Dilma Rousseff.[xxiii]

Was the Brazilian economy deliberately destabilized, as the Chilean economy was in 1973, in order to pave the way for a coup?

2016 – After two years of constant leaks to the media associating Dilma Rousseff with Petrobras corruption,

Operation Car Wash fails to provide any proof. The damage to her image is already done, though, and she is impeached for the non-impeachable offense of "fiscal pedaling", legalized by the Senate one week after her removal from office, in a process in which it is subsequently revealed that congressmen were bribed for their votes. The new coup government immediately begins selling off Brazil's offshore petroleum reserves at below market rate to US petroleum companies like Exxon and Chevron and announces $300 billion in tax abatement for foreign oil companies working in Brazil.

Did Anglo media organizations such as the New York Times deliberately work to damage Rousseff's image during the lead up to the coup?

July 2017 – Flanked by Patrick Stokes and Brazilian General Prosecutor Rodrigo Janot (who is now working with US officials in Colombia), US Acting Assistant States Attorney Kenneth Blanco gives a speech about Operation Car Wash at the Atlantic Council.xxiv,xxv

In this speech, Blanco brags about the charges made against former President Luiz Inacio Lula da Silva, saying that it puts Brazil and the US at the "forefront" of the world's fight against corruption. During the speech he says that the investigation was made more agile by continual "direct communications" with the Brazilian Car

Wash prosecution team, avoiding the bureaucratic slowdowns caused by official protocol. In Brazil it is a crime for government officials to communicate informally with foreign government officials without following protocol. As a result of this speech, Lula's defense team files a motion for dismissal which is currently moving through the court system.

What did the DOJ and Sergio Moro's team talk about during all of these illegal communications?

April 2018 – During an election year in which he is leading all the polls for the presidency, Lula is arrested on corruption charges that he committed "undetermined acts", with no material evidence presented. Like Ted Stevens in 2008, the case is entirely built on a plea bargain testimony by a convicted criminal who changed his story several times in order to get sentence reduction. Like the Stevens case, Lula's defense team accuses the prosecution of preventing them from presenting evidence beneficial to the defense. Like the Stevens case, the prosecution has leaked incorrect and misleading evidence to the media, including lying about the value of the apartment and the reforms.

Did the US Government help build a frivolous case against Lula so that he could be prevented from retaking the presidency and undoing the privatizations that are directly benefiting US industries? As in the cases of Iran, Iraq, Syria, Libya and Venezuela, was petroleum the motive for US support for regime change in Brazil?

i United States Department of Justice. "Odebrecht and Braskem Plead Guilty and Agree to Pay at Least \$3.5 Billion in Global Penalties to Resolve Largest Foreign Bribery Case in History". Accessed January 23, 2019, http://www.justice.gov/opa/pr/odebrecht-and-braskem-plead-guilty-and-agree-pay-least-35-billion-global-penalties-resolve

ii Cararine, C. (2017, October 27). Leilão do pré-sal: a vez das petroleiras americanas. *Carta Capital.* Retreived from https://www.cartacapital.com.br/economia/leilao-do-pre-sal-a-vez-das-petroleiras-americanas

iii Câmara aprova MP do Trilhão para o setor de petróleo. (2017, February 12). *Terra.* Retreived from https://www.terra.com.br/noticias/climatempo/camara-aprova-mp-do-trilhao-para-o-setor-de-petroleo,b916076970027e0f906d09ba873478f90w2bzgtc.html

iv Boeing fica com 80% da divisão de jatos comerciais da Embraer por US\$ 3,8 bi. (2018, July). *Folha de São Paulo.* Retreived from https://www1.folha.uol.com.br/mercado/2018/07/boeing-propoe-pagar-us-38-bi-a-embraer-para-ter-80-de-nova-empresa.shtml

v For example: Romero, S. (2015, March 20). Brazil's Slumping Economy and Bribery Scandal Eat Away at Dilma Rousseff's Popularity. *New York Times.* Retreived from www.newyorktimes.com2015/03/21/world/americas/brazils-slumping-economy-and-bribery-scandal-eat-away-at-dilma-rousseffs-popularity.html

vi Sharmani Peries. Interview with Mark Weisbrot. (Television interview, July 29, 2018). Retreived from https://therealnews.com/stories/the-role-the-us-played-in-reversing-latin-americas-pink-tide

vii Mier, B. (2018, March 10). The US and Lawfare: Meet the Latin American Leaders Under Investigation. *Brasil Wire.* Retreived from http://www.brasilwire.com/the-us-and-lawfare-meet-the-latin-american-leaders-under-investigation/

viii Coatsworth, J. (2005, Spring-Summer). United States Interventions, What For? Revista: Harvard Review of Latin America. Retrived from https://revista.drclas.harvard.edu/book/united-states-interventions

ix Black, J.K., (1977). *United States Penetration of Brazil.* Philadelphia: University of Pennslavania Press.

x Menezes, F. and Jannuzzi, P. (2018, March 26). Com o aumento da extrema pobreza, Brasil retrocede 10 anos em dois. *Rede Brasil Atual.* Retreived from https://www.redebrasilatual.com.br/cidadania/2018/03/com-o-aumento-da-extrema-pobreza-brasil-retrocede-dez-anos-em-dois

xi Aumenta a mortalidade na infância com governo Temer. (2018, May 15). *Brasil de Fato.* Retreived from https://www.brasildefato.com.br/2018/05/15/aumenta-a-mortalidade-na-infancia-com-governo-temer/

xii Mortes de gestantes aumentam no Brasil; piores índices estão na Região Norte. (2018, July 27). *Diário do Pará.* Retreived from https://www.diarioonline.com.br/noticias/para/noticia-526743-.html

xiii AFL-CIO Executive Committee. (2018, July 26). *Defending Democracy in Brazil [Press Release]*. Retreived from https://aflcio.org/about/leadership/statements/defending-democracy-brazil

xiv Amy Goodman. Interview with Glen Greenwald. (Television Interview, April 19, 2018). Retreived from https://www.democracynow.org/2018/4/9/glenn_greenwald_brazils_right_wing_jailed

xv Maia, G. (2018, August 20) Lula tem 37,3% e Bolsonaro, 18,8%, diz pesquisa CNT/MDA. *UOL Noticias*. Retrevied from https://noticias.uol.com.br/politica/eleicoes/2018/noticias/2018/08/20/pesquisa-mda-presidenciaveis-campanha.htm

xvi Savage, C. (2011, November 21). Court-Appointed Investigator Offers Scathing Report on Prosecution of Senator Stevens. *New York Times*. Retreived from https://www.nytimes.com/2011/11/22/us/politics/no-charges-recommended-against-prosecutors-in-ted-stevens-case.html

xvii United States of America. Department of State. By Kubiske. (2009, October 30). Cable 09BRASILIA1282_a. Retrievied from https://wikileaks.org/plusd/cables/09BRASILIA1282_a.html

xviii Watts, J. NSA accused of spying on Brazilian oil company Petrobras. (2013, September 9). The Guardian. Retreived from: https://www.theguardian.com/world/2013/sep/09/nsa-spying-brazil-oil-petrobras

xix Stokes, P and Lloyd, Z. (2017, December 12). 40 Years Of FCPA: Cross-Border Efforts And Growing Risk. *Law 360*. Retreived from https://www.gibsondunn.com/wp-content/uploads/2017/12/Stokes-40-Years-Of-FCPA-Cross-Border-Efforts-And-Growing-Risk-Law360-12-12-2017.pdf

xx Jeronimo, J. (2016, January 21). Obras paradas: o outro lado da Operação Lava Jato. *Istoé*. Retreived from https://istoe.com.br/402288_OBRAS+PARADAS+O+OUTRO+LADO+DA+OPERACAO+LAVA+JATO/

xxi Nader, V. (2017, June 21). Efeito Lava Jato fez construção cortar 500 mil vagas em 2015, diz IBGE. *O Estado do São Paulo*. Retreived from https://economia.estadao.com.br/noticias/geral,efeito-lava-jato-fez-construcao-cortar-500-mil-vagas-em-2015-diz-ibge,70001853492

xxii Costas, R. (2015, December 2). Escândalo da Petrobras 'engoliu 2,5% da economia em 2015. *BBC Brasil*.Retreived from https://www.bbc.com/portuguese/noticias/2015/12/151201_lavajato_ru

xxiii Mier, B. (2017, September 25). How Manufactured Economic Crisis in Brazil Paved Way for a Soft Coup. *Upside Down World*. Retreived from http://upsidedownworld.org/archives/brazil/manufactured-economic-crisis-brazil-paved-way-soft-coup/

xxiv Morando na Colômbia, Janot vira embaixador da Lava-Jato. (2018, March 5). *O Valor*. Retreived from https://www.valor.com.br/politica/5362113/morando-na-colombia-janot-vira-embaixador-da-lava-jato

xxv Atlantic Council. (2017, July 19). *Lessons From Brazil: Fighting Corruption Amid Political Turmoil* [video file]. Retreived from https://youtu.be/rR5Yiz84b5c

A Holy War

By Daniel Hunt

From 9% in 1991 to 30% of the population in 2017, the rapid expansion of Neo-pentecostalism in Brazil since its arrival in the 1970s has caused unease amongst socially liberal sectors of society.i Rarely spoken about is how the story began fifty years ago, and how the country is increasingly living with the repercussions of decisions made far away.

In 1969, then New York Governor, and soon to be Vice President, Nelson Rockefeller, was dispatched to Latin America in the capacity as special envoy for President Nixon. The visit was to assess what was seen as the failure of Kennedy's so called "Alliance for Progress" initiative in the region.

In <u>United States Penetration of Brazil</u>, Jan K. Black writes:
"It is interesting to note that in 1969, the year when U.S. economic assistance was suspended for a few months in "cosmetic" protest against the dramatic tightening of the dictatorial noose signified by the dissolution of the Congress in December 1968 and the promulgation of the Fifth Institutional Act (AI-5), the number of Brazilian policemen brought to the United States for training almost tripled that of the previous year. The number of Brazilian military trainees in the United States also increased that year and was, in fact, higher than at any other time in the post war period.

The marked expansion of the training program also coincided with an increase in documented reports of the systematic torture of political prisoners and of the murders of petty criminals, as well as alleged subversives, carried out by the "Death Squads," reportedly composed of off-duty policemen. (New York) Governor Nelson Rockefeller, as President Nixon's special envoy in Brazil and other Latin American countries in 1969, was uninformed, unconvinced, or unconcerned about these reports. Rockefeller recommended that "the training program which brings military and police personnel from the other hemispheric nations to the United States and to training centers in Panama be continued and strengthened."ii,iii

The training program to which he referred was that of the notorious School of the Americas, which is now both re-branded and re-tooled as WHINSEC. This agency was central to the re-configuration of Latin American militaries as glorified police forces, equipped for internal rather than hemispheric defence, since the 1960s.

Despite official US rhetoric against the Brazilian dictatorship's increasingly egregious human rights abuses, Rockefeller's visit Latin America signified an intensification of US support for anti-communist dictatorial regimes who were friendly to US economic investment. On his tour, under robust military security, Rockefeller was met with violent anti-imperialist protests in almost every city he visited, which were often subject to media blackout.

Following his southern trip, Nelson prepared the

Rockefeller Report on Latin America, which, among its other recommendations, identified Catholic liberation theology as a threat to the national security of the United States.

Under the heading 'The Church', the report states that "Modern communications and increasing education have brought about a stirring among the people that has had a tremendous impact on the Church, making it a force dedicated to change – revolutionary change if necessary. Actually, the Church may be somewhat in the same situation as the young – with a profound idealism, but as a result, in some cases, vulnerable to subversive penetration; ready to undertake a revolution if necessary to end injustice but not clear either as to the ultimate nature of the revolution itself or as to the governmental system by which the justice it seeks can be realized."

In a section 'Changes in the Decade Ahead' the report warns "Clearly, the opinion in the United States that Communism is no longer a serious factor in the Western Hemisphere is thoroughly wrong. We found almost universally that the other American republics are deeply concerned about the threat that it poses to them – and the United States must be alert to and concerned about the ultimate threat it poses to the United States and the hemisphere as a whole."

It goes on to predict that "Growing nationalism, across the spectrum of political groupings, which will often find expression in terms of independence from U.S. domination and influence..."[iv]

To counter that threat to US interests, he recommended

the export of a socially conservative counterpoint to left leaning Liberation Theology. At its core, the problem that liberation theology represented for the US centered on its endorsement of collective action to challenge structural inequality, something which, Rockefeller implied, smacked of communism. The US found its antidote for liberation theology in Protestantism, exported to Latin America by North American missionaries as early as the late 19th century. However, the Protestantism that took root in Brazil was not the progressive social gospel of mainline denominations like Episcopalians, Presbyterians, or Methodists. This new variety of Protestantism was Evangelical, in that it emphasized a deeply personal relationship with God and aggressive proselytization. In many cases, it was Pentecostal or, by the 1970s, Neopentecostal, meaning that it promised a transformative experience of the Holy Spirit, which would manifest itself in believers' lives through "signs" like speaking in tongues and faith healing. Some Neopentecostals were also adherents of an emerging "prosperity theology," promoted in the US by televangelists like Oral Roberts, which preaches that faithful Christians can expect not only spiritual salvation but material prosperity.

In contrast to liberation theology, evangelicals, Neopentecostals, and adherents of prosperity theology preach an intensely individualistic faith. Rather than challenging its adherents to fight against entrenched power structures and challenge injustice, Latin American evangelical Protestants teach that spiritual, physical, and financial salvation are accomplished individually. Liberation theology seeks to transform unjust structures. Evangelical Protestantism promises to equip believers to succeed within those structures. God blesses the righteous - the poor simply haven't believed or worked hard enough.

It isn't difficult to see how this meritocratic theology squares with the interests of the imperialist power where it originated. What could possibly be less threatening for US hegemony in Latin America, in religious terms, than a theology that is, for all intents and purposes, a product of the American dream? Work/pray hard, be a good citizen/churchgoer, and America/God will take care of the rest. If things don't work, well, you should have worked/prayed harder. The problem could not possibly be with the system itself. Above all, American evangelicalism is a denial of structural inequality in favor of individual responsibility – just like liberal and neoliberal economics.

Eight years after Rockefeller's visit, in 1977, the pioneering prosperity theology-based Universal Church of the Kingdom of God (UCKG) was founded in Brazil by Edir Macedo, who had recently had a Neopentecostal conversion experience. In addition to preaching a particularly blatant version of prosperity theology that tied financial blessings from God to donations made to the church, Macedo also lauded the philosophies of Nelson's grandfather John D. Rockefeller.v The church's first service was held on July 9 that year, in a suburb of Rio de Janeiro to a congregation of 200. Forty years later its membership in Brazil stands at at least 2 million and the church has founded congregations around the world, particularly in Africa, Latin America, and North America. And the UCKG is only one of dozens of similar groups that have sprung up in Brazil since the 1970s, usually in poorer regions and neighborhoods, and preaching, nearly without fail, an extremely conservative social message that focuses on respecting church and state authority, glorifies the individual over the collective, and emphasizes the accumulation of wealth as a sign of God's favour.

Meanwhile in 1979, the first Committee of Sante Fe document advised the incoming Reagan administration that it had to do something decisive about the threat posed by Liberation Theology. The administration heeded the advice, and responded both militarily and ideologically. Reagan's military strategy against liberation theology ushered in what Noam Chomsky describes as the first religious war of the 21st century. It was the war of the United States against the Catholic Church in Latin America whose bishops, as noted earlier, had together dared to affirm a "preferential option for the poor" as their official position.vi

It was at this time, with the return to a multi-party system in Brazil, that the Workers Party, or PT was formed by a coalition of trade unionists such as future President Lula da Silva, Marxist intellectuals, and key figures from Brazilian liberation theology like Leonardo Boff and Frei Betto. The PT initiated the *Diretas Já* movement which brought about the end of military rule in 1985.

By 1987, the Latin American Military Chiefs of Staff meeting in conference in Mar del Plata, Argentina, devoted several pages of their final report to liberation theology and the threat it posed to regional stability. The targeting of adherents of liberation theology contributed to thousands upon thousands of deaths across the continent. By the 1990s, with the Southern Cone re-democratised, and given a neoliberal fever by the Bush

Senior administration and IMF, these new Evangelical Churches and missionaries had spread rapidly across the region. At this time some of the earliest allegations of CIA connivance in evangelicalism's expansion appeared.

Thy will be done

The book by Gerard Colby & Charlotte Dennett <u>Thy will be done: The Conquest of the Amazon: Nelson Rockefeller and Evangelism in the Age of Oil</u> is an exhaustive investigation of the growth of Neopentacostalism in Brazil, and its relationship to Nelson Rockefeller, US Corporate interests, and their exploitation of the Amazon.<u>vii</u> It was triggered by the authors' trip to Brazil in 1976 to investigate a missionary organization called the Summer Institute of Linguistics (SIL), also known as the Wycliffe Bible Translators, Rockefeller & USAID had funded, ostensibly to translate the Bible into hundreds of indigenous languages the world over.

Wycliffe was founded by William Cameron Townsend who the authors accuse of destroying indigenous peoples' cultural values to abet penetration by U.S. businesses, employing a "virulent brand of Christian fundamentalism that used linguistics to undermine the social cohesion of indigenous communities and accelerate their assimilation into Western culture". The authors argued that SIL was effectively a scouting party that surveyed the Amazonian hinterlands for potential sources of opposition to natural resource exploitation such as cattle ranching, clear cutting and strip mining, among native populations. SIL had actively whitewashed massacres of Indigenous groups by Brazil's Military Regime and even allowed its Jungle

Aviation & Radio Service (JAARS) base in the Ecuadoran Amazon to be used by Green Berets who were combing the forest for signs of armed insurgency.

The book became a target for criticism from none other than Lincoln Gordon, a personal friend of the Rockefellers and US ambassador to Brazil in 1964, when he conspired with the coup plotters. In response, co-author Gerard Colby said to *Folha de S. Paulo* newspaper in 1996, "After the coup, not only was Brazil's destiny undergoing immense change, but the Amazon and The Indians were opened up to even greater genocide.viii And Nelson Rockefeller knew what was happening inside the country. What does he do? He travels to Brazil in 1969, meets directly with the military leadership, receives the National Intelligence Service report ... and next you see Nelson asking for support for what he calls the 'new military' to be the vanguard of development. A Military that would promote things like the Transamazonica Highway. Not surprisingly, in 1972, you read in the New York Times Nelson's cousin, Richard Aldrich, who was then the president of the Brazil-United States Chamber of Commerce, enthusiastically stating 'This road is terribly important for the development of the interior. It is already bringing people and will make raw materials much more accessible to the outside world.'"

In Uruguayan author Eduardo Galeano's The Open Veins of Latin America, he talks about a US-Brazil agreement in 1964 which permitted US Air Force planes to fly over and photograph the Amazon rainforest:
"They had used cintilometers to detect radioactive mineral deposits by the emission of light wavelengths of variable intensity, electromagnetometers to radiograph

the topsoil rich in non-ferrous minerals, and magnetometers to discover and measure the iron. The reports and photographs acquired in the reconnaissance of the extension and depth of the secret riches of Amazonia were put in the hands of private firms interested in the matter, thanks to the good services of the United States Geological Survey. In the immense region was proven the existence of gold, silver, diamonds, gipsite, hematite, magnetite, tantalium, titanium, thorium, uranium, quartz, copper, manganese, lead, sulfates, potassium, bauxite, zinc, zirconium, chrome and mercury."[ix]

War of the Saints

Some compare the expansion of Neopentecostalism in Brazil to other implanted religions elsewhere, such as the Saudi-sponsored spread of Wahabbism in the Middle East, and with it has grown a radical militancy. Those practicing popular Afro-Brazilian religions such as Candomblé and Umbanda have found their places of worship attacked and burned around the country. This situation has developed in parallel to the influence that tax-exempt, often extremely corrupt evangelical churches have developed in politics, as they now control the Mayorship of Rio de Janeiro, Brazil's second-largest city, and are on the brink of winning the state's governorship.[x] In a context in which Rio de Janeiro's evangelical churches have been accused of laundering money for the drug trafficking gangs, all elements of Afro-Brazilian culture including *Caipoeira*, *Jango* drumming and participation in Carnaval parades have been banned by the traffickers in many favelas.

During preparations for the 1992 Earth Summit in Rio de Janeiro, the Rockefeller Foundation created LEAD (Leadership in the Environment and Development). One of the Brazilian politicians most closely associated with LEAD/ABDL would be Marina Silva. A Workers' Party member and Minister of the Environment in Lula's first administration, Silva had been an adherent of Catholic liberation theology for almost two decades, converting to evangelicalism in the mid- 1990s after a period of illness.

According to their website LEAD have "been recruiting talented individuals from key sectors and professions all over the world to be part of a growing network now standing at over 2400 leaders, who are committed to changing the world.xi Every one of our leaders is a graduate of LEAD's Fellows Training Program, an intensive and demanding program designed to enhance leadership ability, strengthen sustainable development knowledge and foster the relationships that will continue to support our Fellows in their work. This cross-sectoral, cross-cultural program has been at the heart of LEAD activities across the globe. [...] Since 1992, more than 500 professionals have been trained in Brazil, Canada, China, Former Soviet Union, Europe, India, Indonesia, Mexico, Nigeria, Pakistan and South Africa." The Brazilian branch of LEAD (ABDL) was one of the first, founded in mid-1991 and the *Gazeta Mercantil* wrote at the time, that "The Rockefeller Foundation intends to invest US $5 million in the next five years in training environmental leaders, with The purpose of preparing opinion makers capable of having a broad view of environmental problems and their economic implications."xii All Binger, LEAD's international director, said with surprising frankness, "we hope that in ten years many of the fellows will be acting as ministers of environment and development, university rectors and CEOs."

The growing Evangelical power base traded support for policy concessions throughout the 1990s and 2000s, supporting Lula and Dilma Governments but it was not until 2010 that they had a potential Presidential candidate of their own – Marina Silva, her platform a marketable synthesis of evangelical Christianity, environmental campaigning and Wall Street friendly liberalism. Initially, she accepted the vice presidential candidacy for the Brazilian Socialist Party (PSB), a party that is socialist in name only.

Heiress to COA Member Itaú Bank, brother of Rockefeller's Trilateral Commission member Roberto, Neca Setubal, was responsible for 84% of funds to Marina Silva's institute in 2013.[xiii] Former president of Citibank Alvaro de Souza ran the fundraising for Silva's 2010 election campaign. Ex-US Chamber of Commerce, Souza had previously served on the boards of such companies as Gol and AmBev, and was chairman of WWF Brazil. In 2008, the WWF, and its President Emeritus, Prince Philip Duke of Edinburgh, awarded Silva with a medal, championing her work on Amazon conservation.[xiv]

In the lead up to the 2014 election, David Rockefeller's corporate lobby for the Americas, AS/COA, which specialises in both propaganda and grooming future leaders in the region, hosted an event featuring PSB presidential candidate Eduardo Campos and Silva.[xv] Campos would die in an air crash soon after, after which Silva was promoted to the top of the ticket. The subsequent focus of AS/COA on the candidacy of Silva reflected a belief that she was Wall Street and the Obama administration's favoured candidate.xvi Marina received an international campaign of media beatification to match, in which she was marketed as the "genuinely progressive" alternative to Rousseff, despite the social conservatism inherent in her evangelical faith that led her to vacillate on issues like LGBT and women's rights.xvii

In 2018 , Marina's support evaporated - she received less than 1% of the vote in the first round of presidential voting. Most of her evangelical base transferred its support to the neo-fascist , Jair Bolsonaro, with the overt endorsement of some of the largest and most influential Neopentecostal churches.

And the same northern neoliberals who once backed Marina Silva joined Neopentecostals in their support for Bolsonaro. The candidate has been holding off-the-record meetings with AS/COA since 2017 (at the latest), along with his "Chicago boy" economic advisor and potential Finance Minister, BTG Pactual/Millenium Institute's Paulo Guedes.xviii These meetings coincided with Bolsonaro's Damascus-road conversion to the rhetoric of free market and minimal state, to follow his 2016 appeal to the evangelicals with a show baptism in Israel's River Jordan.

Deliverance

The supposed "nationalist" Bolsonaro promised the US Government their wish list of demands for his Presidency, sacrificing sovereignty for power in age-old colonial tradition. His "green and yellow" nationalism masks support for mass privatisation of Brazilian assets, and opening up of the Amazon to exploitation in cooperation with foreign corporations. It is no coincidence that the Wall Street Journal endorsed the neo-fascist candidate, as they did Chilean dictator Augusto Pinochet.<u>xix</u>

During the first decade of the millennium, the so called "Pink Tide" of left and centre-left governments which swept to power across Latin America had liberation theology at its core. A high water mark of this unprecedented regional independence came at the Summit of the Americas in Mar del Plata in 2005, when Brazilian President Lula, Venezuela's Hugo Chavez, and Argentina's Nestor Kirchner joined together to reject David Rockefeller's proposed Free Trade Area of the Americas, to the chagrin of the Bush administration. At this time, efforts to re-assert US-influence in its "backyard" intensified and since the 2009 coup in Honduras, the Pink Tide's reversal has to a significant extent been powered by the support of evangelicals, who represent a fast-growing percentage of the population in most of the region.

In 1956, newly elected president Juscelino Kubitschek promised Brasil "50 years progress in 5". In contrast, Jair Bolsonaro has said he wants to take Brazil back 50 years, to the time of the Rockefeller report, when human development outside what the US Government called "islands of sanity", such as São Paulo, was close to zero.

Since Bolsonaro's pivot to the evangelicals, he has built an alliance with UCKG's Edir Macedo, now a billionaire with twenty-three TV stations, forty radio stations, two major daily newspapers, a real estate agency and a health insurance company. In 2008 Macedo published a manifesto for transforming his church and empire into genuine political power.xx His main TV Network, *Record*, and its online portal *R7* have been transformed into propaganda platforms for Bolsonaro – effectively his own *Fox News* during the election, and reminder of his threat to arch commercial and cultural rival's *Globo's* public concession, thus keeping them too in line.xxi

Now he proposes militarised schooling and creationism in the curriculum. Many find baffling how an open enthusiast of torture can be readily supported by Christian organisations, and some Catholic organisations have joined progressive evangelicals in protests against Bolsonaro, with his support of torture as a rallying point.

The churches' own massive money laundering schemes, in particular the involvement of national saboteur and architect of Dilma Rousseff's impeachment, Eduardo Cunha, makes further mockery of the candidate's anti-corruption rhetoric, and the hegemonic media must take responsibility for a 15 year campaign to make the Workers Party synonymous with corruption, a popular perception which the extreme right now exploits. They were the only political organisation with a national structure capable of beating what Brazil now faces.xxii
Neoliberal pundits talk inevitability of a Bolsonaro presidency without mentioning the surreal distortion and collective hysteria feeding his support, nor the imported nature of his Neopentecostal base. They do not indicate that a US-backed war on corruption wiping out candidates and clearing the way has enabled the ascent of a neo-fascist.xxiii Instead they blithely characterize Bolsonaro's rise as a specious frustration with PT corruption and concern about crime.

Whatever the election result, there is growing, compelling evidence that Brazil is being prepared for a military takeover. Regardless, if the electoral support of Neopentecostalism is decisive, it will bring with it authoritarian rule, an extreme regressive cultural conservatism, and a revival of those 1970s new military development projects in the Amazon, opening it to unprecedented exploitation.

Of course, there is not a straight line from Rockefeller to SIL/WBT to Macedo to Silva to Bolsonaro. Yet it is clear that over and over during the last half century, the interests of evangelical Protestantism and US imperialism have converged, while liberation theology and efforts to secure Brazilian sovereignty over its resources have been pushed to the margins. It is undeniable that the US saw liberation theology as a threat and that its desire for resource extraction in the Amazon found a willing partner in Townsend's Bible translators. It is no coincidence that the individualistic, prosperity-driven faith of Macedo's UKCG and other Brazilian Neopentecostal churches has so much in common with neoliberalism's rejection of the state and society in favor of the individual, for they are both imported from the US – the former from the tent revivals of the Midwest, the latter from Washington's economic and political powerbrokers. In the Amazon, the marriage between evangelicalism and imperialism sought to stifle indigenous opposition to resource extraction. In Brazil's cities today, the marriage between Neopentecostalism and neoliberalism has produced candidates and an electorate that believe that prosperity is the product of meritocratic individual effort. Believers conditioned to unquestioningly accept the voice of their pastor as the voice of God seldom hesitate to accept as equally authoritative the voice of a would-be dictator like Bolonsaro. The same vengeful God who in church promises damnation to the disobedient now promises to smite in this life LGBT people, petty criminals, and indigenous people, and anyone else who crosses Bolsonaro.

This outcome would represent the fruit of a fifty year project to distort and dominate Brazilian social, political, economic and cultural life through an implanted religion, with the reward of unfettered access to its natural riches for foreign capital and not God, but the interests of the United States, above all.

i Mariani, D. and Ducroquet, S. (2017, November 6). *A expansão evangélica no Brasil em 26 anos. Nexo.* Retrieved from https://www.nexojornal.com.br/grafico/2017/11/06/A-expans%C3%A3o-evang%C3%A9lica-no-Brasil-em-26-anos

ii Black, JK. (2009). Updated Epilogue for United States Penetration of Brazil. *Brasil Wire.* Retrevieved from http://www.brasilwire.com/united-states-penetration-of-brasil-epilogue/

iii Brown, H. (2014, December 10). The U.S. Spent Decades Teaching Torture Techniques To Brazil. Buzzfeed. Retreived from https://www.buzzfeednews.com/article/hayesbrown/the-united-states-spent-decades-teaching-torture-techniques

iv United States. Congress. Senate. Committee on Foreign Relations. Subcommittee on Western Hemisphere Affairs. (November 20, 1969). *Rockefeller Report on Latin America : hearings before the United States Senate Committee on Foreign Relations, Subcommittee on Western Hemisphere Affairs, Ninety-First Congress, first session* Washington: US GPO.

v Macedo, E. (2011, September 5). Tither: John Rockefeller. *Bishop Emir Macedo Blog.* Retrieved from https://blogs.universal.org/bispomacedo/en/2011/09/05/tither-john-d-rockerfeller/

vi Committee of Santa Fe. (2005, December 9). *Sourcewatch.* Retrieved from https://www.sourcewatch.org/index.php/Committee_of_Santa_Fe

vii Gerald Colby and Charlotte Dennet. (1996) *Thy Will Be Done: The Conquest of the Amazon : Nelson Rockefeller and Evangelism in the Age of Oil.* New York:Harper Collins.

viii De Sa, N. (1996, August 18). Uma rede de intrigas na América Latina. *Folha de São Paulo.* Retrieved from *https://www1.folha.uol.com.br/fsp/1996/8/18/mais!/7.html*

ix Galeano, Eduardo. (1973). *Open Veins of Latin America.* New York: Montly Review Press.

x Tavares, J.B. (2016, May 17). Qual será o motivo da perseguição do Candomblé no Brasil? *DW Brasil.* Retrieved from https://www.dw.com/pt-002/qual-ser%C3%A1-o-motivo-da-persegui%C3%A7%C3%A3o-do-candombl%C3%A9-no-brasil/a-19263438

xi https://www.lead.org/

xii Gazeta Mercantil. (November 6, 1991).

xiii Talento, A. and Odilla, F. (2014, September 7). Herdeira do Itaú bancou 83% de instituto de Marina. *Folha de São Paulo.* Retrieved from https://www1.folha.uol.com.br/poder/2014/09/1512207-herdeira-do-itau-bancou-83-de-instituto-de-marina.shtml xiv World Wildlife Fund. (2008, October 28). *Amazon's champion Awarded WWF's Duke of Edinburgh Medal* [Press Release]. Retrieved from https://www.worldwildlife.org/stories/amazon-s-champion-awarded-wwf-s-duke-of-edinburgh-medal

xv A boycott of Americas Quarterly and AS/COA, and why it is needed. (2018, February 22). *Brasil Wire*. Retreived from http://www.brasilwire.com/boycott-americas-quarterly-and-ascoa/

xvi Pignotti, D. (2014, September 6). Samuel Pinheiro Guimarães: EUA apostam em Marina. *Carta Maior*. Retreived from https://www.cartamaior.com.br/?/Editoria/Politica/Samuel-Pinheiro-Guimaraes-EUA-apostam-em-Marina/4/31754

xvii Echoes in the Echo Chamber: Brasil, Elections, Media and the Ghost of 1964. (2015, March). *Brasil Wire*. Retrieved from http://www.brasilwire.com/echoes-in-the-echo-chamber-ghosts-of-64/

xviii Pinochet via Fujimori: Wall Street's New Man in Brazil, Jair Bolsonaro. (2018, September 10). *Brasil Wire*. Retrieved from http://www.brasilwire.com/wall-streets-new-pinochet/

xix ibid

xx Figueredo, V. (2018, April 26). O Plano do Poder do Bispo Macedo. *Fórum*. Retrieved from https://www.revistaforum.com.br/o-plano-de-poder-do-bispo-macedo/

xxi Deslandes, G. (2018, April 19). Globo: Evangelical Ascendion, a Threat to its Hegemony. *Brasil Wire*. Retrieved from http://www.brasilwire.com/globo-evangelical-ascension-a-threat-to-its-hegemony-part-3/

xxii Greenwald, G. (2018, October 20). In Jair Bolsonaro's New Brazil, Far-Right Evangelical Billionaire Edir Macedo's Media Empire Is Being Exploited to Investigate Journalists — Including The Intercept. *The Intercept*. Retrieved from https://theintercept.com/2018/10/20/in-bolsonaros-new-brazil-far-right-evangelical-billionaire-edir-macedos-media-empire-is-being-exploited-to-investigate-journalists-including-the-intercept/

xxiii Hidden History: The US "War On Corruption" In Brasil. (2018, January 28). *Brasil Wire*.

The Wholesale Attack On Brazilian Sovereignty: An Interview With Celso Amorim (Part One)

By Brian Mier

For the past 25 years, Celso Amorim has been Brazil's most important diplomat, serving as Foreign Affairs Minister in the governments of Itamar Franco (1993-1995) and Luiz Inacio Lula da Silva (2003-2010), and Minister of Defense for Dilma Rousseff (2011-2015). Born in 1942 in the port city of Santos, Amorim graduated at the top of his class at the Rio Branco Institute, the Brazilian government's diplomacy school, in 1965. This earned him a scholarship to the Diplomatic Academy of Vienna, where he spent 3 years, followed by 3 years at the London School of Economics studying under Ralph Miliband. After working for several years as a Portuguese literature professor at the Rio Branco Institute he was invited to head *Embrafilme*, the Military Government's film agency, in 1979. Shortly afterwards, he was fired for financing the film *Pra Frente, Brasil*, by Roberto Farias, which shows scenes of political prisoners being tortured by the Military.i

Nominated as the International Affairs Secretary in the Science and Technology Ministry in 1987 by President José Sarney, Amorim served in every subsequent government until Michel Temer took office in 2016. His tenure as Lula's Minister of Foreign Affairs was marked by Brazil taking an active role on the international stage. Under Amorim's guidance, Brazil expanded its role in Mercosur, Unasul, IBSA and the BRICS, became more active in the UN Security council and improved trade relationships with countries in Africa, Asia and the Middle East. In a 2009 article in Foreign Policy, David Rothkopf called him, "The World's best foreign minister".ii

I spoke with Celso Amorim on May 16, 2018. The interview was edited for readability.

I would like to ask you about a concept called sovereignty, because I don't think most people in the United States pay much attention to the word. What is sovereignty, why is it important and what did Lula's government do to increase Brazilian sovereignty?

Well, I hope you don't want me to go into the history of the concept of sovereignty since the 16th Century more or less, when it was established. It's really the capacity to determine your own destiny- up to a point of course because everyone lives in the World and the circumstances of the World are also influential. But it is, at least, to be able to guide your own country in a way that corresponds to the interests of your people. Basically I think that is what sovereignty means. That you can face external pressures in a way that is not submissive. Of course you have to negotiate very often but you have to define your own priorities according to your own interests and the interests of your people. Of course this implies some control over your natural resources. The United States is very conscious of what sovereignty is because when a Chinese company decided to buy an important technology company in the United States, President Trump vetoed it. So sovereignty is this. There are some assets which are essential to the capacity to determine your own destiny, of course taking into account the circumstances of the World. I think this is what we want. In order to do that of course you need to have a foreign policy that is able to be affirmative of your views and to defend this policy, enabling you to face any possible threat that may exist.

How do you think Lula's government strategy towards the question of sovereignty differed from, for example, those of Fernando Henrique Cardoso or Itamar Franco?

Very simply. I'll give you an example because I think it's better to exemplify than to try to define. Lula's attitude in relation to the deep water petroleum reserves in which he established the government role for Petrobras is one case of preserving our natural resources. Another example was his authorizing the development of a nuclear propelled submarine which would be able to be vigilant about our very long coast. One has to keep in mind – sometimes we forget – that Brazil has the longest Atlantic coastline in the World. I would say that in foreign policy, which I was more active in, his government contributed to build a more multi-polar World in which each country is not necessarily subject to anyone's hegemony. How did he do that? I would exemplify this with the integration of South America which is now being abandoned by the present government, because even if Brazil is big, it's not big enough to face the big blocks like the United States, which is a block in itself, China, which is a block in itself, or the European Union. The integration of South America was important, relations with other countries in the South, including in Africa and also India and so on, and we also contributed to the creation of BRICS which somehow gives greater balance to international relations. These are some examples but, regarding economic relations, I could also mention our attitudes vis a vis the Free Trade Area of the Americas (FTAA) that was being pushed by the United States, our attitudes in relation to the DOHA trade rounds in which we completely reversed the trend to have a very negative agreement from the point of view of developing countries. Well, these are some examples of sovereignty, and of course this was all based on greater social justice which increased the government's legitimacy. I say legitimacy not only because it was elected, but also because it had the actual support of the great majority of the Brazilian people, especially as Lula worked to reduce inequality in Brazil.

How does this approach differ from the Michel Temer's

Government policies?

In almost every respect, the Temer government is doing exactly the opposite. Internally it is, of course, taking measures which increase inequality instead of decreasing it, like the new labor laws and the freezing of expenditures in health and education by constitutional amendment, which is something that is absolutely unheard of anywhere in the World as far as I know. And externally there is a foreign policy which in the best moments is just nothing and in the worst moments is doing things like contributing to the disintegration of South America by deactivating Unasul, which was a big achievement during the Lula government, and by not having any initiative in relation to the BRICS and other groups like IBSA (India Brazil South Africa). They are diminishing our presence everywhere – even in relation to Palestine and Israel by not having an independent attitude. They have a very submissive attitude which tends to give more importance to one or another internal lobby than to the real interests of peace in the World. So these are some examples, but I could add some others, for instance by allowing Embraer to go into a merger with Boeing – of course everyone knows who will dominate the result of this merger – so these are some examples. I could go on and on.

During the time that you served as Minister of Foreign Relations for the Lula administration and Defense

Minister for Dilma Rousseff, what are a few policies that Brazil implemented that, in your mind, pleased the US Government? What are a few policies that you think may have angered them?

First of all, our preoccupation was not to please or to not please anyone. Our preoccupation was to pursue our own interests in solidarity with other countries, especially in our region, in other developing countries in our region and in Africa. By doing so, we may have frequently displeased the United States. For instance there was our attitude in the WTO meeting in Cancun 2003 during which Brazil led the resistance to an agreement [the FTAA] that would have been detrimental to developing countries. But having said that six months later Bob Zoellick, who was the chief negotiator from the United States, got in touch with me to see what kind of agreement could be possible, what was the kind of position that could be formed in favor of an agreement. So even when we displeased the United States we didn't do that just to annoy them – we were pursuing our interests. And I think that was, to a large extent, understood. So much so that when, for instance, Bush called for this Summit of the G20, I can not be sure if it was the first but one of the first people he called was President Lula to say, "I'm thinking of having this G20 meeting in order that the important countries can see how we can deal with the World economy after the Lehman Brothers crisis." This is one example. There have been other cases, though, in which the United States actually was interested in the presence of Brazil, like the Annapolis Conference for the Middle East, the Palestine/Israel question. Brazil was one of the very few developing countries to be invited. I had a good dialogue with Condoleezza Rice in that respect. Of course we didn't agree on everything but we talked with each other respectfully. Later on, President Obama actually asked President Lula to help broker an agreement with Iran. We helped. We obtained exactly what had been requested from Iran. We brokered it together with Turkey. And when it finally came out it was an achievement. But in May 2010 – I can not say to my surprise because they already had given signals – to our disappointment the United States, led then by Secretary of State Hilary Clinton I am sure, preferred to pursue a role of sanctions and negative actions and dismantled the effort that they themselves had asked us to implement. So was the United States angry? I'm not sure. And bringing Cuba to the OAS. It was in Brazil that Cuba participated in all the forums that exist in South America and Latin America and the Caribbean for the first time. It happened in late 2008. So that was a step that made it necessary to also have Cuba in the Summit of the Americas. Obama himself recognized that. But later on, Trump went in a different way. So it's very difficult to say. It's not our task to know what will please the United States and what will displease the United States. Our task – and this is part of sovereignty – is to pursue our own interests and to a larger extent also the interests of other countries like ours, other developing countries, starting with South America.

I can tell you what actions by the United States displeased us. One of them was refusing the agreement that they had asked us to promote with Iran. Certainly what displeased us – I was no longer Foreign Minister but I was the Defense Minister – was the spying on our President, the spying on our oil company, the spying on our Ministry of Energy. So these are some examples of things that displeased us. But even so we did not break our dialogue with the United States because, of course, the United States is extremely important. It's still the most important country in the World.

I asked this question because, as we know, there was a Coup d´Etat in Brazil in 2016.

Yes.

And one of the things leading up to the Coup was the Lava Jato investigation (Operation Car Wash) and its paralyzation of the Brazilian engineering and construction industry, which cased 500,000 immediate layoffs and a drop in GDP in 2015. And we know that Lava Jato is a joint operation between the US Department of Justice, the FBI and the Public Prosecutors team from Curitiba led by Sergio Moro, which, according to a motion for reversal filed by Lula's defense team in

March, 2018, is based on illegal informal communications between the Brazilian judiciary and the US Department of Justice.

Yes.

So we know that there was some involvement of the United States in events which led up to the Coup and Lula's imprisonment. What reasons would the United States have to want to be involved in all of this?

I can give you a very simple example from the old Chinese proverb that a picture is worth 1000 words. There was a cover of the American issue of *the Economist* which showed an upside down map of the Americas. South America was on the top and the rest was below it. The title of the front page article was "Nobody's Backyard". I think that the simple fact that, when it appeared in 2009 or 2010, the planners and the intelligence people in the United States... I think when the intelligence people had one of their regular meetings which I suppose they have in spite of the lack of coordination sometimes, they saw that map saying that South America and Latin America is no longer the United States' back yard and it is promoting things like the BRICS, like independent meetings with Arab countries, having meetings on their own, creating Unasul without the patronage of either the US or Europe... I think all that – I wouldn't say anger, necessarily – I think all these things suddenly raised eyebrows in Washington and someone said 'well we have to put these things right, put these guys where they belong, which is in the back yard.' I'm not saying that everything was planned by the United States. It's very difficult to say and I have no evidence for that, but certainly there was this cooperation that was mentioned even by Kenneth Blanco from the Department of Justice. He said that there was very informal cooperation with the judiciary in Brazil, which is a scandal really because if you have agreements related to justice or to law enforcement they have follow the rules. And following the rules implies going through the appropriate channels. Informal cooperation is a way of exerting direct domination over less conscious actions. That is what happened. I was the Foreign Minister and I could see it all the time, not only the American Ambassador – I'm not saying it was only the US but the US are more powerful – trying to go around the Foreign Ministry. They would say, "Oh, the Foreign Ministry is very bureaucratic, it's very obstructive." Of course we were – we were the front line of sovereignty. So when you raise these questions I think you are probably right. I don't have many pieces of evidence that I can draw on, but certainly this proof of the informal cooperation is important. The spying, of course, was not innocent. Do you think they spied on Dilma because there was a risk of a communist government? There was nothing like that. They spied because they were interested in things that were around the Oil industry and, later on, the nuclear energy industry and of course all the cases that were related to those industries. The case that there was very strong cooperation between US officials and Brazilian officials in *Lava Jato* is very convincing. The real objective of the *Lava Jato* investigation is removing not only Dilma and not only Lula as a person, but it's a project, a project for a country in which sovereignty occupied a central place.

Was financing engineering companies like Odebrecht through the Brazilian National Social and Economic Development Bank (BNDES) an integral part of Brazil's foreign policy?

Not Odebrecht in particular but, of course, support for all the Brazilian engineering companies abroad was a very important aspect of our presence in Africa and our presence in South America and those things created jobs in Brazil, contrary to what a large part of the Brazilian elite believed. So I have no doubt that all these instruments which are linked to Brazilian sovereignty and the capacity of Brazil to be present in other places in the World were destroyed on purpose. It's impossible to have... It's not only Odebrecht, it's all the Brazilian construction companies, which were certainly the most dynamic sector of Brazilian industry acting abroad, that were affected. Now, another important company, Embraer, is being swallowed by Boeing. And the lending arm of BNDES was curtailed. What BNDES was doing, actually, was like any bank in Europe generally does in terms of bringing special conditions to loans for activities in very poor or vulnerable countries. So this is part of the wholesale attack on the pillars of Brazilian sovereignty. It is not only the foreign policy that is formulated in the Foreign Ministry but also the concrete means through which this foreign policy is exerted. And this certainly includes the engineering companies. Not only them, but Embraer also, as I mentioned before. But let us say the solutions or the ways they chose to attack were different but with a similar result in that Brazil is now much weaker in its presence abroad. And BNDES of course is part of that as well.

The PT is a left or center-left political party and the Democratic party in the United States is considered by some people to be center-left. Obama once called Lula "the man" and praised Brazil a lot but at the same time his government was illegally spying on Brazil, listening to Dilma Rousseff's telephone conversations and spying on the petroleum industry. Do you think that the PT governments of Dilma and Lula made a mistake in trusting the democrats too much?

I don't think this is the problem. I don't even think that Obama had full control over what happened with his hidden government or whatever you call it – deep government – in the United States, which involves the intelligence community plus maybe some sectors of the defense industry. So Obama probably didn't know. Of course he came to know afterwards. I think these things happen independently. I'm not saying anything new. I lived in the United States in the 1970s and in other periods. I read, for instance, the *Ellsberg Reports* and the *Pentagon Papers*. Many things that happen do so without the knowledge of the President of the United States. So Obama did not necessarily determine those actions. I'm not saying this to excuse Obama. Of course Obama also disappointed us in other ways. I mentioned the agreement on the Iranian nuclear program. But I think these things are the doings of a deeper state, which exists in the United States, which sees things from a very geopolitical security point of view and, as I mentioned to you before, when they saw this cover of *the Economist* they were not happy. That's not the idea. It's not Brazil that has to be leading South America. It must be the United States. That's part of the ideology of the deep government. I think Obama tried to have a more conciliatory view, certainly not breaking with the deep government but trying to find different ways and I think it is very significant, for instance, that in the Summit of the Americas that took place in Trinidad and Tobago in 2009, he asked for a meeting with Unasul – the same Unasul that is being destroyed now by our own government, without the United States having to fire even a shot in that. So you have to see these things as part of a two-fold movement. Part of it is this deep government in the United States which of course has links to financial capital, which has links with the military establishment and of course the intelligence agencies which I mentioned. You have to see this also in the light of this very passive, even submissive attitude of the Brazilian elite which doesn't want Brazil to be assertive in international affairs. Which prefers to see Brazil like a good subordinate of the United States. It's always been like that in South America. Before we discussed integration seriously with Mercosur and later on with Unasul and other initiatives, the main competition between Brazil and Argentina was to see who was the United States' best friend instead of trying to be friends with each other. Of course we should be friends with the United States as well, but defending our own interests first.

i Elio Gaspari. *A Ditadura Acabada.* (Rio de Janeiro: Intrínseca, 2016).
ii Rothkoph, D. (2009, October 7). The World's Best Foreign Minister. *Foreign Policy.* Retreived from https://foreignpolicy.com/2009/10/07/the-worlds-best-foreign-minister/

The U.S. "War On Corruption" in Brazil

By Daniel Hunt

Despite public ignorance, and its root in the media blind spot on this matter, US involvement in Brazil's Anti-Corruption Operation *Lava Jato (Carwash)*, which has already resulted in $3bn payout to North American investors, is not some fringe theory, as some like to pretend – US Acting Attorney General Kenneth Blanco has publicly boasted about it himself:

"It is hard to imagine a better cooperative relationship in recent history than that of the United States Department of Justice and the Brazilian prosecutors. We have cooperated and substantially assisted one another on a number of public matters that have now been resolved, and are continuing to do so on a number of ongoing investigations. The cooperation between the Department and Brazil has led to extraordinary results. In just the last year alone, for example, the Criminal Division's Fraud Section and the Brazilian *Lava Jato* task force have cooperated and coordinated resolutions in four FCPA cases: Embraer, Rolls Royce, Braskem, and Odebrecht. Odebrecht is particularly noteworthy due to its breadth and scope. Indeed, just this past week, the prosecutors in Brazil won a guilty verdict against former President Lula da Silva, who was charged with receiving bribes from the engineering firm OAS in return for his help in winning contracts with the state oil company Petrobras. It is cases like this that put Brazil at the forefront of countries that are working to fight corruption, both at home and abroad."i

With the fall of its allied Washington consensus governments to the so called pink tide at the turn of the century, US primacy in the region was genuinely threatened for the first time in generations.ii Many lauded this as Bush Jr's failure, and the United States "losing" the region permanently, as if assuming there would or could be no response. In answer to these defeats, parallel to the War on Terror in the Middle East and War on Drugs already present in the region, a new front, a "War on Corruption" opened up across the continent, becoming part of official foreign policy in 2002, just prior to Luiz Inácio Lula da Silva taking the Brazilian Presidency at his fourth attempt. Around the same time, a new rebranded hemispheric agency called WHINSEC would replace notorious exporter of torture, the School of Americas, with expanded scope, and was tasked with bringing the continent to heel via its own police forces and militaries.iii

Then in Government, Cuban-born cold warrior and former Office of Public Diplomacy propagandist Otto Reich, with characteristic hubris, took credit for encouraging a new focus on corruption in Latin America while assistant Secretary of State under George W Bush.

"Corruption is the single largest obstacle to economic development in Latin America in my opinion. It distorts the market system, which is the only system that works - socialism we know does not work[...]We in the United States Government, we implemented a policy in the year 2002...where we decided to aggressively go after corrupt people, both in government, and private enterprise - we don't differentiate - and to revoke or deny access to the United States of people who are involved in corruption, believe me it is as the military would say, a "target-rich environment". " Reich told C-Span. iv,v

This was embraced in Washington as a new method to force political-economic realignment and "win back" the continent, especially having seen David Rockefeller's baby the Free Trade Area of the Americas (FTAA) brought down by an alliance of Argentina's Nestor Kirchner, Venezuela's Hugo Chavez, and Brazil's Lula at the Mar del Plata conference in 2005.vi,This was an escalation, and the US Government was, according to cables, fearful that the regional trade bloc, Mercosur, and its parallel military institution, Unasur, would be consolidated.vii

Lava Jato's inquisitor judge Sérgio Moro's first recorded visit to the United States was in 1998, on an exchange programme with Harvard University, to study anti money laundering practices in Brazil's domineering hemispheric neighbour.<u>viii</u> That year the US stood accused of multi-faceted interference in Brazil, to guarantee the re-election of its favoured candidate, the pro-market former dependency theorist, Fernando Henrique Cardoso.<u>ix</u> Currency crash, IMF bailout followed, and cut-price privatisations continued.

In 2004, following graduation from University of Paraná, Moro published the paper "Considerations of Mani Pulite", his interpretative thesis on the 1990s Italian (with US-cooperation) anti-corruption probe which decimated Italy's political order, in particular its centre-left, and paved the way for both political emergence of Silvio Berlusconi, the most corrupt leader in its history, and a wave of privatisations of its massive public sector nicknamed "the pillage of Italy".<u>x</u> ,<u>xi,xii</u> Mani Pulite, in particular its use of the media to whip up public indignation in support of convictions, served as the prototype for Moro's own operation *Lava Jato*, launched a decade after his paper. US officials' open admission of involvement was all but ignored in Italy, as it has been in Brazil.

Also in 2004, the *Mensalão* scheme of cash for votes in Congress was being uncovered. It developed into a media scandal so great it almost gained traction enough to trigger the impeachment of then President Lula, despite originating under previous administrations.<u>xiii</u> Lula was not charged, but it did result in prison for some of his closest party allies. A private spy agency, Kroll, which operates a revolving door with the CIA, was implicated in attempts to ensnare Lula when caught spying on communications of Government staff.xiv ,xv In 2010 it was also exposed as a recruiter of Latin America based journalists to spy on behalf of oil giant Chevron, its client.xvi It would, almost unbelievably, then go on to be given the contract for running the CPI (Parliamentary Inquiry) into state-controlled Oil Company Petrobras, which would provide the seeds for Operation *Lava Jato*.xvii Somewhat perversely, architect of Dilma Rousseff's impeachment Eduardo Cunha (whose prosecution was delayed until after Rousseff was gone) would later suggest using Kroll to shut down *Lava Jato* before it reached the coup plotters themselves.xviii The company was more recently in the news after being hired by Hollywood mogul Harvey Weinstein to smear his victims.xix

Following Lula's re-election, in 2007 with the new US "War on Corruption" displacing clumsy attempts to spread its spurious War on Terror to Brazil, Moro would visit the US again, this time on an official State Department fellowship, the "International Visitor Leadership Program", liaising with U.S. agencies and institutions responsible for combating money laundering.xx

Then, in 2009, Judge Moro appears in leaked State

Department cables, speaking at a joint event with the US DOJ under the banner "Project Bridges" in Rio de Janeiro.xxi Outlining an operation similar in configuration to the future *Lava Jato* – ostensibly set up to investigate illicit funding for terrorism – the event coordinators talked about creating a partnership between the Department of Justice and the Brazilian judiciary to investigate corruption. The cable talks about how task forces could be set up in cities such as Campo Grande or Curitiba, which they identify as having a strong fervour for action on corruption. Those cities are known for their conservatism and default opposition to then governing centre-left Worker's Party. Curitiba and Campo Grande are also amongst the most enduring power bases of de-facto heirs to the dictatorship Government, ARENA, now called "Democratas", which despite a collapse in its vote between 2002 and 2014, is now in Temer's Post-Coup coalition, and enjoying life in Government for the first time in almost 20 years.

Around the same time as the Rio de Janeiro conference in 2009, new Secretary of State Hillary Clinton gave an address to the Council of the Americas in New York, which now feels prescient. In her speech to the David Rockefeller-founded Wall Street lobby, a grinning Secretary Clinton promoted a theme that "the ballot box alone is not enough" in Latin America, and that "sustainable democracies do more than have elections". While pointedly reaffirming her commitment to democratic "ideals", she suggests a "independent, capable judiciary" and "vibrant civil society" are what is really needed in the region for its democracies to mature.<u>xxii</u>

The speech is all the more remarkable coming off the back of US loss of influence in the hemisphere following electoral defeats of its favoured candidates, and that in the intervening decade since, the US Government has gone on to bet on the most powerful, unelected arm of government in Brazil – the Judiciary – which is predominantly white, male and conservative, and now nicknamed the Dictatorship of the Toga.

Clinton's predecessor John D. Negroponte (Council of the Americas Chairman Emeritus), as outgoing Director of National Intelligence, identified "Democratisation in Latin America" as a primary threat to US National Security, alongside Chinese Military expansion and Iran's Nuclear programme – on which Lula, along with Turkey's Erdogan, later broke from UN security council's shackles and negotiated a deal directly.<u>xxiii</u> ,<u>xxiv</u> Negroponte also lamented high oil prices as a gift to governments who do not support US interests. By this point, along with Mercosur, the worldwide multipolar bloc of China, Russia, India and Brazil, BRIC (later BRICS following addition of South Africa), was being consolidated as a direct challenge to US hegemony, in particular the continuing reliance on the US dollar. Brazil, along with Russia, Venezuela and Iran, would later, under

Barack Obama's administration, fall victim to Negroponte's desired policy of encouraging low energy prices in order to throttle competitors' Oil-dependent economies.xxv US Presidents and their approach to public relations change, objectives do not. Between the mandated freeze of *Lava Jato*, those low energy prices, and change in law enabled by the removal of Dilma Rousseff, Petrobras, despite record production, lost its monopoly on Brazil's massive offshore oil reserves which are being sold off for cents to foreign producers such as US Chevron & ExxonMobil, UK's BP & Shell, and Norway's Statoil, at an estimated loss of R$1 trillion – funds once earmarked by Dilma Rousseff for a revolution in public education & health investment, deemed Brazil's "Passport to the future".xxvi ,xxvii,xxviii,xxix

As publicly available cables cease in mid-2010 we do not know what level of collusion there was between Moro and the United States Government in the intervening years prior to *Lava Jato's* official inception in early 2014, but his endorsement or presence at think tanks featuring current and ex-USG personnel such as CFR, Wilson Center, AEI, AS/COA (Council of the Americas), and NATO adjunct Atlantic Council – which launched its own Latin America wing in 2013 – are at the least an indicator of continued collaboration, as is the level of unanimously positive international media coverage, unprecedented for any foreign judge, lawyer or legal operation (an often excruciating parade of grey men in suits which would otherwise generate no outside interest). Those organisations come complete with their own patronage networks of journalists, scholars, thought leaders and promoted commentariat.

Although she was never officially implicated beyond innuendo, Moro's selective and accelerated pursuit of figures from her Workers Party supplied the essential media pretext for elected President Dilma Rousseff's impeachment, only for her to be replaced by her actually proven corrupt PMDB vice, former US informant Michel Temer.xxx We can see in leaked 2011 emails from "Shadow CIA", Stratfor, that the wider intelligence community were already betting that Temer would take office during Rousseff's first term, and become the "bulldog" they needed to push through their Wall Street-prescribed reforms – against the will of the Brazilian electorate.xxxi This desired outcome was finally delivered in 2016, with tacit support from the Obama Administration in the form of Clinton's replacement Secretary of State John Kerry and 2009-13 US Ambassador to Brazil Tom Shannon, who by then had returned to State Dept Bureau of Hemispheric affairs, having taken a demotion for his tenure in Brazil.xxxii,xxxiii Shannon was replaced in Brazil by Liliana Ayalde, who is now at Southcom overseeing the rollout of US Military presence across the continent, having been earlier implicated in Paraguay's 2012 Coup while serving as Ambassador there.xxxiv Obama's VP Joe

Biden recently boasted of manipulating Ukraine's Judiciary by blackmailing the Government into firing their Prosecutor General in late March 2016, a few weeks before the Congressional vote on Dilma Rousseff's impeachment – now revealed to have had votes secured via bribes to congress people.xxxv,xxxvi

Even before the impeachment was officially concluded, accelerated privatisations, decimation of workers rights and overhaul of the pension system, all demanded by Wall Street, were hastily set in motion by the interim Government.xxxvii Temer himself admitted in a speech to the Council of the Americas that the real reason for Dilma Rousseff's removal was her refusal to implement the capital-friendly "Bridge to the future" policy platform, which brought with it a 20 year constitutionally protected freeze on investment in public health & education, tying the hands of any near-future social democratic government. Science and Technology funding was also slashed.xxxviii,xxxix In 2017, with Rousseff gone, Attorney General Janot addressed the economic elite at Davos, and eulogised *Lava Jato*, which he described as "Pro-Market" – a clear political/ideological position that both its protagonists and ardent supporters insisted it did not have.xl

Whether by accident or design, Moro helped change the course of Brazil's political history. His continued pursuit of former President Lula – the single politican popular enough to reverse what Temer has done – on a flimsy charge without material evidence, which has been admonished by Brazilian legal scholars and the international legal community alike, now threatens democracy further, with the clear 2018 front-runner facing a decade in jail, with a dangerous precedent set.<u>xli</u> <u>xlii</u>

Whatever theoretical long-term advantages *Lava Jato* was supposed to bring, with Temer's Brazil institutionally and morally adrift, government decision making processes are increasingly captured with the unholy trinity of bribery, blackmail and violence.

Now imagine if you will that Moro was a Prosecutor-Judge (if such thing existed) from the United States and his training, fellowship and collaboration was with Russia. US media, and that of the Anglosphere at large, would go into meltdown.

The emergence of more evidence is inevitable, but it can already be established on the basis of what is available that despite denial and obfuscation, Sérgio Moro has, in collaboration with various wings of the US Government and its expanded apparatus, aided the removal of an elected President, convicted a former President, and future candidate – all of the same party – and with that significantly contributed to a change in Brazil's political direction, away from social democratic, mildly redistributive developmentalism, and towards discreet re-colonisation as authoritarian client state or neoliberal viceroyalty. This comes combined with a new US Military presence on Brazilian territory which was simply unthinkable just a few years ago.<u>xliii</u>

While transnationals scramble for its riches, delivered to them by an *entreguista* elite whom in his seminal <u>Open Veins of Latin America</u> Eduardo Galeano christened the "commission-agent bourgeoisie", ordinary Brazilians go about their daily business unaware that they are now akin to a population on the losing side of a kinetic war.

i The Atlantic Council. (2017, July 19). *Lessons From Brazil: Fighting Corruption Amid Political Turmoil*[video file]. Retrieved from https://youtu.be/rR5Yiz84b5c

ii Sankey, K.(2016, July 27). What Happened to the Pink Tide? *Jacobin*. Retrieved from https://www.jacobinmag.com/2016/07/pink-tide-latin-america-chavez-morales-capitalism-socialism/

iii Livingstone, G. (2010, November 18). The School of Latin America's Dictators. *The Guardian*. Retrieved from https://www.theguardian.com/commentisfree/cifamerica/2010/nov/18/us-military-usa

iv United States Government National Security Archives. (2001, March 2). *Public Diplomacy and Covert Propaganda: The Declassified Record of Ambassador Otto Juan Reich*. Retrieved from https://nsarchive2.gwu.edu/NSAEBB/NSAEBB40/

v C-SPAN. (2007, February 15). *Amb. Otto Reich on Corruption in Latin America* [video file]. Retrieved from https://www.youtube.com/watch?v=QThtmecq228

vi TeleSur. (2015, November 4). Today Marks the 10th Aniversary of the FTAA Defeat [video file]. Retrieved from https://www.youtube.com/watch?v=Qohoajtr2Gk

vii Pearson, T. (2011, March 8). US Feels Threatened by MERCOSUR Consolidation and Venezuela's 'Generosity' in the region. *Venezuela Analysis*. Retrieved from https://venezuelanalysis.com/news/6052

viii Locatelli, C. (2017, June 24). Moro, Lava Jato e Interesses dos EUA. *Jornalistas Livres*. Retreived from https://jornalggn.com.br/noticia/moro-lava-jato-e-interesses-dos-eua

ix Johnston, J. (2015, June 8). Why is the US Government still Hiding what it did to Brazil in 1998? *Center for Economic and Policy Research Americas Blog*. Retrieved from http://cepr.net/blogs/the-americas-blog/why-is-the-us-government-still-hiding-what-they-did-to-brazil-in-1998

x Moro, S. (2004, July-September). Considerações sobre a Operação Mani Pulite. *Direito Penal*. Retrieved from https://www.conjur.com.br/dl/artigo-moro-mani-pulite.pdf

xi Sachelli, O. (2012, August 29). Ci fu una regia occulta degli Usa dietro Mani pulite? Le rivelazioni dell'ex ambasciatore americano. *Il Giornale*. Retrieved from http://www.ilgiornale.it/news/interni/ci-fu-regia-occulta-degli-usa-dietro-mani-pulite-rivelazioni-833119.html

xii Bortolotti, B. (2005, August 11). Italy's Privatization Process and it's Implications for China. *Fondazione Eni Enrico Mattei*. Retrieved from http://ageconsearch.umn.edu/bitstream/12189/1/wp050118.pdf

xiii Freitas, S. (2006, May 9). OAB Desiste de Pedir Impeachment de Lula. *Folha de São Paulo*. Retrieved from https://www1.folha.uol.com.br/fsp/brasil/fc0905200604.htm

xiv Welcome to the Murky World of Kroll Inc- the Private CIA. (2005, June

25). *The Sydney Morning Herald.* Retrieved from https://www.smh.com.au/business/welcome-to-the-murky-world-of-kroll-inc-the-private-cia-20050625-gdlkpn.html

xv Alencar, K. (2006, May 29). Elo entre Kroll e CIA será investigado em inquérito da PF. *Folha de São Paulo.* Retrieved from https://www1.folha.uol.com.br/fsp/brasil/fc2905200604.htm

xvi Cuddehe, M. (2010, August 10). A Spy in the Jungle. *The Atlantic.* Retrieved from https://www.theatlantic.com/international/archive/2010/08/a-spy-in-the-jungle/60770/

xvii Nascimento, L. (2015, October 23). Deputada pede à PGR que Kroll devolva dinheiro recebido da CPI da Petrobras. *Agência Brasil.* Retrieved from http://agenciabrasil.ebc.com.br/politica/noticia/2015-10/deputada-pede-pgr-que-kroll-devolva-dinheiro-recebido-da-cpi-da-petrobras

xviii Rosa, A. (2017, April 12). Eduardo Cunha queria contratar a Kroll para tentar conter a Lava-Jato. *O Valor.* Retrieved from https://www.valor.com.br/politica/4935878/eduardo-cunha-queria-contratar-kroll-para-tentar-conter-lava-jato

xix Farrow, R. (2017, November 6). Harvey Weinstein's Army of Spies. *The New Yorker.* https://www.newyorker.com/news/news-desk/harvey-weinsteins-army-of-spies

xx Taylor, M. (2017, March 24). What US Policymakers can Learn From Brazil's Anticorruption Gains. *Council on Foreign Relations.* Retrieved from https://www.cfr.org/report/what-us-policymakers-can-learn-brazils-anticorruption-gains

xxi United States of America. Department of State. By Kubiske. (2009, October 30). Cable 09BRASILIA1282_a. Retrievied from https://wikileaks.org/plusd/cables/09BRASILIA1282_a.html

xxii US Department of State. (May 13, 2009). *Council of the Americas: Secretary Clinton* [video]. Retrieved from https://www.youtube.com/watch?v=Cdh5xRwNTEg

xxiii Hassan, G. (2004, June 4). Who is John Negroponte? *Counterpunch.* Retrieved from https://www.counterpunch.org/2004/06/04/who-is-john-negroponte/

xxiv C-Span 2. (2007, January 31). John Negroponte: Democracy is a Threat to America [Video]. Retrieved from https://www.youtube.com/watch?v=cK2wDEKP2JE

xxv Steve Inskeep. Interview with Barrack Obama (television interview, December 29, 2014). *NPR.* Retrieved from https://www.npr.org/2014/12/29/372485968/transcript-president-obamas-full-npr-interview

xxvi Quantos empregos custa a Lava Jato? (2017, March 27). *Carta Capital.* Retrieved from https://www.cartacapital.com.br/economia/quantos-empregos-custa-a-lava-jato

xxvii Petrobras Closes with Record Production 2016. (2017, January 14).

Panama Offshore. Retrieved from https://www.panoramaoffshore.com.br/
en/petrobras-fecha-2016-com-recorde-de-producao-2/

xxviii Militão, E. (2017, October 31). Estudos apontam perda de R$1 Tri em renuncia fiscal apos leião do pre-sal. *UOL*. Retrieved from https://
economia.uol.com.br/noticias/redacao/2017/10/31/estudos-apontam-perdas-
de-r-1-tri-em-renuncia-fiscal-com-leilao-do-pre-sal.htm

xxix Calgrao, F. (2013, October 22). Riquesa do pre-sal será passaporte para o futuro, diz Dilma. *UOL*. Retrieved from https://economia.uol.com.br/
noticias/redacao/2013/10/22/riqueza-do-pre-sal-sera-passaporte-para-o-
futuro-diz-dilma.htm

xxx Janowski, P. (2016, June 16). Wikileaks uncovers interim President Michel Temer as former US informant. *COHA*. Retrieved from http://
www.coha.org/wikileaks-uncovers-interim-president-temer-as-former-u-s-
informant/

xxxi Wikileaks Global Intelligence Files. (2013, February 13). Re: discussion – Rousseff is deathly ill [email communications]. Retrieved from https://
wikileaks.org/gifiles/docs/30/3020371_re-discussion-roussef-is-deathly-
ill-.html

xxxii Kerry, J. (2016, August 5). Remarks after meeting with Brazilian Foreign Minister José Serra. US Embassy and Consulate in Brazil [website]. Retrieved from https://br.usembassy.gov/remarks-meeting-brazilian-foreign-
minister-jose-serra/

xxxiii Weisbrot, M. (2016, April 22). Washington's dog-whistle diplomacy supports attempted coup in Brazil. *Huffington Post*. Retrieved from https://
www.huffingtonpost.com/mark-weisbrot/washingtons-dog-whistle-
d_b_9757652.html

xxxiv Kozloff, N. (2012, July 12). Behind the Paraguayan Coup. *Al Jazeera*. Retrieved from https://www.aljazeera.com/indepth/opinion/
2012/07/201278122117670811.html

xxxv Council on Foreign Relations. (2018, January 23). *Foreign Affairs Issues Launce with Former Vice President Joe Biden* [transcript]. Retrieved from https://www.cfr.org/event/foreign-affairs-issue-launch-former-vice-
president-joe-biden

xxxvi Cunha recebeu R$ 1 mi para 'comprar' votos do impeachment de Dilma, diz Funaro. (2017, October 14). Folha de São Paulo. Retreived from https://www1.folha.uol.com.br/poder/2017/10/1927138-cunha-recebeu-r-1-
mi-para-comprar-votos-do-impeachment-de-dilma-diz-funaro.shtml

xxxvii Mier, B. (2018, January 17). The rolling coup: how Michel Temer is turning Brazil into a banana republic. *New Socialist*. Retrieved from https://
newsocialist.org.uk/brazil-post-coup/

xxxviii Temer: impeachment occoreu porque Dilma recusou "Ponte para o Futuro". *Carta Capital*. Retrieved from https://www.cartacapital.com.br/
politica/temer-impeachment-ocorreu-porque-dilma-recusou-ponte-para-o-

Year of Lead

Part two

Lula, Political Prisoner

The Break From Democracy Opened the Door for Fascism

By Luciana Waclawovsky

On March 27, 2018, the second to last day of Lula's whistle stop tour of southern Brazil, two buses in his caravan were attacked with gunfire. One of the final buses in the convoy was full of journalists. Lula was in the convoy's first bus.

Violence against the convoy started in Rio Grande do Sul where a rally was met with stones, eggs and clubs, and blocked from proceeding in some towns. The situation was so extreme that in one town in Rio Grande do Sul, a supporter of Lula was horsewhipped while he was trying to walk towards an event where Lula was speaking.

The violent and barbaric images that circulated widely in the social media networks shocked the nation and sent a warning sign about the advanced level of hate speech that is underway.

For the historian and professor at Joaquim Venancio Polytechnic school, André Dantas, we are experiencing a rise of fascism. He notes that the number of groups that are using fascist language and political personalities that publicly adopt this narrative are growing in Brazil.

"In the classic fascist experiences, the general acceptance of hate speech proceeded the configuration of a fascist State. Today, we don't have this type of government in power, although public figures who adapt a fascist posture are present in the legislative and executive branches", he said.

During Lula's tour, which started on March 19, the omission of authorities in relation to the convoy, which included two ex-presidents of the Republic, was blatant. During a press conference on the night of March 27 after the buses had been shot at, Gleisi Hoffmann, national president of the Workers Party (PT) and a senator from Parana state, demanded action from local and national security authorities. All of them had been informed of the convoy's route.

"The violence against the convoy had been increasing and the authorities were informed about what was happening. Before the journey we sent a request to Brazilian Public Security Minister Raul Jungman explaining the route and asking for security support. We also sent the information to the Parana State Government and spoke with its Military Police Chief. The fact is that they did not provide any protection. The level of violence and hatred reached a point in which we need a public statement from the authorities to know what they think about everything that is happening. Will politics now become a wild west show in which people shoot at each other?"

In the opinion of Paraiba Federal University (UFPA) political science professor Rodrigo Freire, what happened is the result of the deterioration of Brazilian democracy, supported by the commercial media, the judiciary and the legislative branch to remove a legitimately elected Brazilian president. He says that the groups which attacked the convoy in the Southern region of the country are formed by privileged members of the upper middle class: ranchers and plantation owners who feed off of this daily hatred in the corporate news outlets.

"A Pandora's box is opening", he says. "For Brazilian democracy, the Pandora's box was the coup." "Now the *golpistas* can no longer control the hatred and it is transforming into fascism".

Historian André Dantas says that moments of deep economic and political crisis are fertile ground for the expression of class hatred, which intensifies most deeply among young members of the middle class. In this sense, he says that separatist movements like "the South is my nation" and national fronts calling for the return to military dictatorship are attracting followers and are becoming socially accepted in a manner that didn't previously exist.

> "There is no doubt that the intimidation of a character such as the ex-president is clearly fueled by class hatred because Lula effectively represents a discourse that the right wants to politically destroy through illegal means, ripping up the constitution in an attempt to block his candidacy. It is a strategy. Extreme right groups of fascists are using other tools, but the objective of class hatred is the same. They are distinct tactics used within the bourgeoisie."

Rodrigo Freire says that the scale of violence is serious and relies on the collaboration of politicians from various spheres of government. "There are several videos circulating in the social media of the convoy passing with people throwing eggs and rocks in front of police who do nothing. A Senator from Rio Grande do Sul state made a hate speech inciting violence against the rallies. We are not only talking about a political manifestation which is important to guarantee democracy," he said, "but one with participation from two Ex-Presidents of the Republic. The state is obligated to provide security, and this is not what we are seeing."

Freire says that city councilwoman Marielle Franco (PSOL-RJ), who fought for human rights and had a strong level of discourse in favor of women, Afro-Brazilians and favela residents was killed without having suffered any threats. "The signs are bad and the assassination of Marielle was a message to people who defend the objectives of the left. It shows that we are all, some more than others, exposed and insecure."

He said that the period of democracy which began with the 1988 Constitution was, in general, successful, as there was an expansion of rights and citizenship which we had never seen before in Brazil.

"It was a virtuous period which suffered a break in 2016 and since then we have been living in a period of de-democratization. We hope that the 2018 elections occur normally and that Lula will be able to run for office like all the other candidates and that, starting in 2019 this current state of exception will come to an end through the popular vote. But at the moment we are living in a transition towards dictatorship."

Lawfare and the Political Imprisonment of Luiz Inácio Lula da Silva: An interview with Valeska Martins

By Brian Mier

On July 8th, 2018, Brazil's 4th Regional Federal Court Chief Judge Rogerio Favreto ordered ex-President Luiz Inacio Lula da Silva's immediate release from prison.<u>i</u> From a vacation resort town where he was enjoying his holidays, Judge Sergio Moro, a lower court judge and hero to the Brazilian far right who has been working closely with the US Department of Justice for several years, immediately ordered the Federal Police to disobey the release order.<u>ii</u> It was just one more chapter in a Kafkaesque process which has resulted in the imprisonment of the center-left former president on frivolous charges with no material evidence. And it has happened during an election year in which Lula is the undisputed front-runner for the presidency, despite being held in solitary confinement and barred from giving interviews for the past three months.<u>iii</u>

During a press conference at the Geneva Press Club on July 3, British barrister and Queen's Counsel Geoffrey Robertson and Lula's defense lawyer Valeska Texeira Martins revealed that, although the Brazilian government recently requested the UN Human Rights Committee to halt its investigation into ex-President Lula's arrest, it was rejected and the investigation is moving forwards.<u>iv</u>

The UNHRC is looking at whether Lula was denied his

right to a fair trial with an impartial judge. Issues that contributed to the Committee's decision to investigate the case include the fact that Judge Sergio Moro admitted to breaking the law by illegally wiretapping Lula's defense lawyers but was allowed to continue presiding over his own investigation. The Committee is also investigating whether Lula's political right to campaign is being denied, as other candidates are publicly criticizing him and he is not being allowed to respond.

Meanwhile, the Anglo press has continually published misinformation about Lula's case, have given misinformation as to why he is in jail, and have not clarified the fact that he is officially registered by the PT Party as its pre-candidate for the presidency.

Lula's defense lawyer, Valeska Martins contends that Lula is victim of a political persecution masked in legal processes which she calls Lawfare. In the following interview, she explains why.

What is Lawfare?

The law can destroy reputations, it can destroy assets, it can destroy freedom and it can end people's lives. So when it is misused it is extremely violent. Lawfare is the abuse and misuse of the law in a violent manner to conduct political persecution. We are able to identify all of the dimensions, tactics, and strategies typically used in Lawfare in the persecution of Lula. The prosecutors did not produce one single piece of evidence or one single logical accusation against him, even on that day when they invited all the mainstream media outlets to a hotel and made that sensationalist PowerPoint presentation with the clear intention of achieving a political goal. The fact is that making someone a defendant or putting him under criminal investigation is already a form of punishment. Basically it is a battle, a legal war with the goal of dehumanizing and defaming a political enemy. So, when people say we are politicizing the defense, this is a lie because, in reality, this is a technical diagnosis. When we understand that, technically speaking, there is no material evidence, that the accusations are illogical, that the legal arguments are misrepresented, we come to the unequivocal conclusion that we are dealing with a process of Lawfare.

Do you think that the foreign journalists understood the judgment against Lula?

It is easy to get lost in the details and just repeat what the prosecutors say, ignoring the defense, or to get stuck in a 'he said she said,' because the language is very technical. This causes a huge barrier for people who are trying to understand how this political persecution is taking place. The biggest problem with Lawfare is the following: a political fight is transferred into the legal realm so the only people who understand what is happening are lawyers and judges. Due to the technical nature of legal jargon, reporters have problems making any kind of critical analysis. It is literally lost in the translation.

When Lula was arrested on April 7th, most English language newspapers that covered the story falsely insinuated that his arrest was connected to a bribery scheme involving Petrobras.v Although prosecutors mentioned this to the press in 2016, this charge was not included in Lula's judgement, which condemns him for

It is completely unequal. We have been holding national and international press conferences for two years now, since the beginning of the case. We have carefully explained and shown all of the material evidence and all of the testimonies and explained, in minute detail, everything that enables us to show former President Lula's innocence beyond the shadow of a doubt. The fact is that the foreign press ignored us and constantly repeated an accusation that was made long ago, in September 2016. After that accusation was made there was a trial. During the trial prosecutors were unable to prove that Lula committed one single act of corruption. This is why the sentence convicts him for 'undetermined acts'. This alone is something that you would think would draw the attention of the international press, because no other country in the world convicts people for 'undetermined acts'. They are unable to explain what the act of corruption was. In relation to Petrobras, we have continually repeated the fact that Judge Sergio Moro himself admitted, in his decision regarding the motion for clarification, that he never said or accused former President Lula of receiving any illicit funds from Petrobras. This statement should annul the Thirteenth Court's jurisdiction over the case and the entire case should be dismissed. When you have a trial in a court that has no jurisdiction over it, the case is dismissed. Another reason why there is no "Petrobras connection" to Lula's arrest is that there are no acts of corruption – he wasn't convicted for corruption, he was convicted for undetermined acts. In relation to the apartment, they were unable to prove ownership and they even speak of an "attribution" – a concept which does not exist in legal terms. There is no such thing as the "attribution" of an apartment in Brazilian law. So I wish that the press would start acting more critically and conduct critical analysis of the facts surrounding the case. After all, the facts overturn any and all accusations of money laundering and corruption against former President Lula, which in turn transforms this entire proceeding into an unfair trial. Consequently, they shouldn't have the authority to put him in jail or bar him from running in the elections.

Are they showing any more fairness, in your opinion, in the way they are writing about the new accusations against Lula?

It is the same *modus operandi* and this is a common Lawfare tactic: the prosecution presents so many allegations and convoluted charges against a political rival that it becomes difficult for journalists to address or even understand them. The new charges are related to the building where the Lula Institute operates and Lula's frequent use of a country house and they are using the same methodology from the previous case.

There is a huge legal irregularity in all of the *Lava Jato* cases involving Odebrecht Engineering Company: the Company's MyWebDay accounting software system and the way Sergio Moro's task force is using it. At first the prosecutors said they didn't have the system, then they said they had it, then they said they didn't have it. Finally, they said they were "recreating" what was in the system and were making it publicly available. This is when we discovered that they had created the entire system themselves and that it was not the original system used by Odebrecht. They created it with different security parameters, opened it in places where it shouldn't have been opened without taking security measures and new archives may have been inserted into or deleted from it. The *Lava Jato* task force are using this system as the basis for all of their accusations, not only in Brazil but across Latin America and Africa. The system has obviously been corrupted but journalists, including foreign ones, are not asking any questions about it. They are also using Excel spread sheets in the trials. Where do they come from? Are they reliable? How can they use these Excel spreadsheets in countries like Brazil, Ecuador and Peru to convict people for crimes without explaining to anyone where they come from? The defense teams from all of the different cases have been explaining this all along in regular press conferences, so it seems like there hasn't been much desire on the part of journalists to establish any kind of certainty related to these cases. Instead, they seem to just repeat everything the prosecutors say at face value.

Odebrecht Engineering Company was one of the largest employers in Brazil when the **Lava Jato** *investigation froze its operations in 2015, causing around 500,000 immediate layoffs in the construction industry. This had a negative effect on the Brazilian economy. Why do you think that Odebrecht was not treated as too big to fail, like Goldman Sachs and Volkswagen were when executives in those companies were embroiled in mega-corruption scandals? Why was the approach in Brazil* *different from the US and Germany?*

It is hard to explain the reasons behind this different approach but, without a doubt, the company should have been kept in full operational mode and the jobs should have been preserved. If the executives did anything illicit, they should be punished. This is what every civilized country around the world would do with a company that is as strategic for its economy as Odebrecht was for Brazil. After all, it was not only important in the engineering and defense industries, but it held a 50% share in the petrochemical giant Braskem which will now also be dismantled and alienated. In other words, they are dismantling a company that was an internationally competitive, national symbol. Regardless of who committed any illicit acts, the company itself should not have been punished in this manner, without a doubt. We can see that there are ulterior motives behind the way these corruption accusations are being used to dismantle certain companies that are strategic for Brazil. I think we will have to talk more about this in the future when this story is really unveiled. Brazilians should demand an explanation from the Government for why they are dismantling these companies. Even if the judiciary is to blame and has created this situation, the Government should be treating these companies as too big to fail, as the US does. Today we have some answers but we continue to have a lot more questions about the *Lava Jato* investigation and what its real goals were.

What are some of these questions?

For example, regarding the informal cooperation between the US Department of Justice and Brazilian public prosecutors, what evidence was exchanged? What was its role in building the case and convicting President Lula, which American prosecutors spoke about in 2017 at the Atlantic Council?<u>vi</u> I think we need to understand this. Brazil needs to understand more about this informal cooperation which has been happening since the beginning of *Lava Jato*.

Another question is why the *Lava Jato* investigation is allowed to operate unlawfully. It is an operation that is, exceptionally, not required to comply with general regulations. *Lava Jato* has extensively violated peoples' human rights and the task force engages in illegal behavior without any fear of reprisal or suspension. For example, a total of 227 bench warrants were issued. These are 227 testimonies that were illegally and unconstitutionally taken by force. So what is happening to these 227 people? These were 227 acts of violence. The police and the prosecutors pulled these people out of their houses at 6 AM to give depositions that they were not legally obliged to make.

In a recent article Tacla Duran, who is a former lawyer from Odebrecht, accuses the *Lava Jato* task force of excluding or destroying evidence beneficial to the defense.<u>vii</u>

In the United States this is a violation of the Brady Rules. US Department of Justice officials have been caught before violating Brady Rules in the United States. Do you think that, if this really happened, the idea to destroy evidence beneficial to the defense came from the Americans in the DOJ?<u>viii</u>

Regarding what happened in the United States, I'm not

familiar with those cases. I think that Tacla Duran can and should be heard as a witness in the case against former President Lula. He talks about the destruction of evidence and explains how the MyWebDay system information is not trustworthy and how it should not be used as evidence in any legal proceeding related to Odebrecht. What we see in our case are obstacles to requesting evidence. We requested a forensic expert report in order to follow the money in Lula's case. It would serve as evidence for the defense because it would show no connection between Petrobras and any asset or monetary value in any of his bank accounts. So we requested this forensic report and it was denied. When we found out about the bonds that had been issued and the fiduciary assignment agreement, which would definitely explain the ownership of the apartment, we specifically requested these documents to be included in the case files. They would prove the president's innocence once and for all. This was also denied. So we have serious problems obtaining key evidence. We don't have a Discovery system here in Brazil like you have in the United States, so obtaining exculpatory evidence is practically impossible if you don't have an impartial prosecution. The judge has the power to deny access depending on what you request. Another challenge for us has been to find out exactly what we have to request. We discovered a large amount of evidence on our own through due diligence in the Notary Public offices, but it was all completely ignored by the court. The evidence was not addressed in the judgment of conviction. It was simply ignored. We definitely see that exculpatory pieces of evidence have been hidden in our case, something which is a violation of the Brady Principle in the United States. This is exactly what we see in the case regarding the beach apartment, where the Federal Police and Federal Prosecutors conducting the investigation do not bring the exculpatory evidence into the files, seriously harming the defense. Concerning Odebrecht, we were not allowed to access the evidence through full and unrestricted access to Odebrecht's systems. Even in the hearings, we aren't allowed to ask questions to the witnesses according to the logical objectives of the defense. Some of our questions were denied for no reason, with no justification, which violates the principle of the equality of arms. This lack of equal treatment between the defense and the prosecution and the lack of rules, including procedural ones, seriously compromises the work of the defense, not only Lula's but of any defendants' in Brazil.

A recent news story came out saying that the* Lava Jato *prosecution team wiretapped your office phones. Is this a crime in Brazil?

It is a crime in Brazil and anywhere in the world. This is what happened: in 2016 they bugged our central telephone line, which relays the conversations of 25 lawyers, our office staff and our clients. When the phone company found this out they sent Judge Moro a notice and he ignored it. Then the telephone company sent Judge Moro a second notice and, once again, he ignored it. When this went public back in 2016, Sergio Moro was admonished by the Supreme Court for illegally tapping and leaking confidential phone conversations between lawyers and clients. Moro said it had been a mistake and that he would destroy the audio files if the procedures returned to his jurisdiction. Two years later, when the case returned to his jurisdiction, we were surprised by the fact that he deliberately gave access to all the audio files for all of the defendants' lawyers, including our phone calls. I believe that audio files of 411 of our conversations were made available. We fought for them to be destroyed because they contained confidential information about our lawyers, other employees and our clients. To our surprise, when we sent a lawyer over to listen to the files and verify what was in them, he found a chart that a Federal Agent had used, based on our phone conversations, to map out every potential move that would be made by the defense. For example, "Cristiano Martins spoke with the lawyer Nilo Batista and they decided that if X happens they will file a petition for *habeas corpus*. If Y happens they will file a petition for a writ of mandamus." They mapped out Lula's defense so that they could anticipate all of its moves. There is no precedent like this in the world. There is no other precedent like this in any civilized country. There is a case in Spain where a judge wire tapped a lawyer and he was suspended for 11 years. The idea that they were allowed to monitor the defense through its central phone line and anticipate its strategy by mapping out its moves – this is something that really needs to be explained and somebody needs to held accountable for it. The *Lava Jato* task force has to explain how this type of monitoring, which enables them to anticipate every move of the defense, can be acceptable in a democracy. No State that operates according to the rule of law allows this type of behavior. You do not abide by the rule of law when this type of defense rights violation is allowed to happen. We complained about this to the United Nations and the Brazilian Bar Association (OAB) and we are waiting for reparation. There are many examples of the *Lava Jato* team breaking the law. Some of them really stand out but they are all equally violent and crass.

Why wasn't Judge Moro pulled off the case if he admitted he broke the law?

In March 2016 the story broke and the audio recordings [between President Dilma Rousseff and Lula] were released. At that time, 19 lawyers filed a complaint against Judge Moro in the 4th Federal Regional Court (TRF-4) and there was that famous, 13-1 judgment, in which they ruled that Judge Sergio Moro, due to the exceptionalism of the *Lava Jato* case, did not have to follow the general rules. Therefore, the court authorized the *Lava Jato* task force to operate outside of the law, as a trial of exception. The *Lava Jato* operation was authorized by the TRF-4 to operate above the law. Raul Zaffaroni, the famous Argentinian legal scholar and Inter-American Human Rights Court Judge, describes this decision by the TRF-4 as an international legal scandal. There is no other precedent in the world in which a court has allowed a prosecutor/judge to act illegally or above the law. And the ruling was made by thirteen judges to one.

What do you think will happen to Lula now? Some people say that he could be released soon. Do you think they will keep him in jail until after the elections?

He should not even be in jail. The TRF-4 used a precedent to automatically arrest Lula after the second appeal. The precedent they cited, however, is from a Supreme Court ruling which does not mandate automatic imprisonment. It speaks of the "possibility of imprisonment" after the second appeal is denied, only if it is justified. In that case we filed a *habeas corpus* against this order with the Superior Justice Court and, afterwards, the Federal Supreme Court. We had 10 justices discussing the general concept of the possibility of arresting someone after the second appeal but nobody was talking about the actual *habeas corpus*. [Supreme Court Minister] Rosa Weber was the only justice who addressed the actual *habeas corpus*. So there was a distortion in the judgment and we have appealed to have it reanalyzed. Regardless, the arrest warrant was issued before we had exhausted all legal remedies before the Appellate Court (TRF4). We understand that Lula's imprisonment was absolutely arbitrary. Furthermore, his arrest is having nefarious consequences for the Nation. A report came out in the press the other day stating that, in São Paulo alone, 14,000 people have now been arrested because of the ruling on ex-President Lula which enabled imprisonment after the second appeal is denied. Last week we filed two precautionary measures so that a stay motion could be imposed on the special appeals that we filed with the Superior Justice Court and the Federal Supreme Court. The special appeals aim to reanalyze the constitutional violations that occurred during the prosecution. We are asking the Supreme Justice Court to consider the measure due to the clear violations of federal laws, and the Federal Supreme Court to consider the measure as result of the clear and gross violations of Lula´s constitutional guarantees. We are hopeful because this procedure was full of irregularities from start to finish and the proof of innocence is extremely blatant. All of the evidence points to ex-President Lula's innocence. Regarding his right to run for office, our Constitution speaks of barring political rights only after all of the appeals processes have been denied and there is a final ruling. There is another law, called ficha limpa which could be used to justify denying his rights. I will not go into whether it is constitutional or not but in any event all international treaties which speak of barring people from running for office always speak of removal of political rights only if preceded by a fair, independent and impartial trial. It is clear that ex-President Lula did not have a fair, impartial and independent trial. This is why we filed a complaint to the UN Human Rights Committee, which functions as a World Court for many nations [like Brazil, which signed the Optional Protocol] and this is why it has agreed to analyze the case and rule on whether Lula can run for office. So now we have a situation in Brazil in which if they deny Lula's political rights through this unfair process and he is not allowed to participate in the elections, a World Court may rule that the electoral front-runner was illegally removed. It is a very worrying situation for the legitimacy of democracy in Brazil. His imprisonment is already violating his right to campaign. All of the other candidates are traveling around Brazil, doing interviews. Some of them are making false accusations against Lula and he is not being given the right to defend himself.

If he were guilty of anything, he would also deserve a fair trial, but President Lula is the victim of injustice because there is not one piece of material evidence against him. But when everyone says there is no proof its wrong. We on the defense don't say that there is no proof because we proved that he is innocent. The existing material evidence proves his innocence. So we have a lot of hope and we will continue fighting until justice is made so that his freedom is decreed and so that he can run for office, which is his right.

i Luiz Inácio Lula da Silva.(2018, July 8). *TRF4 determina fim de prisão illegal de Lula* [press release]. Retrieved from https://lula.com.br/trf4-determina-fim-de-prisao-ilegal-de-lula/

ii Stokes, P and Lloyd, Z. (2017, December 12). 40 Years Of FCPA: Cross-Border Efforts And Growing Risk. *Law 360*. Retrieved from https://www.gibsondunn.com/wp-content/uploads/2017/12/Stokes-40-Years-Of-FCPA-Cross-Border-Efforts-And-Growing-Risk-Law360-12-12-2017.pdf

iii Pesquisa de Ibope: Lula 37%; Bolsonaro 18%; Marina 6%; Ciro 5%; Alckmin 5%. (2018, August 20). *Globo*. Retrieved from https://g1.globo.com/politica/eleicoes/2018/noticia/2018/08/20/pesquisa-ibope-lula-37-bolsonaro-18-marina-6-ciro-5-alckmin-5.ghtml

iv Geneva Press Club. (2018, July 5). *Geoffrey Robertson* [video]. Retrieved from https://youtu.be/YMjZ7xOK904

v *Cowie, S. (2018, April 3). Brazil court to rule on former President Lula's jail term. The Guardian.* Retrieved from https://www.theguardian.com/world/2018/apr/03/brazil-supreme-court-luiz-inacio-lula-da-silva

vi The Atlantic Council. (2017, July 19). *Lessons From Brazil: Fighting Corruption Amid Political Turmoil*[video file]. Retrieved from https://youtu.be/rR5Yiz84b5c

vii Duran, T. (2018, June 14). *Há quatro anos, poder paralelo da "lava jato" influi na política e na economia do país. Conjur.* Retrieved from https://www.conjur.com.br/2018-jun-14/ricardo-tacla-duran-poder-paralelo-lava-jato

viii *National Association of Criminal Defense Lawyers. (2012, March 15). Misconduct Report on Ted Stevens Prosecution: 'Systematic Concealment of Exculpatory Evidence' [press release]. Retrieved from https://www.nacdl.org/NewsReleases.aspx?id=23788&libID=23757*

The attack on Lula and threats to Brazil's democracy

By Alfredo Saad Filho

Luiz Inacio Lula da Silva was the most influential trade union leader in Brazil in the 1970s and the most important leader of what was known as the new unions that emerged under the military dictatorship. The new unions were centered on the durable consumer goods industries that had been building in the previous 20 years, and in the state owned enterprises and the state sector. Between the late 1970s and the early 1980s, Lula led some of the largest and most influential workers strikes in Brazilian history. He was also the leading founder and then president of the Brazilian Workers Party, the PT, in the early 1980s. Interestingly and despite the dominant media discourse and image back then as well as now, Lula was never a socialist of any description. He was always a social democrat, always a trade unionist and always a negotiator. And he is impressively good at reaching agreements across economic and political divides and this has been essential for his later trajectory.

As the main leader of the PT Lula fought and lost three presidential elections in 1989, 1994 and 1998. Each time the PT fought a more moderate campaign, trying to appeal more and more to the political center and to the middle class. By the time of the elections in 2002, Lula and the PT put together a very broad coalition. This coalition included formal sector workers in the lower sectors of the civil service which was the traditional base of support of the PT, plus chunks of the middle class. It also included a large chunk of the internal bourgeoisie which is a fraction of capital that is not very closely connected to finance or international capital. They were represented in that program by Vice President José Alencar, a leader of the textile industry and a politician of the center right – a nationalist. During 2002 Lula was rising in the opinion polls and that created a lot of turbulence in the exchange rate and the market for the domestic public debt. This led Lula to create a document that became known as the Letter to the Brazilian People, four months before the election. The letter essentially committed his administration to maintaining neoliberal economic policies, those policies that had been imposed by then President Fernando Henrique Cardoso of the PSDB, the main rival of the PT back then as well as now. The letter was effective. Lula was elected and he appointed as President of the Central Bank a very prominent international banker and member of the PSDB, Henrique Mierelles. Mierelles would then become Minister of Finance after the coup – the Minister of Finance under Michel Temer – but this was all in the very distant future. In appointing Mierelles, Lula was trying to negotiate an agreement with finance, with international capital and with the Brazilian elite. He would not change macroeconomic policy but he wanted to be able to do some social policies, he wanted to be able to distribute income at the margin, and he wanted to be able to reduce poverty. This is what Lula's first administration tried to do until reality interfered in two ways.

First Lula's administration discovered that neoliberal macroeconomic policies, fiscal austerity, high interest rates, inflation targets, an independent central bank, free international flows of capital, and so on, are incompatible with rapid economic growth. You just can't have growth with these policies.

Second, his administration also discovered that in Brazil political moderation does not bring peace. The problem for the PT was not that the government failed to deliver growth in the beginning of the 2000s, Cardoso also failed to deliver growth and of course Michel Temer is failing right now. Growth is not a problem for the political right in Brazil. The problem was that the mainstream media, the judiciary, the upper middle class and the financial elite resented their dislocation from the State and from the inner circle of power. And so, they decided to destroy Lula. And to do this, in 2005 they invented the *Mensalão* scandal, a story about the PT paying a monthly stipend for Deputies and Senators to vote for the government in Congress. And this was never proven. But the scandals started and it showed that it can be very difficult to prove that you did not do something, especially if it didn't happen but the media and the courts are determined to show that you did it. The *Mensalão* tarnished the image of the PT, nearly led to Lula's impeachment and destroyed Finance Minister Antonio Palocci and José Dirceu, the chief strategist of the PT and other party leaders as well. Lula managed to recover only because of his support among the poor and among the industrial elite in the country.

Lula was reelected in 2006, and then proceeded to implement much bolder, much more interesting economic policies in line with this new base of support. He was also very very fortunate because Brazil was riding on a global prosperity brought by the commodities boom in the early and mid 2000s. The economy was growing faster and the government had money, money to raise the minimum wage to raise pensions, to raise transfers and benefits to implement more ambitious social policies, to introduce bolder industrial policies and to support what they called "the National Champions". This was a selected group of large companies that would be following the example of Japanese and South Korean conglomerates and then drive growth, innovation and exports. These were firms like Petrobras in oil, Odebrecht in construction, JBS in foods, OI in telecoms and etc. It is no coincidence these are exactly the firms that the *Lava Jato* investigation and the coup against the PT have been trying to destroy. The policies implemented by the second Lula administration were successful and Brazil saw very significant improvements in employment creation, formalization of labor, distribution of income, education and social indicators. Lula's popularity rose to unprecedented levels and when he stepped down from the presidency in 2010 his approval ratings were above 80%. He was the most popular politician in republican history in Brazil.

Dilma Rousseff, Lula's chosen successor, was not so fortunate. The World economy had been in crisis since 2008 and Brazil was hit heavily from 2011. Dilma Rousseff could not keep the economy going and she could not keep her coalition together. The government essentially collapsed. The story of the PT administrations was that under favorable economic conditions and under favorable political circumstances they could deliver a virtuous circle of growth with political stability and gains in distribution. But those administrations were limited. They were limited in five ways.

The first is that they were attached to neoliberal policies

and this was made to guarantee credibility with capital, but credibility is not a symbolic attribute. Credibility in this case is a consequence of the limitations that neoliberal policies impose against distribution of income and against social inclusion. When Lula and Dilma tried to change those policies the media and the economic elite turned against them.

Second, the moment was limited because high interest rates and a currency that was valued too high meant that any income growth at home would leak abroad in the form of higher imports. The consequence was deindustrialization in Brazil, the loss of jobs, the re-primorization of the economy and the growth of agribusiness at the expense of industry. The economy created millions of jobs but they were bad jobs and those jobs did not correspond to the demands of the middle class and they did not correspond to the aspirations of the rising working class that was now, because of Lula's policies, going to university. There were no jobs for them.

Third, lack of investment and weak industrial policy contributed to a productivity gap that was intractable in the country and the government was unable to upgrade the infrastructure. They were unable to catch up with the advanced Western economies, then they were unable to keep up with the rising East Asian economies, and then they were unable to accompany China. Brazil is now locked underneath all these countries in the international division of labor and for this reason alone there is no prospect of sustained economic growth in the country for the coming years, maybe the next generation.

Fourth, the economy suffered because of the deterioration

of the global economic environment after the crisis and the impact of quantitative easing in the advanced economies. Brazil simply did not have a way to neutralize that. If you are locked underneath much larger, much richer and much more dynamic economies you get all the weight of their adjustments and you can't adjust yourself.

Finally, the PT was committed to political stability but stability depended on the ability of the administrations led by the PT to deliver economic gains to almost everyone, which was possible only in times of global prosperity.

Eventually policy mistakes, an adverse global environment, the economic slowdown, the strength of the opposition and a succession of corruption scandals- all of them planned and organized – paralyzed the government. Dilma Rousseff was overwhelmed by what I like to call an alliance of privilege, including the social groups at the top of society, and she was overthrown by a civilian judicial coup in 2016. Since then, the administration, led by Michel Temer, has been restoring orthodox neoliberalism through severe fiscal contraction, a huge attack on labor and a dismantling of the skeletal welfare state that exists in Brazil. The income and employment gains that had been achieved under the PT have evaporated by now. Also worrying is that the far right has recovered a mass base in the country for the first time since the early 1960s. Despite all this and perhaps because of it, Lula remains the most popular politician in Brazil. He leads all the opinion polls as a potential candidate for the presidential elections scheduled for this October so preventing his election has become the priority for the coup now, and the priority for several judges and public prosecutors and the almost entire mainstream media in the country. So we find now that Lula is a political prisoner in Brazil and Lula must be supported and he must be defended because of who he is and because of what he means for Brazil.

In contrast with most people in Michel Temer's inner circle including Temer himself, Lula was never caught with stolen money, he was never caught with illegal bank accounts, he was never proven guilty of corruption or anything else. He's not a rich man. He was never caught on tape suggesting that somebody should be killed. All this is on Temer and his friends. Lula is innocent of all that. His crime was to be a worker and a political leader in an elitist country. His crime was to be popular in a country of awful politicians. His crime was to be an outsider from the elites who had governed the country for 500 years and because of that Lula and Dilma were presumed guilty and were punished despite the absence of proof while politicians in power now are innocent despite the evidence of guilt.

What is happening in Brazil is scandalous. It is scandalous to politicize justice in this way. It is scandalous to have the US government guiding policy and the judicial prosecution of Lula. It is scandalous to have the judicial process turned into a spectacle for TV. It is scandalous to invite the military back into politics. Brazil is rolling back to the 1950s now. The conspiracy of the elite has turned Brazil into a banana republic. The challenge now is the challenge to confront the coup. The challenge is to rebuild a democratic movement that will clean up the political system, that will clean up the judiciary, that will reform the media, that will put the media, the judicial system and the State at the service of political freedom, at the service of legal equality and at the service of substantive democracy. This is the challenge that we have to confront now.

This speech at SOAS, University of London, was transcribed and edited for readability by Brian Mier

Why we don't give up on Lula's candidacy

By Gleisi Hoffmann

Lula is innocent. We know about his life and how it is dedicated to the Brazilian people. And we know the faults, failures and arbitrary elements of the legal process which condemned him. Police, public prosecutors and biased judges acted with political motives, in collaboration with *Rede Globo* and the big media companies, to remove Lula from the electoral process. Lula was imprisoned in a rushed and illegal procedure, before his appeals process had finished. It was a decision that will definitely be annulled in the near future.

Lula carries with him the hope and confidence of the most expressive portion of the Brazilian people, who want to vote for their greatest leader this October, despite the persecution and his arbitrary imprisonment. The vast majority of the population knows that the haste to arrest Lula served the needs of his political opponents, who do not accept the electoral victories of the PT.

This perception is confirmed by all serious, quantitative and qualitative studies. The majority of people interviewed believe that the arbitrary imprisonment serves the needs of the powerful, who want to gain more for themselves without Lula in the government. The sectors of the judiciary are playing the game of Lula's adversaries and want to appear important. And the media spends too much time attacking Lula and only shows one side.

Lula's supporters, who are a wide majority in all polls, hope that PT and its directors will defend him and guarantee the viability of his candidacy to fill the political hole that exists without him, in an election that is happening in such a difficult and troubled moment in the life of the Nation.

The imprisonment of Lula has not changed, in any way, the right of the PT to register his candidacy on August 15. Whatever happens, there is no legal way to defer Lula's candidacy in advance, contrary to what the *Globo* pundits are saying.

Even a supposed provisional act of ineligibility can be reversed at any time, according to the law and precedents in the electoral courts and the Supreme Court, even after the election. This is what guarantees Lula's right to be a candidate, according to the opinion of electoral law specialist and legal scholar Luiz Fernando Casagrande Pereira. It is an opinion which, to date, has not been disputed.

If Lula is innocent, if the majority of the people want to vote for him, if the Constitution guarantees his political rights, why would we not present him as our candidate? Not doing so would be playing the game of his tormentors, who want an election without Lula and are trying, through this maneuver, to give an air of democratic normality to a dispute that would be flawed by the absence of Brazil's greatest popular leader.

It will not be us, the PT, who will hand over and give up on our leader!

And for those who try to anticipate a supposed ineligibility, mentioning the *Ficha Limpa* (clean slate) law, observe Article 26 C and its legal precedents. Whenever any plausible motion is filed against a conviction, ineligibility has to be suspended. Recently Lula's defense filed motions in the Federal Supreme Court and the Federal Supreme Justice Courts against the decision of the 4th Federal Regional Court. Even those who believe the decision of the 4th Court is defensible recognize that Lula's motions present legally plausible theses.

We know the political and historic responsibility that we have to the Nation. For this reason, we will continue with Lula's candidacy to the end. The PT has always known to walk the road together with the people, and it won't be at this moment that we will orient ourselves on evaluations made from outsiders.

Lula is much greater than the prison that is holding him, as a human being and a leader. After 30 days in prison Lula continues present on the national political scene. They have not been able to remove him from the day to day events of the country, or normalize his imprisonment or make him invisible.

We respect and recognize the legitimate rights of all other candidates, mainly those of the left and center left, with whom we maintain permanent dialogue. We will be together, without a doubt, to the end of the electoral process. But due to his experience, his legacy, and popular opinion, it is Lula who will peacefully fix this country and restore the dignity of the Brazilian people.

Translated by Brian Mier.

Chapter Nine - Lula, Political Prisoner

Celso Amorim on Lula's political imprisonment

Part two of an interview with Brian Mier

Lula was arrested 38 days ago on charges with no material evidence. Do you think there are going to be free elections this year?

I took the initiative of launching a manifesto called "Elections without Lula are a fraud". It is a manifesto that was signed by many intellectuals in the United States, by people like Noam Chomsky, by many other intellectuals in Europe, by Nobel Prize Laureates, by ex-Presidents and ex-Prime Ministers. The polls show that the candidate favored by the Brazilian people is Lula, by far. He wins in all scenarios in the second round, and in the first round he has twice as many votes as the second place candidate. He is certainly the one who is preferred by the people. So I think that all our efforts should begin towards making it possible for Lula to be a candidate. I know it's an uphill battle, especially from the judicial point of view because this didn't happen all at once. It is a process that went through the impeachment of president Dilma but went all the way, focusing on Lula. Just this week Judge Moro- it's an incredible thing even from the point of view of appearances – the man who conducted the investigation and convicted Lula, is receiving a prize in the Brazilian-American Chamber of Commerce. Is that a coincidence? I don't know. In politics I don't believe in coincidences, everything is related somehow. So I think this is the most telling fact and the most telling image of what is happening now in relation to Brazil. The Judge is being rewarded for the good service he made. I'm not saying that he got money or anything like that but he is being recognized as the man of the year because he was able to put Lula in prison. In Latin there is an expression, *et quid prodest*, 'who profits from it'. So I think the prize gives the answer.

Some outlets in the American and English media are saying that Guilherme Boulos is the heir to Lula even though he is only polling at 0.5%. What will happen if Lula is not allowed to run?

Well I think this is still speculation. Of course it is important in politics to speculate, but I think we have to focus on the task of the moment. The task of the moment is still trying to have Lula run and starting his campaign. There is no law that prevents him from campaigning. Although physically he is in prison, he is an idea, he's an image and it's very interesting that with him in prison he still has twice as much support as the second place candidate. It is almost unheard of. If you think of similar examples they have to do with colonial or semi-colonial situations like South Africa or India in the times of Gandhi. Lula is a unique case.

Can you think of any Western democracy in which someone in prison, who has been in prison for 5 weeks now, was ever, by far, the most preferred candidate of the people? I think this is something that has to come through and be understood even by the judges even if they are formally following what the law prescribes. This goes totally against the central idea of democracy, which is people's sovereignty. Sovereignty has two faces. We spoke a lot about it externally, the sovereignty which is preventing other countries or other nations or other centers of power from dominating your country. But there is the internal face of sovereignty, which is the fact that the government has to reflect what the people want. That is the principal that Jean Jacques Rousseau established of the people's sovereignty. And what is happening in Brazil is a frontal attack against people's sovereignty. I hope at some point, because there are still some stages to go, even people in the judiciary who have been negative or hesitant may see that this is the best thing for Brazil, irrespective even of some particular interests. Lula is not actually a firebrand revolutionary. He wants reform, he wants to have a society that is more equal in which Afro-Brazilians and women are all treated appropriately and have equal opportunities but he is not someone who wants to destroy private property. He showed that.

So I hope people will see that, and see that the best solution is to free Lula – it's difficult, you may think that I am too idealistic but anyway maybe I am – and to allow him to run for office. And then of course if someone else wins, OK. But I think he will win.

Lula Must Be Allowed To Run For President: An Interview With UN Human Rights Committtee Vice President Sarah Cleveland

By Brian Mier

On the two year anniversary of the coup against Dilma Rousseff, on August 31, 2018, the Brazilian Supreme Electoral Court (TSE) disqualified Luiz Inácio Lula da Silva's candidacy for the presidency. Like so many measures taken by Brazil's unelected, elite and conservative judiciary, since illegitimate president Michel Temer took office and increased their salaries by 41%, the TSE's move literally broke the law. On August 17th, the UN Human Rights Committee issued a ruling that demanded that the Brazilian government allow Lula to run for the presidency. Brazilian Law MP 311, which was ratified by Congress in 2009, declares all rulings by the UN Human Rights Committee as legally binding in Brazil. Therefore, in barring Lula's candidacy, the TSE broke both International and Brazilian law.

On the eve of TSE's historic ruling of exception, I interviewed UN Human Rights Committee Vice President Sarah Cleveland about the repercussions of a possible lack of adherence to the UN order by the Brazilian government, for a web TV program on the Brazilian news channel Brazil 247. The following transcripts of our conversation have been edited for readability:

It seems like most of the cases reviewed by the UN Human Rights Committee are more related to things like torture, violence and things like that, but this case seems unique because its dealing with an ex-president of one of the largest nations in the world. What prompted you guys to look into Lula's imprisonment?

A case comes in front of the Human Rights Committee the same way for all cases, which is that the country has to be a party to the Treaty that gives us the authority to hear the case and an individual has to submit a case to us claiming their rights under the international covenant on civil and political rights have been violated. You are right in that most of the cases we get involve issues related to torture or the death penalty but we also get claims involving arbitrary detention and unfair trial proceedings and those are the basis for Mr. Lula da Silva's claim. His specific claim at present involves article 25 of the Covenant on Civil and Political Rights, which protects the right of all individuals in Brazil to participate in political proceedings and elections.

How long did you spend looking over the case and what were some of the deciding factors that made you decide to rule in the way that you did?

Mr. Lula da Silva, I should clarify, has a case pending before us. On top of that case he requested that the Committee issue what are called Interim Measures to protect his rights to political participation while his claim is pending, so the only thing that the Committee has decided right now is his request for interim measures. That involves his request that while he is in prison and while his appeals in the domestic courts in Brazil are pending, challenging the correctness of his conviction, that he should be allowed to stand for election as president and that he should have access to the media and to members of his political party in that regard. So that is the only thing that the Committee has addressed at present. Sometime next year it will actually address the underlying merits of his claim.

When you announced this interim decision, the Brazilian Federal Government said that the UN Human Rights Committee only has an advisory role in relation to Brazil. But we know that Brazil is a signatory to the UN Second Optional Protocol [for Civil and Political Rights] which seemingly would give the UNHRC some kind of legal authority over the Brazilian government on human rights cases. What is your opinion of their assessment that they do not have to abide to this decision of yours?

You are exactly right and we disagree with them on this point because, as you said, Brazil is a party to the Second Optional Protocol which gives the Human Rights Committee the authority to hear claims by individuals that Brazil has violated their human rights under the Covenant. And Article 1 of that Treaty obligates Brazil to comply in good faith with the individual complaint procedure that the Treaty establishes. Brazil has committed to allow the Human Rights Committee to hear such cases and as part of that obligation it means that Brazil is required to participate in good faith in that process. So Brazil can't take an action against Mr. Lula da Silva or another person who has a claim pending before the Committee that would irreparably harm that person's rights or render their claim moot while the case is pending. Basically what the interim measures say is that there is a risk that Mr. Lula da Silva's rights will be irreparably harmed while the case is pending before the

Committee and therefore we have requested that Brazil take action to ensure that that doesn't happen. We consider this request legally binding on Brazil as a matter of International law.

What will happen to the Brazilian government and what will happen to the election process if they simply decide to ignore you guys on this?

If they ignore us, Mr. Lula da Silva still has his underlying case pending before us alleging violations of his rights and he could come back to us and request an opinion from the Committee that Brazil had violated its obligations under the Optional Protocol by ignoring our interim measures request. So Brazil will be in violation of its international treaty obligations if it ignores the interim measures request. We ourselves are not a sanctioning or enforcement body, we would not impose something like economic sanctions on Brazil. But depending on Brazilian domestic law Mr. Lula da Silva might be able to bring a claim in the domestic courts that his rights under the treaty have been violated and, as I said, Brazil would be in violation of its international legal obligations with all the implications that follow from that.

What do you think would happen to the reputation of Brazil on the world stage if it just started ignoring its responsibilities to the UN?

It is a very dangerous position for any nation that wants to be considered as a country that complies with human rights and the international rule of law. Countries like Brazil ratify human rights treaties because they want to be considered human rights compliant. I would say in particular with respect to interim measures issued by the Human Rights Committee, countries in general do comply with those. We issue interim measures asking countries not to execute people who are facing the death penalty, not to deport people to situations where they may face torture, and countries generally do comply with them, particularly countries like Brazil that care about their human rights reputation.

Would there be any chance that the UNHRC could invalidate the elections if they are held without granting Lula the right to run?

We wouldn't invalidate an election. We could conclude, if the claim were brought before us, that the process by which an election was conducted violated an individual's rights under the Covenant. We have had cases like that before in which election procedures were not consistent with Article 25 of the Covenant. So that would be the way in which we would raise questions about the domestic legal process for the election. Here the specific problem is that Mr. Lula da Silva argues that he cannot be denied the ability to stand for election if he has been wrongfully convicted. And the Human Rights Committee did recently have such a case involving the former President of the Maldives who had been, in our view, wrongfully convicted and therefore wrongfully denied the ability to participate in the election.

And what happened in that situation?

We recently issued the decision. It just happened this year so the Maldives have six months to respond to us on how they are implementing it and we have not heard back yet.

In the case of your decision regarding Lula, people have complained, for example, that in Brazil there are mass murderers and drug traffickers who give television interviews from behind bars. Lula has been barred of all contact with journalists. Is this something that factored into your decision in the ruling that this represents a violation of his rights to run for office?

Yes, exactly. One of his claims was that he was being given extremely limited access – only to his family. And therefore one of the requests that the Committee made to Brazil was that he must be given appropriate access that would allow him to stand for election while he is in prison, including access to the media and access to his political party. Now he also asked for us to request that he be released from prison in order to participate in the election and we did not make that request.

Why not?

Because he has been convicted in a domestic court in Brazil and he has a challenge to that conviction pending. The interim measures request that he submitted to us did not attempt to or seek a determination from the Committee regarding his guilt or innocence and that is not something that we would be in a position to assess at this stage anyway so, in order to protect his political rights – which was a specific request before us – we simply asked that he be given access to his party and to the media in prison. I should add that the other element to the request was that he should have this access and he should be allowed to stand for election as a presidential candidate while his challenge to his conviction was pending in the domestic courts. In other words he has appeals pending that have not been addressed and until those appeals are addressed through fair judicial procedures, the Committee requested that he should have the right to stand as a presidential candidate.

I know that there are probably a lot of things that you can't speak publicly about regarding Lula's case because it is ongoing. But what are some of the factors that prompted you to start this investigation? I know that it was a provisional ruling that he has to be allowed to run for office, but in the general case that you are looking into regarding Lula's imprisonment. What were some of the factors that prompted you to decide to review it?

We don't make the decision. An individual submits a case to us and then we have a procedure by which we register the case if it states a potential violation of the Covenant. We then provide the claim and the information that the individual has submitted to the state party for their response. Then we receive a response from the individual and then a Committee will actually decide the underlying merits of the case. That process is underway but that process is initiated by the claimant – in this case by Mr. Lula da Silva – and not by us. We don't go out looking around the world for cases, so he brought the case to us and he brought the case for interim measures to us. A request for interim measures is always an urgent procedure because the basic claim is that there is a risk of irreparable harm, in this case pending the October elections in Brazil and so that was the reason that the Committee took this action at this time.

What kind of time frame to you have for the final ruling?

We are expecting to decide on the underlying merits of his claim sometime next year.

It does not look like the Brazilian government is very interested in following this decision. If they don't respect the decision, what would happen, hypothetically speaking, if next year you rule that Lula did not receive a fair trial and that he should be immediately released from prison? How would this effect the election results in an election in which Lula was not allowed to run?

That is the risk of irreparable harm and that is why the Committee has taken this action now and as I said if Brazil doesn't comply then it is in violation of its international legal obligations. If the Committee ultimately found that Brazil had violated Lula's rights and it was something that had been done in the past and could not be undone, then the Committee would ask Brazil to provide Mr. Lula da Silva with reparations including compensation and ensuring his ability to stand for election as a candidate in the future and also to take steps to ensure that violations like this did not occur in the future as a general matter. I am speculating now because I don't know what would happen and I don't know exactly what the Committee would say, obviously, but these are the types of requests that we make to states in this kind of situation and this is essentially what we said to the Maldives recently.

Year of Lead

Part three

A storm gathers

Wall Street's new man in Brazil

By Daniel Hunt

New York Times, July 1993. In an article called "Conversations/Jair Bolsonaro; A Soldier Turned Politician Wants To Give Brazil Back to Army Rule", James Brooke interviewed a 38 year old Congressman. Brazil was struggling, a President gone, in the third year of directly elected Government since the coup of 1964, and the already infamous former Army Captain was proposing a return to Military Rule.

This may have sounded outlandish but just 4 years previously, declassified documents reveal that if the 1989 election had not gone the right way, Brazil's Military establishment and the United States already had contingency plans for another Coup to set things right. It is safe to assume that a Latin American politician featured in the *New York Times* is already on the US Government's radar.[i]

Brooke wrote:
"Applying to politics the boldness he once displayed as an army parachutist, Congressman Jair Bolsonaro plunged into uncharted territory a few weeks ago when he strode to the podium of Brazil's Chamber of Deputies and called for the closing of Congress. 'I am in favor of a dictatorship,' he bellowed in a speech that rattled a country that only left military rule behind in 1985. 'We will never resolve serious national problems with this irresponsible democracy. Everywhere I go,

people embrace me and treat me like a national hero,' Mr. Bolsonaro asserted. 'The people in the streets are asking for the return of the military. They ask, When are you coming back?'[ii]

"But to many defenders of Brazilian democracy, the Bolsonaro phenomenon represents a flashing yellow light — a sign that people are growing impatient with democracy's failure to curb inflation and deliver a better style of life, and a warning that politicians on the authoritarian right are eager to take advantage of this mood, and to cultivate it. The Fujimori Model. Today a new and less odious model for Latin American authoritarianism has emerged in Peru's President, Alberto K. Fujimori. Faced with congressional deadlock last year, Mr. Fujimori, a civilian, ordered the Peruvian Army to close the country's Congress and its courts. One year later, Mr. Fujimori rules with a compliant, one-chamber Congress."

During the interview, Bolsonaro was enthusiastic about the strategy of Fujimori, and even then, 25 years ago, was lauding political corruption as the element that would enable a return to military rule:

"'I sympathize with Fujimori,' the Brazilian congressman continued, 'Fujimorization' is the way out for Brazil. I am making these warnings because the population is in favor of surgery.' Political surgery, Mr. Bolsonaro continued, would involve closing Congress for a defined period of time and allowing Brazil's President to rule by decree. The justification for such a constitutional break, he said, would be 'political corruption' and Brazil's inflation, which is now running at 30 percent a month. With Congress often deadlocked in battles among its 21 parties, Brazil's press has displayed an increasing fascination with the Fujimori model. In the last month, Brazilian newspapers, magazines and television news programs have carried long interviews with the Peruvian leader. 'Fujimori put 400,000 civil servants in the street,' Mr. Bolsonaro asserted. 'How could we ever do that here?'"<u>iii</u>

The congressman was equally enthusiastic about the wave of neoliberal privatisations then sweeping the region and the world:

"When it held power in the 1960's and 1970's, the Brazilian military vastly expanded Brazil's state sector, implanting a welter of state-run companies and monopolies. Today, Mr. Bolsonaro said, the leaders of the armed forces favor bringing the state back to basics: defense, education and health. 'I vote for every privatization bill that I can,' Mr. Bolsonaro said. 'It is the left that opposes privatization. They just want to preserve their government jobs.'"

25 years later, Jair Bolsonaro is leading the Presidential polls. He lies in a hospital bed, connected to all manner of tubes and devices, after suffering an apparent assassination attempt.

New Normal

The weather vane for gauging opinion in the corridors of power is Anglo corporate media. In 2017 came the first public signs that Jair Bolsonaro was becoming acceptable to investors, and what followed was a concerted attempt to normalise his candidacy.

For a long time he looked like an anti-establishment outlier, yet has been part of their armoury for years – break glass in case of emergency.

Bolsonaro has never been "Brazil's Trump" as some foreign media have depicted over the past year. Despite he and his supporters' protestations he is an actual fascist, former Military and unlike the US President, is far from being a billionaire, nor a reality TV host.

Any depiction of the Bolsonaro as an outsider is wide of the mark. Jair has been a federal deputy for 27 years, his sons Eduardo, a federal deputy since 2015, Flávio, a state deputy since 2010, and Carlos, a city councillor since 2000. The family has 13 apartments worth R$15 million, and a summer house in Angra dos Reis. Jair and Eduardo pocketed over R$ 700,000 in housing rental allowance despite owning two apartments in Brasilia. Jair's estate alone is worth R$2.3 million. Eduardo's personal estate grew by 432% between 2014-2018.

In articles in publications like_Rupert Murdoch's *Wall Street Journal* and the *BBC*, his normalisation accelerated through 2018. "Outspoken comments", "Arch-Conservative", "Law and Order campaigner", "Hardline candidate" have been the kind of euphemisms used for Bolsonaro's neofascist politics.iv v

Human Rights dominate narratives on foreign governments when it suits, but Israel and Saudi Arabia are clear examples of how easily such rhetoric is disregarded when it is in North Atlantic interests to turn a blind eye. His public remarks from anyone else, God forbid a leader like Venezuela's Maduro, would draw unanimous condemnation. Somehow they're now acceptable coming from a politician who promises to let capital run free.

Never underestimate the levels of human suffering that Wall Street, and those whom blithely serve its interests, are prepared to accept.

Blood Waltz

On September 4, speaking at a campaign rally in Acre, an excited Bolsonaro called for the machine gunning of Workers Party members. Brazilian Prosecutor General General Raquel Dodge deemed that no crime had been committed, and that no harm had been done.

Two days later, whilst being carried on the shoulders of supporters through the city of Juiz da Fora in the state of Minas Gerais, an assailant approached the Presidential Candidate and plunged a knife into his abdomen. Although initially reported as a surface wound and not a threat to his life, he arrived at hospital with, according to his son, "40% blood loss" and multiple injuries to his intestines, liver and other organs. Some of these claims were later debunked.

His attacker, Adelio Bispo de Oliveira, was immediately depicted by Bolsonaro allies as a Worker's Party militant. The rumour spread quickly, and risked sparking retaliatory attacks. Coup loyalist newspaper *Estadão* emphased that he described himself as "moderate left", effectively a euphemism for the PT. It was also reported that between 2007-2014, he had been affiliated to the PSOL party, who immediately denounced the attack as did all the other candidates and parties.

The attack amplified fears of a wider demonisation of the left in general, which always spikes at election time. In 1989, just prior to the election, businessman Albinio Diniz was kidnapped and it was blamed on Lula's Workers Party.vi The timing of the kidnapping, so soon before the election, meant that the PT could not respond to the accusations through the media, due to a compulsory ban on campaigning for the final 24 hours ahead of voting. Lula would lose the election to Fernando Collor.

Bolsonaro's vice, General Mourão, reacted to the attack with a chilling, "If you want to use violence, we are the professionals of violence." Bolsonaro campaign coordinator Gustavo Bebianno, leader of the PSL party to which Bolsonaro belongs, said simply "now it is war".

In a video from his hospital bed Bolsonaro whimpered, "I've never hurt anyone". In the first photo of the Presidential candidate conscious since arriving for treatment at São Paulo's Albert Einstein Hospital he made his trademark "Two Gun" hand gesture.

His son Flavió posted on social media, "a message for these thugs who tried to ruin the life of a guy who is the father of a family, who is the hope for all Brazilians: you just elected the president, it will be in the first round".

In a country where candidates and top government officials have been known to die in plane crashes at key moments in the political conjuncture, where a President elect suddenly died before taking office, and where the leading candidate has been jailed with no material evidence, people do not necessarily believe what they see on the news. The fact that Bolsonaro met with the owner of *Globo*, the largest media conglomerate in Latin America, 2 days before the knife attack, and that the video footage shows no blood, has led a large percentage of the Brazilian population to conclude that the incident was simulated or exaggerated to some extent. Regardless of whether this is the case or not, and we may never know, the fact is that *Globo* has used the incident to alter its portrayal of Bolsonaro from a right-wing fringe outlier to a hero – even a martyr, during the 15 minutes of airtime they gave to the knife attack.

Wall Street was watching, and there was a sharp rise in the Real against the Dollar as news broke of an attack, which was immediately interpreted as increasing his chances of election. On September 10, White House spokeswoman Sarah Sanders confirmed that members of the Trump administration had "reached out" to Bolsonaro.<u>vii</u>

In Plain Sight

A watershed moment for Bolsonaro came just one day before his stabbing, on September 5, 2018, and was quickly forgotten in its wake.

It was a column for *Folha de São Paulo* by Brian Winter, editor of *Americas Quaterly*, the magazine of Wall Street lobby and think tank AS/COA (Americas Society/ Council of the Americas). COA's main patron is Chevron, but the corporate membership is a who's who of US Corporations, Banks and Investment funds. The *Folha de São Paulo* column openly admitted for the first time, for a wealthy Paulista readership, that Wall Street now supported the Presidential Candidacy of Jair

Bolsonaro. And this was from the horse's mouth, as "Wall Street" in effect equals the membership of the Council of the Americas, the actual organisation for which the author works.

Winter wrote, "there is, finally, the moral element. How can investors support a candidate with positions such as those of Bolsonaro on women, minorities and human rights? That's the easy question. I know many honest people on Wall Street who feel repulsed by Bolsonaro. But they admit in private conversations that there is no room for feeling. As one told me, 'my job is to make sure the bonds get paid on time. As for the rest-it's up to the Brazilians to decide.'"viii

For those familiar with the history of AS/COA, the handwringing tone of the column should have come as no surprise. Pulitzer winning investigative journalist Seymour Hersh wrote about it in his book Price of Power, detailing its role in the build up to the 1973 Chilean coup which left Salvador Allende dead and brought Augusto Pinochet to power.ix

Bolsonaro's "Brain"

AS/COA met with Bolsonaro and his advisors in 2017. What followed was a road to Damascus style conversion to the public rhetoric of free markets and the minimal state. Yet, whereas prior he had been depicted as a some kind of economic nationalist, it was clear as early as the 1993 *New York Times* interview, that he was always staunchly pro-privatisation.

Despite this long held commitment to free markets, he

admitted publicly in a TV Interview that he doesn't understand anything about economics, and that's where his "guru" Paulo Guedes comes in.

Wall Street investors see the Bolsonaro/Guedes combination like Pinochet and the Chicago Boys. Neoliberalism at the point of a gun. Guedes was a founder of what became BTG Pactual Bank, and actually worked in Chile under Pinochet. He describes that genocidal dictatorship as "an intellectual point of view". x

Since becoming part of Bolsonaro's team in 2017, Guedes has described the former soldier as the representative of an abandoned Brazilian middle class, and they have worked to consolidate support amongst the Bullet, Bible & Bull congressional caucuses, with a promise of carte blanche for agribusiness violence against Indigenous communities and Social Movements. With a nod to extractive multinationals he said "where there is indigenous land, there is wealth beneath it".xi

In 2017 Guedes embarked on an international mission to improve Bolsonaro's image with investors and foreign media. It appeared to have had some effect.xii

Bolsnaro openly supports torture and his congressional vote for Dilma Rousseff's impeachment was marked by a demented eulogy to the man, Carlos Brilhante Ustra, responsible for her brutal and sexual torture in the early 1970s. He has twice made rape-related threats and remarks to PT Congresswoman Maria do Rosario, for which he was convicted. He has made racist remarks at public events for which he has been convicted. He is an outspoken homophobe, denier and apologist for violence and murder of LGBTQ Brazilians. He has said that "30,000 Brazilians needed to be killed for the country to function".

Yet in the eyes of Wall Street, he is still preferable to a Social Democrat.

Patriotism

Filmed on a trip to Miami in 2017 saluting the United States flag, it was not the first time Bolsonaro's "nationalist" credentials had been questioned. On July 9, 2013, the country was still gripped by mass protests that appeared to spring from nowhere. Just prior to the explosion on the streets, whistleblower Edward Snowden released documents showing United States surveillance of Brazilian government, law enforcement and strategic companies.xiii In congress that day, Bolsonaro all but dismissed the revelations. He was joined by PSDB's Nilson Leitão and by the Dictatorship-heir party Democratas and their future Congressional President Rodrigo Maia.

The minutes of that congressional session in Brasília report that the plenary approved, by 292 votes to 86 and 12 abstentions, a motion proposed by the PT and signed by the leaders of the PMDB, the PV, the PSOL and the PCdoB to repudiate the US government for the espionage of US intelligence agencies on companies and people:

"Deputies stressed that the motion was a response to the gravity of the allegations made by former CIA technician Edward Snowden, that the National Security Agency (NSA) maintained offices in Brazil to monitor the communication of companies and Brazilians.

"It is a manifestation of the Legislature, which cannot be omitted, it is not a diversionary maneuver, but the position of Parliament," said the leader of the PV, Deputy Sarney Filho (Maranhão).This was reinforced by the leader of PSOL, Deputy Ivan Valente (São Paulo).

The proposal for a motion of repudiation led to divergences in the plenary. Deputy Jair Bolsonaro (PP-RJ) said the attitude was premature and stressed that the US is a major trading partner. The minority leaders Nilson Leitão (PSDB-Mato Grosso), Ronaldo Caiado (DEM-Goiania), and Deputy Rodrigo Maia (DEM-Rio de Janeiro) complained that the motion aimed to divert focus from the country's problems."xiv

It is a historical curiosity that such unprecedented US spying on Brazil – a friendly nation – which was a story broken by Glenn Greenwald and quickly identified as a fundamental sovereignty issue on the left, was dismissed entirely by Bolsonaro and prominent figures from Democratas, whose party ancestry is ARENA - the Dictatorship government.xv

It is critical for the outside world to understand that this new-look, market-friendly Bolsonaro is only in a position where victory is theoretically possible because of former President Lula's contested imprisonment. That imprisonment has been aided through informal (and illegal) collaboration between the US Department of Justice and Brazilian Federal Police, discussion of which is an Anglo media taboo.xvi

If investors truly believe that a fascist's victory in such an obvious sham of an election would protect their assets, they massively underestimate the Brazilian people, and should think again. If, somehow Jair Bolsonaro is elected President of Brazil, we should be under no illusion – there will be blood.

i Brizola 1989: The coup that never was. (2017, February 22). *Brasil Wire*. Retrieved from http://www.brasilwire.com/brizola-89-the-coup-that-never-was/

ii Brooke, J. (1993, July 25). Conversations/Jair Bolsonaro; A Soldier Turned Politician Wants To Give Brazil Back to Army Rule. *New York Times*. Retrieved from https://www.nytimes.com/1993/07/25/weekinreview/conversations-jair-bolsonaro-soldier-turned-politician-wants-give-brazil-back.html

iii ibid

iv Pearson, S. and Trevisani, P. (2018, August 21). Ex-Army Captain Upends Brazil's Election With Law-And-Order Campaign. *Wall Street Journal*. Retrieved from https://www.wsj.com/articles/ex-army-captain-upends-brazils-election-with-law-and-order-campaign-1534843801

v Watson, K. (2018, April 2). Brazil's rising tide of young conservatives seeks change. *BBC*. Retrieved from https://www.bbc.com/news/world-latin-america-43414315

vi Em 1989, sequestro de Albino Diniz foi relacionado ao PT e desmentido logo apos eleições, mostra pequisa. *Rede Brasil Atual*. Retrieved from https://www.redebrasilatual.com.br/blogs/blog-na-rede/2010/09/em-1989-sequestro-de-abilio-diniz-foi-relacionado-ao-pt-e-desmentido-logo-apos-eleicoes-mostra-pesquisa

vii United States White House. (2018, September 10). *Press briefing by press secretary Sarah Sanders and CEA chairman Kevin Hasset* [press release]. Retrieved from https://www.whitehouse.gov/briefings-statements/press-briefing-press-secretary-sarah-sanders-cea-chairman-kevin-hassett-091018/

viii Winter, B. (2018, September 5). Por que tanto gente

em Wall Street torce por uma vitoria de Bolsonaro? *Folha de São Paulo.* Retrieved from https://www1.folha.uol.com.br/poder/2018/09/por-que-tanta-gente-em-wall-street-torce-por-uma-vitoria-de-bolsonaro.shtml

ix Hersch, S. (1984). *Price of Power.* New York: Touchstone

x Winter, B. (Fall 2015). Good by to the status quo: why change is coming to South America. *Americas Quarterly.* Retrieved from https://www.americasquarterly.org/content/goodbye-status-quo-why-change-coming-south-america

xi Fascist Bolsonaro: "Where there is indigenous land, there is wealth beneath it." (2017, April 6). *Brasil Wire.* Retrieved from http://www.brasilwire.com/fascist-bolsonaro-where-there-is-indigenous-land-there-is-wealth-beneath-it/

xii For example: Biller, D. and Luchessi, C. (2018, April 2). Chicago boy helps calm bankers' fears about Brazilian election wild card. Bloomberg. Retrieved from https://www.bloomberg.com/news/articles/2018-04-02/chicago-boy-helps-calm-bankers-fears-about-brazil-wild-card

xiii Veja os documentos ultrasecretos que comprovam espionagem a Dilma. (2013, September 2). *Globo.* Retrieved from http://g1.globo.com/fantastico/noticia/2013/09/veja-os-documentos-ultrassecretos-que-comprovam-espionagem-dilma.html

xiv Camara dos Deputados do Governo Federal Brasileiro. (2013, July 10). *Câmara aprova moção de repúdio ao governo dos EUA por suspeitas de espionagem* [press release]. Retrieved from http://www2.camara.leg.br/camaranoticias/noticias/RELACOES-EXTERIORES/447266-CAMARA-APROVA-MOCAO-DE-REPUDIO-AO-

GOVERNO-DOS-EUA-POR-SUSPEITAS-DE-ESPIONAGEM.html

xv Greenwald, G. (2013, July 7). The NSA's mass and indescriminate spying on Brazilians. *The Guardian*. Retrieved from https://www.theguardian.com/commentisfree/2013/jul/07/nsa-brazilians-globo-spying

xvi Mier, B. (2018, August 20). US DOJ and Operation Car Wash: Facts and Questions. *Brasil Wire*. Retrieved from http://www.brasilwire.com/us-doj-and-operation-car-wash-facts-and-questions/

Elections 2018: possible scenarios

By Marcos Arruda

Understanding a very complex historical situation, like that of Brazil today, is not an easy task. What will happen to Brazil if Fernando Haddad or Ciro Gomes win the election? What challenges will they face? And what if the winner is Jair Bolsonaro, the extreme right-wing candidate promoted by the mainstream media and a public angered by the hate syndrome created against Lula and the PT? These are some of the issues that I examine in this article.

Capital's Historic Bloc and its Neoliberal Extremism

There are two opinions about the most urgent challenge of these elections: one, the need for a "shock of order" presented by the mainstream media, which says that the current situation, is a big mess. They focus on corruption and violence as the only facets of the country's reality, and of police and military interventions as the only way to combat them. The other opinion recognizes that violence is part of the current reality but that inequality of income, wealth, and access to decent living conditions affects the lives of the population with much more virulence and are themselves a form of violence. Policies that contribute to deepening inequality are neither denounced nor opposed by the mainstream media. Nor does the media raise crucial questions about the systemic nature of these inequalities. Never do they examine how these inequalities arise structurally from the globalized oligopolistic capitalist system. Public debt already exceeds R $5 trillion (roughly US$1.2 trillion) and annually sucks a large portion of public budget expenditures (roughly US $ 100 billion), guaranteeing usurious gains to its approximately 10,000 creditors, according to economist Marcio Pochmann. And this debt remains unaudited. The fact that the six richest billionaires hold the same wealth as the poorest half of Brazil's population is an indisputable indicator of the barbaric character of Brazilian capitalism.

The "Bridge to the Future" economic project represents the global offensive of capital aiming to install a neoliberal revolution throughout the Americas. According to *golpista* President Temer, President Dilma's refusal to carry out this project was the main reason she was ousted in a parliamentary coup in 2016. The ultra neoliberal government resulting from this coup has ensured that capital is the main beneficiary of its reforms. In the current elections, former captain Jair Bolsonaro, former governor Geraldo Alckmin, and banker Henrique Meirelles are the main representatives of these interests. It is therefore likely that the electoral victory of the Center-Left candidates will open a stage of intense pressure on them to continue pushing neoliberal economic reforms, offering in return the guarantee of respect for governability; a kind of Pax Americana. If not, the new government will risk provocation, slander, and actions aimed at creating instability, fear and chaos. That is, an environment conducive to a military coup or other coercive regime.

Lula's leadership and the threat of Bolsonaro

The evolution of the electoral process reveals some peculiar characteristics of this election:

– Not even the pro-coup big media doubts that the Workers' Party's (PT) 'natural' candidate, former President Lula, if not prevented by the baseless, spurious decisions of Operation Car Wash with the complicity of the Federal Supreme Court (FSC), would win the elections–maybe even in the first round. The respect of tens of millions of voters reveals that Lula remains the most expressive and influential leader in this country.

– The army of lawyers and jurists allied to Congress and the Federal Police who investigated Lula and Dilma failed to present effective evidence of crimes by either one. Judge Moro's decision to convict and imprison Lula had the stamp of political persecution, and he is described as a political prisoner in Brazil and abroad. This does not prevent the mainstream media, in particular the two largest oligopolistic information groups, *Rede Globo* and *Bandeirantes*, from systematic disinformation, slander, half-truths and fake news in attempt to convince the public that the PT is the only Party responsible for the corruption between politicians and big businessmen.

– The fact that the PT allied itself with the chief coup forces throughout its mandates is one reason for its current wear and tear. But what led to the polarization and rise of an extreme right candidate was that the population lost confidence in the traditional way of doing politics. In Brazil this has meant that the Legislative and Judiciary Powers became profitable business centers, and the ministries, government secretariats, and management of State-owned enterprises became bargaining chips. This current political system of rotten powers that has privatized the State must be defeated, for it is a corrupting and corrupt system. It is responsible for the State's failure to fulfill its constitutional mandate, leading to the deepening of inequalities in income and wealth. All major parties have played a part. It is up to the PT and the PDT (the Democratic Labor Party) to make their self-criticisms and inaugurate a new form of governance: the practice of governing with the people.

– The great bourgeoisie does not forgive Lula for his worker-peasant origin. The rotten powers, who also benefited from conciliatory PT governments, chose to betray him. If the PT failed to acknowledge the errors of its mandates, it might still, like the Phoenix, benefit from the extremism of those who tried to exclude it from Brazilian politics. The selective treatment given by Operation Car Wash and the Supreme Court to indict PT politicians, shelving cases of suspected crime from other parties, gained the attention of impoverished classes in Brazil as well as the international media. And, against the will of his enemies, Lula gained a symbolic power of planetary magnitude.

– The erosion of the image of Lula, Dilma and the PT by the coup media did not fully achieve its objective. Lula's popularity continues to grow, especially among the lower-income electorate, which more directly benefited from the PT social programs. The middle classes and an expressive part of the Center-Left joined in. The openly anti-democratic candidate, Jair Bolsonaro, has managed to gain surprising support and with Lula declared ineligible by the Electoral Supreme Court, has maintained the lead in opinion polls. The same candidate leads the rate of rejection by the electorate. Looking closely, we realize that if Bolsonaro visited sectors of the country early in the year and gained increasing support from the military, the media's erosive action against the PT, coupled with Bolsonaro's anti-PT speech, assisted the increasing polarization expressed today in the so-called "wave of hatred." Assisted by propaganda, workers with low purchasing power, women, and large sectors of the middle and high classes, became indignant about the "corruption" and violence attributed to the PT governments and adopted the language of hatred against the PT, Lula, and Dilma. The mainstream media said nothing about the systemic nature of corruption, choosing to focus on the PT as the main culprit in the recessionary policy of fiscal adjustment, which is responsible for the economic crisis that plagues Brazil. This policy, begun under Dilma's rule, was aggravated in a perverse and irresponsible manner by the gang of corrupt politicians who seized the Brazilian State with the coup of 2016.

– The knife attack against Bolsonaro raises serious suspicions. Who does it benefit? First, he was treated as a victim and even as a hero by some (for example: journalist Merval Pereira of *Jornal O Globo* and commentator on *GloboNews* TV). Second, it benefits the interests of the far-Right bloc, who use the long-defunct (and false) banner of anti-communism to spread a visceral hatred toward the PT. The unfounded accusation of PSL deputy General Mourão that a PT supporter was responsible for the attack, followed by the thinly veiled threat that the Armed Forces are the true "violence professionals," is strong evidence that those with Bolsonaro seek to generate a climate of fear and insecurity conducive to military intervention. Bolsonaro's speeches (both old and new) resemble the aggressive Philippine President Rodrigo Duterte. Some speeches reveal his fascist and *golpista* values:

– "I am in favor of a dictatorship" (1993, speech in Congress)i

– "Voting does not solve anything, it does not change anything. This country only changes with … civil war. " "I am in favor of torture." Chico Lopes should hang from the perrot's perch!" [The parrot's perch was a common and cruel torture method of the dictatorship.]

– "Winning the government, we'll kill 30,000, starting with the FHC",

"I would close the Congress, yes. I would make a (military) coup the same day." (1999, Bolsonaro in a TV interview)ii

– "Let's shoot the gang of PT here from Acre" (campaigning in the Acre state in 2018) …

– "I cannot speak for the [military] commanders. From what I see in the streets, I will not accept a result different from my election" (9/28/2018)

On Sep 25, 2018, the results of IBOPE's recently published research clearly agitated right-wing currents. IBOPE revealed that Bolsonaro had stagnated at 28% and Haddad was at 22%. The rejection rate of Bolsonaro continues to rise, already reaching 46% against 30% for Haddad and 18% for Ciro Gomes; the number of women who would never vote for Bolsonaro is now 54%. IBOPE's forecast for the second round is: 43% for Haddad and 37% for Bolsonaro, or 46% for Ciro and 35% for Bolsonaro. Perhaps in response, jurist Miguel Reale Jr., juridical coordinator of the 2016 coup, convened a meeting to propose to the four right-wing candidates–Marina Silva, Henrique Meirelles, João

Amoedo and Álvaro Dias–to give up and recommend their votes give their "useful votes" to Geraldo Alckmin. It did not work. The latest poll reveals the sum of votes from these four candidates is only 13%.

Before closing this article, a new move is appearing to reduce Haddad's chances of victory, through the banning of 3.3 million voters, most of them in the Northeast, where Haddad has greater support. The justification is that they did not complete a biometric re-registration. Judge Luiz Fux illegally cancelled the right of journalists to interview Lula. And IBOPE and Datafolha issued the results in their new weekly poll, inverting the trends in such way that arises suspicion about the integrity of their data. In the meantime, Judge Sergio Moro illegally leaked parts of plea bargain testimony by one of Lula's former Ministers, Antonio Palloci, to the media. What other tricks will they make up to weaken Haddad's candidacy?

US Empire and the subversion of democracy

The U.S. government, mega-companies, and banks were invisible but very real actors in the conspiracy that led to the coup of 2016. They are all part of an entity called AS/COA (Americas Society / Council of the Americas), founded by David Rockefeller to influence politics in Latin America. AS/COA brings together representatives of major U.S.-based transnational corporations and banks. The change in the U.S. empire's interventionist strategy dates from the first decade of this century. The coups of Haiti (2004), Honduras (2009) and Paraguay (2012), toppled the presidencies of Jean-Bertrand Aristide, Manuel Zelaya and Fernando Lugo, respectively, and were performed by judicial means rather than military coups. Considered "soft" coups, these interventions replaced democratically-elected presidents with puppets serving the interests of the U.S. empire.

The 2016 coup in Brazil follows the prototype: lawfare instead of warfare. Philosopher Euclides Mance analyzes in detail this change of strategy of the American capitalist empire in his book, *O Golpe, Brics, Dollér e Petroleo* (The Coup – BRICS, Dollar and Oil).iii

Mance opens the book with two quotes about U.S. involvement in the 2016 media-sponsored parliamentary coup. The first is from the global articulator of the Students for Liberty (SFL) organization, Alexander McCobin, showing how this group, renamed "Estudantes pela Liberdade" in Brazil (who were also the initiators of Movimento Brasil Livre movement), worked across the continent to mobilize middle class youth in ousting the President-elect and achieving the privatization of Petrobrás.

The second opens with the title: "The Brazilian President of BRICS, next target of Washington." Mance quotes F. William Edgdahl: "The reason Washington wants to get rid of Rousseff is clear. As President, she is one of five BRICS leaders who signed the formation of the BRICS Development Bank with a $100 billion capitalization and a reserve currency coalition worth an additional $100 billion. It also supports a new International Reserve Currency to supplement and eventually replace the dollar (as international currency). (...) Brazil is also distancing itself from the Anglo-American domination of the exploitation of its oil and gas."

These and other proof of interventionist action by agents of the U.S. empire in Brazil suggest the need to evaluate the probable positioning of the empire in the 2018 elections process.

An article from *Brasil Wire* quotes journalist James Brooke, who published in the *New York Times* (July 1993) the article, "A Soldier Who Became Political Wants to return Brazil to the military domain."iv The ex-soldier was Bolsonaro. While many comprehend the significant role the U.S. played in the coup of 1964, new documents released by the U.S. government show that the Brazilian military and the U.S. government had plans to carry out another coup in 1989, in case the result of the presidential election was inconsistent with U.S. financial and geopolitical interests. Nothing prevents the U.S. from colluding now to avoid seeing a Brazilian president who cancels the petroleum auctions, puts the Pre-Salt oil deposits in the hands of a fully State-controlled Petrobras, reverses the sales of refineries and other subsidiaries, prevents the privatization of Eletrobrás and the sale of Embraer to Boeing, defends Brazilian minerals, promotes redistributive tax reform and Social Security reform, promotes auditing and renegotiation of the public debt, and imposes limits on the remittance of profits and dividends. In other words, candidates like Haddad.

Possible Scenarios

If Haddad's trend continues, his victory in the second round will give the federal government back to PT. If the winner is Bolsonaro, Brazil will be turned over to the right-wing military, and an age of darkness will once again subsume this country.

Scenario 1 – Haddad and Bolsonaro move to the second round.
The Right divides: most of them pass their votes to Bolsonaro, and a minority rejects Bolsonaro to vote for Haddad. But most voters of Gomes and Boulos, and a large portion from Marina and Alckmin, migrate their votes to Haddad. Something similar could happen if Gomes becomes the candidate with the best chance of beating Bolsonaro. Worried about the likely victory of the PT (or PDT) in the second round, the extreme Right articulates a possible military coup.

a) The national and global political environment is not conducive to a military coup. But it is not impossible for far-Right to mount actions to justify it. There is suspicion that the stabbing of Bolsonaro in early September may have been one of those actions. Other terrorist actions may be launched. If these actions are avenged, a military coup would go from possible to probable. The "hypothesis" of General Mourão, running mate of Bolsonaro, is that a situation of anomie and anarchy would justify a unilateral action of the Army to install a shock of order.

b) The liberal sector of the AS/COA entity is opposed to the coup and insists on maintaining the lawfare strategy and negotiating with those who benefit from a democratic image of Brazil, which after all guarantees the ongoing implementation of neoliberal reforms and protection of U.S. interests in Brazil. Meanwhile, the "hawks" of U.S. foreign policy support a military coup.

c) The far-Right of Brazil and the U.S. hawks prefer that the coup occurs as soon as possible (even before the first round). That's because it will be very difficult to justify the coup after the possible victory of the Center-Left has been consummated.

Scenario 2 – Bolsonaro wins the first round.
The anti-PT group rejoices. Center-Left candidates flock to defeat Bolsonaro in the second round. The far-Right is encouraged to express its violent streak, even though it maintains the "democratic" discourse and works to gain control of the State by the vote. What would it mean if most voters elected an anti-democratic figure and general, both outspokenly in favor of a military coup, ready to violate the Constitution and outlaw democracy? Bolsonaro has insisted that most people want a dictatorship. With the endorsement of these votes, he would be in a position to fulfill his nightmare.

Scenario 3 – Haddad (or Gomes) wins the election in the second round.
a) The economic elites, the mainstream media, and the guardians of the U.S. empire will endure an historic defeat. The return of the PT in national politics will be surprising. Police investigations and prosecutions will continue, reaching the (now former) coup president Temer and the gangs that have occupied the federal government since the coup in 2016.
b) Bolsonaro, defeated, can join the generals in a conspiracy to carry out a coup, in accordance with General Mourão's statement that "we will not accept a PT victory."
c) If they realize that a military coup is not feasible at this time, they will wait for an auspicious occasion to articulate the coup. In fact, a military candidacy is becoming more likely; there are 71 military candidates for government posts in 2018, and perhaps soon a "military bloc" in the legislative bodies will form.

d) For the new president, the greatest challenge will be governance. There is an urgent need to scrutinize the Judiciary, removing judges, prosecutors and High Court Judges, as well as and members of the Public Ministry, whose decisions have damaged current legislation and the Constitution. Even if the new president and his team reconfigure the Judiciary, it is likely that the Legislature will oppose profound changes and insist the new Executive follow the neoliberal agenda. It will count on the support of the mass media, which will continue to present corruption as a normal pathology rather than a systemic vice derived from capitalist ethics.

e) Without a mobilizing action of the population to amend the economic and social disaster of the last 4-5 years, PT or PDT and its allies will not make changes beyond welfare policies.

Scenario 4 – Bolsonaro wins the Presidency.
Unless his victory is questioned, it would mean that Brazil will be engulfed in an era of far-Right rule, perhaps similar to Chile's brutal era of the Pinochet dictatorship (1973-1990), the only way the elites and the U.S. empire could impose an ultra-Right economic program on the country. Paulo Guedes, Bolsonaro's economic aide, was also bred by the Chicago University School of Economics, and advocates an ultra-neoliberal reform aimed at privatizing everything and converting the right to live into a mere commodity.

a) Bolsonaro might implement his promises of making a coup-d'état the next day, "killing 30,000" to begin with and imposing a reign of terror for as long as his hegemony remains. In my opinion this is the least likely scenario.

b) Bolsonaro might be called to order by less extremist leaders of the Armed Forces and the U.S. imperial doves, and would try to reshape the institutions using the law as his main weapon. His economic counter-reforms – beginning with the total privatization of Petrobrás and the Pre-Salt oil and gas deposits, Eletrobrás, the two largest State banks, and the country's underground waters – will require strong alliances in the Congress and a society under control – whether by intimidation or by violent coercion. What challenges would this scenario pose to democracy and to the nation's sovereignty?

It is hoped that the new government learns from both the mistakes and successes of 13 years of PT government, overcomes any populist tendency, re-unites ethics and politics and joins the masses who elect it to create a government with authentic popular participation capable of convincing even opponents that: (1) democracy is much better and more effective than dictatorship; (2) democracy is a holistic project of power, which must encompass the economic, political, cultural and ecological realms; and (3) democracy is like swimming: you only learn by doing.

Major Challenges

Present trends point to the victory of the so-called Center-Left bloc. But this bloc will come to power aware that society is divided, with a strong rejection of the old way of doing politics. This is what explains the polarization in these elections. Many people will vote for PSL candidates simply because they see the need for a radical change in how Brazil does politics, and not because they understand what matters most to the agents of current political power: the continuation of the ultra-neoliberal revolution initiated by the coup of 2016. This was the motivation to bar Lula, the PT and its allies in State power. They are seen as hindrances to the project.

The more likely the victory of Haddad and the PT, the more pressured their government will be to commit to the ultra-neoliberal revolution in order to guarantee some governability. If it is not possible to defeat PT, the Right will join them, as they did in 2002, with the goal of co-opting them to govern within the rules of the neoliberal game, even if they have to tolerate some compensatory social policies. This happened when Lula was elected for the first time, and the PT gave in. The name of the project already under way is Bridge to the Future. The authors of these pressures, from the ranks of the Right, were those who articulated the coup in 2016 – businessmen and bankers, agribusiness, the mainstream media (*Globo* and *Bandeirantes* networks), the Right wing of the Armed Forces and the conservative evangelicals. Along with them, the agents of the American empire: AS/COA, CIA, the Department of Justice of Washington D.C. and the Department of State, whose neoliberal project has a global horizon. AS/COA includes all major U.S.-based transnational corporate groups, including IT, telematics and robotics, petroleum, automotive, chemical, pharmaceutical, food, and armaments production chains. They want to keep the veins of Latin America open, manipulating the sold-out elites, sucking Brazil's riches like vampires and keeping the continent in a pre-industrial condition.

This set of actors is known as Financial-Industrial-Military Complex. Joined with the conservative elites of Brazil, this block initiated with the 2016 coup an ultra-neoliberal "revolution" determined to continue at any price. Will Haddad-Lula-PT allies adhere to it? Or will they be victims of some form of coercion, one that best suits the ultra-neoliberal revolution – a tutored government, murders, terrorist actions in the name of fighting the left, and a military coup? The form doesn't matter. It is important that this "revolution" guarantees a subordinate role to the "sleeping giant" within the planetary geopolitics of globalized capital, led by the U.S. empire, until some climatic/environmental, financial, social or civilizational mega-catastrophe spins the kaleidoscope of history and introduces the Biocene Age. Here, the remnants of humanity may finally realize that they are only one among millions of species of life, whose livelihood must be established in harmony with Nature.

In this context, who will the new government serve? And how can the Brazilian people avoid such a political and social disaster?

> • To avoid accusations of electoral fraud, parties defending democracy, the Brazilian Bar Association (OAB), and other professional and religious bodies should unite to invite outside observers to assist in monitoring the October elections.
> • To prevent a coup, all parties should engage in the defense of democracy by carrying out marches in the streets in defense of their rights, of policies and institutions that make corruption unfeasible, and of Brazil's wealth.
> • Parties and other groups should contact commanders and officials of the three armed forces in order to mobilize them for the defense of representative democracy and the sovereignty of Brazil over its territory, wealth, and culture.

• Shows of resistance from the population abound already. The emergence of women in social networks organizing themselves around #EleNão (#nothim) have flooded the streets of Brazil and other countries, demonstrating a strength, integrity and capacity for unity that inaugurates a new era of Brazilian politics. We need a multiplication of alternative communication media, community radio stations, independent media, and progressive bloggers, and the recovery and strengthening of the public radio and TV networks.

• Elected president Haddad (or Gomes) should not hesitate to call TV and Radio national networks to dialogue with the people; and they should use other instances of direct democracy, such as plebiscites and referenda, to consult the people on matters of national and strategic interest. It is also urgent to break the information monopoly exercised by *Rede Globo* and the Marinho family, a monopoly that would be inconceivable according to the legislation of the countries of North America and Europe, countries the rotten powers ironically so admire.

Winning the election, Haddad will be harshly tested by a reality shock, which will come with the pressure to concede to the interests of big capital. This occurred in 2002, and the PT gave in. It happened again in 2013, and the PT gave in. Will Haddad's millions of voters provide him the courage not to give in? The only way to resist will be to patiently build a new social pact centered on the millions who have chosen him. And this implies a systematic and massive educational and informative work with the majority of workers.

The new government will be nourished by the strategic vision of overcoming all oppression. To ensure the continuity of this transition, people need to be organized and educated for self-management. As a first step, they must focus on the rights and needs of the majority, rescue what's best in the Constitution and the law, and dismantle everything the coup government did to push Brazil backwards. It must adopt policies capable of establishing Brazil's majority not in a project of the future but in one of a new present.

It will also be urgent to dialogue with society about a political reform that will dismantle the systems of corruption and debt, and make possible new rules for making Politics (with a capital P) that rescue its original sense as the art of managing power for the good of all. May this government have the courage to use the power of the Constitution to punish officers of the three armed forces who transgress their constitutional obligations.

On the subjective level, Haddad will have to deepen his knowledge of and harmony with the working people, including the majority of women, indigenous and *quilombola* peoples, public employees, educators, and the artists and scientists who remain in Brazil. This harmony will temper Haddad's heart so that he will be strong enough to resist the pressures and threats of the rotten powers and face these challenges, despite the risks, without abandoning the oppressed women, men and children of our rich Brazil.

Translated from Portuguese by Kathy Swart

i Hunt, D. (2018, September 10). Pinochet via Fujimori: Wall Street's new man in Brazil. *Brasil Wire.*
Retrieved from http://www.brasilwire.com/wall-streets-new-pinochet/

ii Bolsonaro quer matar 30 mil [video]. (uploaded 2016, April 10). *Youtube.*
Retrieved from https://youtu.be/PGTtIGmOY24

iii Mance, E. (2018). *O Golpe: BRICS, Dolar e Petroleo.* Passo Fundo: Saluz.

iv Hunt, D. (2018, September 10). Pinochet via Fujimori: Wall Street's new man in Brazil. *Brasil Wire.*
Retrieved from http://www.brasilwire.com/wall-streets-new-pinochet/

ATENÇÃO

NÃO APOIE
AS MÃOS
NAS PORTAS

Bolsonaro and the institutionalization of Necropolitics

By Guilherme Soares Dias and Juliana Gonçalves

As Brazilian presidential candidate Jair Bolsonaro (Partido Social Liberal/PSL) rises in the polls, more and more cases of political violence and death spread across Brazil. The country will have its second round of elections on October 27th. Fernando Haddad (Partido dos Trabalhadores/PT) has the difficult mission of rallying progressives against an imminent loss of rights and freedom.

Democracy is still a luxury word in Brazil. There have only been 33 years of democratic rule since the last dictatorship. It is a fragile and young democracy which has yet to be solidified for millions of Brazilians, especially Afro-Brazilians and marginalized peoples who, even in the democratic period, were constantly deprived of their rights.

What is happening today is the response of conservative and narrow-minded sectors of society to the social progress made during the PT governments, most importantly under Luiz Inácio Lula da Silva. Under Lula the PT solidified public policies for the poor and marginalized majority, removed millions from below the poverty line and leveraged their social insertion into the middle class – all of this without taking anything from the rich. The banks never made as much money as they did during the PT period.

Even at the time, the advances made in the Lula era triggered a backlash of hate. It was also during this period that the largest black population outside of Africa witnessed its genocide levels surpass acceptable numbers for a democracy. Every 23 minutes a young black man is killed and homicides against black women rose by 54% in Brazil between 2003 and 2013, according to the Faculdade Latino-Americana de Ciências Sociais (FLASCO) Violence Map. If death politics already exist, with Bolsonaro in power they can become institutionalized. In this sense, the possibility of effectively solidifying Cameroonian Sociologist Achille Mbembe's concept of "necropolitics" has never been greater in a democratic society. Mbembe defines "necropolitics" as political action centralized on the large scale production of death at the hands of the state, which decides who should live and who should die.

As political polarization rises in Brazil we see a rise in the violence – which has always mostly affected the bodies of blacks, women, LGBT's, etc. This violence was elevated to new heights with the execution of Marielle Franco, a black, lesbian woman from a favela who was elected to City Council, and her execution represented the synthesis of many targets of violence. Seven months have passed without any answers about the political assassination which marked the arrival of dark times for Brazil.

With the rise of fascism, political killings increased, such as the murder of Master Moa do Katendê in Salvador on October 7th, a few hours after election results established a run off between Bolsonaro and Haddad in the second round. It was also during shouts of "Bolsonaro" and "Yes him" that, according to witnesses, a trans woman named

Priscilla was murdered early in the morning of October 16th.

"Yes him", is an allusion to the hashtag #EleNão (#NotHim). Women created this huge social movement to confront Bolsonaro and became the great hope to stop him. In addition to a massive social network mobilization with millions of followers reproducing the hashtag, public demonstrations took over the streets in cities and towns across Brazil and around the world on September 29th. The many misogynist declarations made by Bolsonaro prove that, more than not respecting women, he views them as enemies.

A divided nation

What stands out in the profile of the newly elected Congress is the intense political party fragmentation and a rightward swing on social issues. Around 141 of the newly elected congressmen are from traditional political families, are evangelical leaders, hardline police officers or celebrities. They are, in the majority, white males. The total votes represents a solidification of polarization between the PSL and the PT, which are now the two largest parties in Congress.

If, on the one hand, far-right candidates took the spotlight repeating Bolsonaro's most barbaric and violent ideas, there were also advances made on the left. Inspired by Marielle, some black women were able to win elections for the first time in different states across the country. Undoubtedly the most emblematic victory was that of Erica Malunguinho, elected to the São Paulo state congress for the PSOL party and the first trans women to be elected to public office in Brazilian history. In this country with its alarming numbers of killings of young black males, and its killings of more LGBTpeople than any other in the world, the election of Malunguinho, who represents various bodies, was a breath of hope. With minimal financing and party structure, with a combative discourse on race issues and a campaign that was nicknamed "The Quilombo" (escaped slave/maroon community), and without fear of criticising failures by the left against Afro-Brazilians, Erica got 55,423 votes and is now building a "Quilombo-Mandate" in one of the main left wing parties in the country.

The class struggle in Brazil is more alive than ever. Erica and Jair, on opposite sides, are potent echoes of the winds of change. She represents the hope for policies that aim to bring the margins into a pluralist and inclusive center. He, incarnating the slave masters, represents the oligarchs who have gained strength in a country, which, in recent years linked citizenship to consumption.

Bolsonaro is the personification of Brazilian fascism

The Brazilian election comes on the back of other elections around the world where the extreme right is gaining space. In the US, after the Barack Obama era, Donald Trump triumphed promising to build a wall on the border with Mexico. Brexit is causing Great Britain to withdraw from the European Union. In France, Marine Le Pen nearly won the elections. In Latin America, the businessman Mauricio Macri won in Argentina, promising austerity reforms and economic growth.

It seems like the world is undergoing a counter-flux

against human rights and that each country in which there were even modest social advances has chosen to go backwards. It is for this reason that Bolsonaro's promise to end race-based quotas in Universities and civil service exams has been so effective. The candidate also promises to end the public school system's gender policy – this is one of his only campaign promises related to education – despite the fact that there has not yet been an effective methodology on this theme implemented by the Brazilian public school system.

Security is another of his key campaign issues, although there have been no clear promises for anything in this area beyond castrating rapists and relaxing gun ownership legislation. His frequent racist, misogynist and homophobic statements are reproduced by his followers. Bolsonaro is viewed as being honest and many of his followers don't believe that he will end rights that affect them in their everyday lives.

The Bolsonaro myth is consolidated through hatred against the PT, but he is also portrayed as not being corrupt and saying what he thinks. He is portrayed as a leader ready to confront everyone and everything to make the country grow and free it from the specter of corruption. But during the campaign the ex-Army captain has shown little disposition to engage in dialogue with anyone and says that he plans on ending all forms of "activism". Some specialists believe that "Bolsonarism" will be a model in which, if he takes office, his supporters will beat up possible opponents to his government.

In the economic field, the financial markets are in an anachronistic moment: the stock exchange rises and the dollar falls every time a new poll comes out showing Bolsonaro in the lead. But his economic policies are a mystery. He has already shown total ignorance on the matter and promises that he will outsource his economic policy decision making to the ultra-neoliberal Paulo Guedes.

Fernando Haddad (PT) promises measures that were practiced by previous PT governments, during which many people in the markets made a lot of money. The fact is that the market has bought into the idea that Bolsonaro is more neoliberal and willing to privatize the state companies with the goal of reducing the public debt. The enigma is whether he will be able to lead a divided country that has left an economic crisis and confronted social disparities which the candidate promises he will ignore.

Can Brazil still be saved?

In 1946 the Bahian banking oligarch Clemente Mariani gave a speech in the Constituent Assembly and, in all of his anti-communist furor, said, "the democracy that we want to install in Brazil is not social or proletariat democracy, but a formal, bourgeois democracy that is based on freedom and not on equality."

That quote sets the tone for what one part of the supporters of Bolsonaro believe in: a democracy on paper and a dictatorship on the streets. Another faction of his supporters openly defend the return of the military to power.

A moment of chaos is never the right time to point the blame, but we should start building a resistance that is different from the guidelines that brought us this incomplete democracy that we live in. Race, gender and class need to be at the center of our concerns when we dream of a democracy which is not so distant from the people that it serves, and that does not guarantee rights to the rich while penalizing the most poor.

In order to make this reflection reality we need to fearlessly face the limits of democracy within capitalism. The Portuguese intellectual Boaventura Souza Santos says that "radicalizing democracy means intensifying its tension with capitalism." We need to work so that this base, abandoned by some sectors, serves as the starting point for the pluralist construction that is so urgent.

Regardless of the results of the October 27th elections, Brazilian democracy will remain in peril. Fascism is a monster that will not want to go back in the closet. Now they know its size. Luckily, we know it to. There is going to be a fight.

This article was translated by Brian Mier and originally appeared in New Socialist.

Paulo Freire and the war on Brasil's public education

By Larissa Jacheta Riberti

"When education is not liberatory, the dream of the oppressed is to be the oppressor".

This quote is from Paulo Freire, one of the most renowned and frequently cited educational theorists in the World. The works he produced during the 20th Century conceived of education as a means to transform people, consciousness and, therefore, society. In the Pedagogy of the Oppressed he writes:

"Who better than the oppressed to be prepared to understand the terrible meaning of an oppressive society? Who feels the effects of oppression more than them? Liberation does not arrive by accident, but by the praxis of the search for it; by the knowledge and recognition of the need to fight for it. A fight that due to the results that it gives to the oppressed, should be an act of love that opposes the lack of love shown by the violence of the oppressors, even when it is full of false generosity".

In one of his most famous projects, Paulo Freire coordinated President João Goulart's National Literacy Plan. Created through Decree number n° 53.465 of January 21, 1964, the program represented an attempt by the Ministry of Education and Culture to coordinate the base level education and adult literacy movements which had been spreading across the country since 1961. According to the decree that started the program, the goal was to facilitate 60,870 cultural circles to teach literacy to 1,834,200 adults, which represented 8.9% of the illiterate population that, in September 1963, numbered 20,442,000 people. These cultural circles were to be implemented in four successive stages (each lasting three months) in all the country's schools. The National Literacy Plan was based on pilot projects which had been developed in the South and the Northeast.

After the civilian-military coup of April 1, 1964, however, the project was interrupted and Paulo Freire was accused of subversion and imprisoned for 72 days. When he got out, he left for exile in Chile, where he worked for 5 years in the Institute for Training and Investigation in Agrarian Reform (ICIRA) and wrote Pedagogy of the Oppressed.

To the surprise of at least the most conscious Brazilians, this would not be the last time that Paulo Freire and his educational theories would be criminalized. The violent times of the Civil-Military Dictatorship, which lasted 21 years, left an authoritarian legacy much deeper than any historian could measure.

The consequence of this legacy is that Brazil is currently holding elections during a moment of growing fascism, with violent rhetoric and promises of restoring authoritarianism coming from the right wing extremist, Jair Bolsonaro.

Protected by impunity, the candidate from the PSL (Partido Social Liberal/Social liberal party), who defeated Fernando Haddad from the PT (Partido dos Trabalhadores/Workers Party), has a long history of giving speeches praising violence, torture and the torturers. He honored one of them in Congress when he dedicated his vote in favor of the legal-parliamentary coup which deposed Dilma Rousseff from the Presidency of the Republic to Carlos Brilhante Ustra, who brutally tortured her during the military dictatorship.

Jair Bolsonaro's speeches also frequently warn of a supposed "communist threat" and mix this paranoia with hatred and opposition to liberatory ideas. In this manner, the right wing extremist candidate includes Paulo Freire and his works in his list of enemies. The construction of a vulgar and incorrect discourse about the educator and his methodology has caused many of the "bolsonarists" to share false information about him, attributing quotes to him that were never made.

The people behind Bolsonaro's campaign have a very clear goal in deconstructing Paulo Freire's philosophy. Freire who preached liberation from the condition of oppression through education, has been intentionally misinterpreted by a presidential candidate and a group of supporters who back a government project that's main proposal in the area of public education is to eliminate what it calls "Marxist indoctrination." For this reason, in one of his announcements over the internet, Bolsonaro promised to "eradicate" Paulo Freire's influence from the national public school curriculum.

The absurdities do not end there. Bolsonaro's education plan also calls for implementing distance learning at all levels of public education, from grammar school to university. It appears to be no accident that the name most cited for Education and Culture Minister in a possible Bolsonaro victory is Stavros Xanthopoylos, the

Getulio Vargas Foundation's former director of online education. This measure clearly shows an attempt by the possible new government to favor private companies offering distance learning courses at "affordable" prices to the population. In another video recorded live during the week after the first round of elections, Bolsonaro said that if he implements distance education he will fire the teachers and cafeteria workers from the public schools.

Bolsonaro's proposals not only reveal an attempt to criminalize critical thinking and limit the public, democratic and universal character of education, they also reveal a dishonest misrepresentation of Paulo Freire's legacy and his real influence on the Brazilian public school curriculum. Supported by an illegal fake news manufacturing network, Bolsonaro has encouraged a false narrative based on a nonexistent "Marxist indoctrination" in the classroom, which is supposedly imposed alongside a so-called "gender ideology".

Paranoia over the supposed existence of 'Marxist indoctrination' and 'gender ideology' is not new. Both were issues that accompanied the resurgence or growth of already existing neofascism in Brazil, identifiable most clearly during the 2013 protests. At the time, it was possible to observe how conservative groups took advantage of the protests that were organized by the Movimento Passe Livre (Free Fare Movement) to pressure for lower public transport costs in the big Brazilian cities – to begin to push for what they called, "the end of corruption".

Encouraging an empty discourse in terms of proposals and without much political direction, these groups were responsible for creating an atmosphere of mistrust of the political class in general, even raising the "out with everyone" banner. The institutional and representative crisis that started at that point had two consequences. First, it caused a growth in anti-PT discourse which expanded after Dilma Rousseff's 2014 re-election and the 2016 coup which deposed her. Secondly, it spurred the growth of new right-wing groups that dishonestly raise the anti-corruption banner but are financed by traditional, corrupt political parties.

This is the case of the Movimento Brasil Livre (Free Brasil Movement/MBL) which arose in 2013 on the tail of that year's protests. Led by youth such as Kim Kataguiri and Fernando Holiday, the movement called itself "non-partisan" in 2013. However, today, both Kim and Holiday are affiliated with Democrats, one of the most conservative parties in the country. In 2016, Holiday was elected city councilman in São Paulo and this year Katiguiri was elected to Congress with one of the highest vote tallies in the state of São Paulo.

Due to its initial false characterization as a non-partisan group, the movement grew in popularity for supposedly rejecting the traditional power bases of a corrupt and non-representative political system. It did not take long, however, for the real interests behind the MBL to come out: the movement was financed by political parties and its main representatives were aligned with traditional hegemonic power sectors.

The MBL was also one of the primary producers of misinformation, fake news and conspiracy theories during the arbitrary process which culminated with the coup against Dilma Rousseff. It was a coup that was proved by a conversation recorded between the Planning Minister at the time, Senator Romero Jucá (PMDB-Roraima), with the former president of Transpetro company, Sérgio Machado.

In the leaked audio, Jucá suggest a plan to Machado to "stop the bleeding in Operation Car Wash." According to the senator, the idea was to remove Dilma Rousseff from power so that the Federal Police investigations could be interrupted. In conclusion he said that they needed to make a "Big national deal, with the Supreme Court, with everything!"

Between the date of her re-election and 2016, when Dilma was definitively blocked from the position of president, the MBL spread a series of lies about her, contributing to a media lynching. One of these lies, which fell on fertile ground, was that Brazil was being converted into a "Venezuela" and that the PT was embezzling public funds to invest in public works in countries governed by "dictators" like Cuba, Nicaragua and Venezuela.

The construction of a discourse about a supposed danger of a communist takeover, something which may remind readers of the Cold War period, is a reality in 21st Century Brazil. All of the fake news spread, not only by the MBL but also by sites such as O Antagonista which are financed by business groups connected to the right wing extremist candidate, have caused the same practical result on Brazilian's mentalities.

In a large measure, this discourse was responsible for creating a generic and vulgar idea that the Brazilian left was dominating educational institutions and policy decision making with the goal of establishing a "communist regime" in the country. As much as the left tried to convince this violent, ignorant "mass" that, in fact, economic policies of the PT in recent years were neoliberal, it is clear that a large part of the Brazilian population was stricken with a collective blindness that blocked them from coolly and rationally analyzing reality.

The situation, exacerbated through WhatsApp chains and social media publications, quickly snowballed. Currently part of the population has reached the point that it is accusing Globo, the TV network that has already admitted it supported the 1964 coup and the civilian-military dictatorship that it installed, of being communist and supporting the Workers Party. Part of this population also faithfully believes that Brazil is on the verge of being converted into a country like Venezuela.

And it is in the midst of this febrile environment, in which a large sector of the population believes that the Brazilian left is creating a megalomaniac project to take power and build a dictatorship, that the criminalization of the memory of Paulo Freire appears.

For Jair Bolsonaro and his followers, the educator exerts a direct "indoctrinating" influence on the public school curriculum. Therefore, the candidate defends a restructuring of the curriculum, in order to "extinguish" the influence of Paulo Freire and his Marxist conceptions about education. In reality, Bolsonaro is planning to eliminate the constructive character of school, replacing it with a conception of education as an essentially technical and bureaucratic practice, in which students don't have the right to critical thinking and free interpretation, that's primary function is training workers for the job market.

Bolsonaro's proposal is also echoed in a new movement called "School without Party". Founded by a lawyer named Miguel Nagib, the movement is based on lobbying to pass laws that will "regulate" teaching in the public school system. The movement also says that it is nonpartisan and supposedly aims to guarantee free thinking for teachers and students.

However, the project is supported by members of the evangelical caucus at the federal, state and municipal levels. It is also relevant to note that the MBL supports the project.

The existence and defense of this project has caused a series of uncomfortable events for teachers. Without support of any scientific analysis to debate complex issues such as freedom in the classroom, the proposal, in practice, was transformed into a simple, pure criminalization of critical discussion and of leftist thought which seeks to break from hegemonic and dominant discourses.

In this form, the movement has few criteria to determine what is or isn't indoctrination – or what the School Without Party even means – but it motivates right-wing parents and students to gratuitously harass teachers for the most varied of reasons. More and more public school teachers are being accused of "Marxist indoctrination" whenever they mention any subject related to the left and are accused of practicing "gender ideology" when they try to discuss issues related to sexuality and homophobia.

It is not hard to see that this project aims to censor and determine the content that its supporters, mostly religious fundamentalists and conservatives, consider ideal. It aims to politicize teaching in public schools according to one party, criminalizing critical thought and persecuting anti-hegemonic discourse, above all in the humanities.

To date, the School Without Party project is moving through several municipal and state legislatures. However, it is a real threat to teachers because the Bolsonaro plan for government promises to adopt the project at all levels of the public school system.

Education professionals are being hunted in Brazil, from the criminalization of Paulo Freire and his ideas, to the attempts to institutionalize the School Without Party, which teachers are calling "the gag order". Our days of freedom of expression and free thinking may be numbered.

Add to this to the fact that the great majority of Bolsonaro voters appear to reject any type of technical or scientific knowledge and, with this, are devaluing the projects which seek to improve and democratize education. In today's Brazil, both Paulo Freire and the nation's teachers are becoming more and more ostracized. Part of the population, moved by lies about the work teachers do and the meaning of education, is building an anti-intellectual mood and an aversion to any liberatory educational methodology without understanding how it functions.

The greater problem is that this refusal of rational engagement – like the belief in the existence of communist indoctrination or the imposition of a gender ideology in schools – has been converted into a project for governance. With the election of Jair Bolsonaro for President, they will face a future of repressed freedom, censorship and criminalization of teaching.

Once again, Brazil's teachers will face dark days like those during the military dictatorship that halted one of the most important literacy programs in our history because it was viewed as a "communist threat". This time, however, we don't have Paulo Freire to defend us.

This article was translated by Brian Mier and originally appeared in New Socialist.

Liberalism without the people: PSDB's electoral funeral

By Ricardo Duwe

In 1975, during the heat of the conflicts over Brazil's re-democratization, the sociologist and future President Fernando Henrique Cardoso raised the question of what commitments Brazilian liberals would have to democracy. According to his diagnostic, they would never show true allegiance to their own principles, because, "in practice, liberals have rarely accepted the burden of liberalism," emphasizing that "it would be tiresome to recall all the times that, when regimes that liberals considered authoritarian (such as Vargas in 1945) or bureaucratic-populist (such as Vargas in 54 and Goulart in 64) were overturned, they themselves were the first ones to appeal to and rely on the mediating quality of the armed forces." For that reason, he concluded that Brazilian liberalism would be a form of castrated liberalism, due to the fact that it would "almost always be afraid of freedom and of effective civil society organization and participation."[i] In other words, his suspicion seemed to suggest that liberalism without the people would be doomed to conservatism and would flirt with authoritarianism.

It looks like the passage of time is proving that the sociologist of the 1970s was correct, and the Partido da Social Democracia Brasileira (Brazilian Social Democracy Party/PSDB) is now a practical example of Fernando Henrique Cardoso's own theory. Everything indicates that the results of the 2018 elections will consolidate the most significant break between the PSDB and the demands of Brazilian society in the history of the party. It is more and more obvious that the dialogue of the party elites with the Brazilian people is falling on deaf ears.

The party members don't understand what they did wrong for the people to prefer, according to the latest poll by IBOPE released on September 24, Bolsonaro's authoritarianism (28%), Haddad's Lulismo (22%), or Ciro's national developmentalism (11%), over their candidate Geraldo Alckmin's icy charisma (8%). On the other hand, the people do not see any reason to believe in the PSDB's promises. After all, it does not do justice to the word social – as the party enthusiastically supported all of the Temer Government's anti-people reforms – nor does it do justice to the word democracy, if the unfortunate role that PSDB leaders played in rejecting the results of the 2014 elections is taken into account, conducted in a manner reminiscent of the worst moments of the UDN when that party denied the victories of Getulio Vargas and Juscelino Kubitchek and the rise of Jango Goulart and Brizola during the 1950s and 1960s.

The four consecutive losses to the PT during the last presidential elections deeply impacted the PSDB, to the point that the party abandoned most of its historic goals and a deep debate about the national reality to become, exclusively, a bastion of anti-PT-ism. Without any concrete proposals to solve Brazilian's problems, and with a deep absence of dialogue with the poor and working class, the only solid discourse of the PSDB during recent years has been to try to propose an inverted self-portrait in relation to the PT: Whatever the PT is, we will be the opposite.

No character better symbolizes what the PSDB has transformed into – this hybrid mixture of anti PT-ism and lack of knowledge of the people's reality – than the image of the ex-Mayor of São Paulo, João Doria. One minute dressed up in a street cleaner's uniform downtown, another moment showing his labor card to the cameras apparently to meet a bizarre need to prove that he once held a steady job, and nearly always surfing on the shallowest kind of anti-PT-ism, Doria is the perfect portrait of the current moment of the PSDB: a party with an identity crisis which no longer knows what its role is within the Brazilian party system to the point that it is desperate because it is no longer able to dialogue with the popular classes in our society.

Regarding the current divide between the PSDB and the people, it is worth remembering that the party arose in the context of Brazilian re-democratization, this being the period of the greatest social mobilization in the modern history of the nation. During the year of its founding in 1988, broad sectors of the Brazilian population were unsatisfied with the path that the New Republic was taking, the influence of President José Sarney, the so called "big center" of the National Constituent Assembly and the chronic inflation problem, which had been exacerbated the year before during the failed *Cruzado II* monetary policy.

Faced with this scenario, PMDB leaders like Fernando Henrique Cardoso, Mário Covas, André Franco Montoro, José Serra, and Luiz Carlos Bresser-Pereira met a popular demand to break from the party and founded the PSDB. Its main promises were to break with the physiology of Brazilian politics and adopt economic practices that mixed liberal proposals of fiscal responsibility and inflation control without abandoning the central role of the State in promoting welfare and income redistribution. These latter proposals were defended by developmentalist actors who were still affiliated with the party at the time, but who would go on to leave it due to disagreements with the conservative turn it was taking, like Ciro Gomes and Bresser-Pereira.

In comparing the past with the current scenario, it may look strange that the international experience which served as the ideal reference point for the recently founded PSDB was the French Socialist Party government led by then President François Mitterand (1981-1995). Mitterand was elected in 1981 by means of a historic coalition between France's traditional left fronts which included his Socialist Party and the Communist Party which had triumphed with a centrist candidate, then – President Valéry Giscard d'Estaing. The election of Mitterand caused great repercussions around the world as his social-democratic government adopted ground breaking policies such as: abolition of the death penalty, taxation of large fortunes, reduction of the work week to 39 hours, a fifth annual week of paid vacation, nationalizing companies, regional decentralization and reduction of the retirement age from 65-60. How many of these measures are defended by Geraldo Alckmin or João Doria in their 2018 electoral campaigns?

In a recent interview in *Estado de São Paulo* newspaper, one of the historic leaders of the PSDB, former Governor and current Senator from Ceará, Tasso Jereissati, publicly admitted to a series of errors made in the recent history of the organization. For Jereissati, big mistakes included: 1) challenging the results of the 2014 elections; 2) voting against the basic economic ideals of the party, "just to be against the PT"; and 3) the greatest error of all – joining Michel Temer's government.

Although the growth of extreme-right fronts is a world phenomenon, in observing the Brazilian case, it is noticeable that most of the former voting base of the PSDB has migrated to the candidacy of Jair Bolsonaro (PSL-Rio de Janeiro). As the PSDB abandoned concrete political proposals, betting all its chips on anti-PT-ism and allying with the worst groups inside the PMDB and the "big center", the party fell into mistrust by the people and this void was rapidly filled with Bolsonaro's authoritarian radicalism. According to data obtained in a September 19 survey in São Paulo state, former governor Geraldo Alckmin only has 13% support and is losing by a wide margin to Bolsonaro, who is leading with 30%.ii

The results of these disastrous and anti-people policies will be collected in the 2018 election. According to current predictions, the PSDB Congressional Bloc will shrink and, even with the most amount of commercial airtime [due to election laws which grant time according to coalition size], Geraldo Alckmin will not make the second round. After 24 years without losing a gubernatorial election in São Paulo, João Doria looks like he will lose in the second round to Paulo Skaf. Faced with this conjuncture and the inability of the party to renew itself, could it be possible to hold an electoral funeral for the PSDB by the end of the year?

A definitively affirmative response to this question would be an exaggeration that would not take into consideration the power that the PSDB will continue to wield within the Brazilian party system after the elections, in which it has a good chance of electing governors in important states like Minas Gerais and Rio Grande do Sul. On the other hand, it is undeniable that, at the moment, the party is experiencing its greatest credibility loss in history. The current image of the party is a deformed and unrecognizable caricature when compared to that what was built on its founding principles in 1988. A comparison with this period is even more meaningful when we remember the fact that in the 1989 presidential elections party founder Mário Covas supported Lula in the second round against Fernando Collor de Mello.

The years passed by and the current context is considerably distinct from 1989. The most likely scenario for the second round will be a run off between Jair Bolsonaro and a candidate from the center-left, like Fernando Haddad or Ciro Gomes. The role of the PSDB in this runoff, independent of what it will be, will have undeniable practical effects on the outcome. But the fact is that, faced with the threat that Bolsonaro poses to the democratic values of the country – values that the founding leaders of the PSDB fought against during the military dictatorship – history imposes a crucial decision to be made, that touches on the traditions of the party, that is if these traditions still provide any moral guidance for its leaders. If the pragmatic and anti-people intransigence of the party elite insists on adapting a position against both Bolsonaro and Haddad or Ciro, the PSDB will, once again, miss the boat of history. This time, the boat will take social democracy and the party traditions with it, leaving the PSDB to fulfill the prophecy that its honorary president made during the 1970s:

Liberalism without the people is doomed to fail.

This article originally appeared in LeMonde Diplomatique Brasil and was translated by Brian Mier.

i Cardoso, Fernando Henrique. (1975). *Autoritarismo e democratização*. Rio de Janeiro: Paz e Terra.
ii IPOPE. (September 19, 2018). Paulo Skaf e Jõao Doria seguem emptados na disputa pelo governo de São Paulo. Retrieved from http://www.ibopeinteligencia.com/noticias-e-pesquisas/paulo-skaf-e-joao-doria-seguem-empatados-na-disputa-pelo-governo-de-sao-paulo/

The fall of Brazil's egalitarian and sovereign democracy

By Marcelo Zero

At the moment that I write this article (October 2018), Brazil is about to elect Jair Bolsonaro as President of the Republic. He is an ex-military officer and politician who is openly fascist, homophobic, misogynist and racist.

Intellectually very limited and with a political career that is absolutely mediocre, Bolsonaro has already publicly declared that "Democracy is good for nothing," and that the only way to solve Brazil's problems is through a new dictatorship that would kill at least 30,000 people. His idol is the great torturer of the Brazilian military dictatorship, Colonel Brilhante Ustra, who used to insert rats in prisoners' vaginas.

Besides this, he has a habit of saying that homosexuality is the result of lack of physical punishment for children and that women should earn less than men. He once told a left wing congresswoman that she "didn't deserve" to be raped because she was ugly.

His Vice Presidential candidate, General Mourão, has made similar declarations. He said in public that Brazil, unfortunately, inherited the "dishonesty" of the black race and the "laziness" of the Indians.

No, these declarations are not fake news. Everything is registered on video. Unfortunately it's all true.

This democratic debacle is developing in the middle of the worst political, institutional and economic crisis in Brazilian history.

President Dilma Rousseff, who was recognized even by her worst enemies as a serious and honest politician, was deposed in an apparent media and parliamentary coup d' etat, based on *a posteriori* claims of illicit conduct. Since there was no crime whatsoever, it was generated in the coup's imagination. A majority ultra-conservative and corrupt Congress was encouraged to ratify the charges as if they were true.

She was replaced by corrupt and profoundly conservative politicians like Michel Temer, who took advantage of the coup to implement the orthodox and socially regressive economic agenda that had been rejected in the 2014 elections. This coup greatly deepened the economic crisis that began in 2015, increased unemployment which now affects nearly 13 million Brazilians and under-employment, which affects around 24 million people. Brazil is returning to the UN World Hunger Map, extreme poverty has returned and the working class was hit hard by labor reforms which removed a series of historic rights.

The worst, however, is the damage to democracy. The coup created a State of Exception which, among other things, imprisoned former President Lula based on a fake conviction without any concrete proof.

The "judgment" was only made to remove him from the elections. According to all polls, Lula was the clear favorite and would have beaten Bolsonaro by a wide margin if he had been allowed to run. It is important to note that the UN Human Rights Committee ruled, two times, that Lula had the right to run for office. However the coup government simply ignored the legally binding UN ruling.

Furthermore, cases of violence against gays, blacks, women and leftist activists have become common on the streets of Brazil. Marielle Franco, a feminist, leftist activist and community leader, was barbarically assassinated. To date, the culprits have not been found. In Bahia, an important cultural leader, Moa de Katendê, black like Marielle, was assassinated after saying that he voted for PT.

The situation in Brazil today forms a stark contrast to Brazil under Lula, when the country developed with the elimination of poverty, distribution of income, and democracy and protaganism on the international stage.

To understand Brazil's abysmal fall one needs to understand the structural weaknesses of Brazilian democracy, the slave master and exclusionary DNA of its social structure and the role that the country plays in world geopolitical conflict.

In post military dictatorship Brazil, disputes generally involved forces from the left and center left against forces of the center-right and right who competed for the vote of the political center and the undecided.

There was a kind of implicit pact by which all the relevant political forces recognized democracy as a universal value that was indispensable to advance national development.

Even with the obvious structural limitations of Brazilian democracy, which denied the majority of the population of its basic political and social rights, there was a practically consensual disposition to deepen it and consolidate it, a natural feeling in a country which had just come out of decades of military rule.

However, this pact, embodied in the 1988 Constitution, was respected in its basic aspects while the left was a controllable minority that served as a legitimizing element to a democracy that was still under construction. Left parties composed a tolerated opposition that was incapable of really contesting power.

In this manner, contrary to what happened in Europe, for example, the Brazilian democratic "stability" was based on a structural imbalance of political power and an absence of any real alternation of power.

Evidently, this scenario changed with the arrival of PT in power in the 2002 elections. Many believed that Brazilian democracy had matured enough to handle a moderate center-left government that was dedicated to promoting social inclusion and eradicating poverty and inequality.

For a brief historic moment, it seemed like we emulated, *mutatis mutandis*, the successful experiences of classical European social democracy. Our democracy appeared to be capable of dealing and negotiating with the distributive conflicts inherent in capitalist economies. Despite much resistance and prejudice, the Lula and Dilma governments managed for a time to promote social inclusion for vast segments of the population and substantially reduced poverty and inequality, in a context of fierce opposition but relative democratic stability.

However, this picture changed suddenly and drastically when the economic crisis, coupled with the pressures of distributive policies on profits, began to affect the interests of big business, especially large financially-owned capital and its allied political sectors.

In a flash, the illusion of maturing Brazilian democracy was thrown to the dirty ground of a banana coup. The historic structural imbalance between the political powers on opposite sides of the political spectrum was reestablished based on force, against 54.5 million votes. It broke with the democratic alternation between the political forces and the pact that was embodied in the 1988 Constitution.

It is no secret to anyone that there is a general crisis in democracies and in the political representation systems, strongly damaged by the inequality caused by neoliberal policies. As Piketty makes clear, 21st Century capitalist accumulation seems less and less compatible with democracy.

However there is a serious aggravating factor in Brazil. To the contrary of what occurs, for example, in Europe, here the traditional right and center right fanned the flames of fascism and bet everything on a rupture of democracy. Our economic and political oligarchies broke with democracy. They broke with democracy and with popular sovereignty. They inflated the most backwards forces in Brazil to conduct a coup against an honest president and put in power what was called the "bleeding class" - a band of corrupt politicians who are mostly rich, white men.

They also heavily engaged with the arrest of Lula, who was the man who was in the best position to oppose rising fascism.

The coup supporters came out to the streets together with Bolsonaro and other proto-fascist groups that were demanding military intervention. They condemned democracy and politics in a general manner. They planned to only "destroy the PT" but they laid the egg of the serpent that would inject mortal poison in all of the democratic institutions. The Temer government transformed into the Brazilian Weimar Republic. The traditional forces of the Brazilian right lost control over the political process. The traditional parties of the center and the right were swept away and the extremist, fascist right assumed political and ideological hegemony over the Coup project.

With the support of the military, of a good part of the judiciary and extensive sectors of national and foreign capital, Bolsonaro became the one to consummate and deepen the 2016 coup's ultra-neoliberal agenda. To do this, he will not hesitate to use force and persecute and repress all and every type of "political activism". This is written in his program for government.

From its current form as a type of semi-democracy and State of Exception, Brazil is expected to slide into a disguised dictatorship, supported by a caste of ultraconservative military and judiciary members.

II- International Context and Imperialist Intervention

These deep, rapid and tragic changes were mainly caused by internal economic, social and political factors. Nevertheless, we cannot rule out, *a priori*, that there are not also international interests committed to destabilizing Brazilian democracy and supporting the conservative economic agenda put in place through the 2016 coup.

Whenever one tries to raise this issue, people try to discredit it as mere conspiracy theory. This is inappropriate. After all, the history of Latin America and Brazil shows that external interference in national affairs has been, and still is, prevalent in our region. A 2005 study published in the *Harvard Review of Latin America* shows that between 1898 and 1994 the US successfully caused regime changes in the region 41 times, which comes out to an average of one every 28 months.[i] It is important to note that this study, published at Harvard University, does not analyze recent possible US interventions such as those in Honduras (2009), Paraguay (2012) and Brazil (2016).

There is, therefore, a long history of interventions, which includes the Brazilian Military Coup of 1964. This suggests that wider and deeper analysis needs to be made of the 2016 parliamentary coup, of Operation Car Wash and its *modus operandi*, and above all, of Bolsonaro's meteoric rise and his fascism.

US interference in Brazil's internal affairs was shockingly evident in the Bolsonaro campaign. There was an overwhelming growth of Bolsonarist fascism in the final stretch of the campaign, fueled by an avalanche of fake news against PT spread over the internet. It is an old tactic, developed by the American and British intelligence agencies, to manipulate public opinion and influence political processes and elections. It was used in Ukraine, the Arab Spring and Brazil in 2013.

Documents released by Edward Snowden prove that the US and UK intelligence services, as well as those from other countries, have specialized and sophisticated units that are dedicated to manipulating information that circulates on the internet and changes the direction of public opinion. There are also private companies which, in collusion with these agencies, specialize in manipulating public opinion. The Bolsonaro campaign has had active collaboration from Steve Bannon, Trump's strategist, and it used and abused these tactics to discredit Fernando Haddad, the adversary of fascism.

The many barbaric messages that were widely distributed through WhatsApp against the PT include the lie that Haddad distributed a "gay kit" to public school children to transform children into homosexuals; that starting from the age of 5, children would have to be delivered to the State to be indoctrinated; and that Haddad himself was a pedophile. The list of dirty lies with grotesque manipulations of photos and videos is enormous and varied.

Bolsonaro's team, made up of people as coarse and unprepared as their candidate, does not seem to have the financial or technical conditions to promote such a massive, destructive campaign.

This is why there have long been suspicions that this overwhelming misinformation campaign had the fingerprint of foreign intelligence agencies, as well as big national and international corporations, committed to promoting this so-called "hybrid war."

This suspicion was confirmed by a story in *Folha de São Paulo*, a newspaper that has no sympathy for the PT, on October 18, 2018. The story revealed that Bolsonaro's social network campaign of lies and hate is being financed by dirty money from big companies that is used to contract tech firms that specialize in boosting information through social networks.

Just one of these companies spent around $3.5 Million USD to spread fake news through the Brazilian social media. Most of the telephone numbers used were based abroad, mainly in the USA. Apparently, this story is just the tip of the iceberg and many actions are continuing without any investigations whatsoever.

In Brazil, this type of activity constitutes a serious electoral crime. However, the Brazilian Supreme Electoral Court (TSE) has been washing its hands of it, and its current President, Minister Rosa Weber, has already received death threats if she refuses to confer victory to Bolsonaro in the second round election.

The commitment of foreign governments and companies to the annihilation of the PT and the Brazilian left, as well as the promotion of the coup and now of a fascist candidate, is not surprising.

There is a lot at play and Brazil is a key country in world geopolitical strategy. The big world geopolitical conflict is clearly defined. On the one side are the big emerging countries and their allies like China, Russia, etc., which are working for a politically multipolar order that is more balanced economically, and on the other is the US and some allies, which desperately try to restore the previously unchallenged hegemony of the great world superpower and impose a unipolar and deeply asymmetrical world order.

Because of this, the new US security doctrine no longer considers terrorism as its top priority. According to Defense Secretary Jim Mattis, the "Mad Dog" who recently visited Brazil, "the great competition for world power, and not terrorism, is now the main focus of US national security."

After the coup, Brazil took a favorable position towards North American geopolitical interests in this great dispute, and transformed itself, once again, into a geopolitical satellite of the USA.

Indeed, with the coup, our country has rapidly passed from being a great international actor – the creator of the BRICS that was courted and respected throughout the world – to a mere pawn of the United States in its struggle for the restoration of hegemony. Brazil created the BRICS but has now become the weak link of the group.

The active and haughty foreign policy which so elevated Brazil on the world stage was replaced by a passive and submissive policy that makes us crawl on the world chessboard as an outcast of international relations. Brazil is now a country that is inexorably sliding toward geopolitical irrelevance, but that can be extremely useful to the US and its allies' strategic interests.

After all it is a country of continental proportions that has one of the world's largest hydrocarbon reserves, the pre-salt petroleum reserves, the planet's greatest biodiversity, abundant mineral reserves, a large availability of arable land, and 14% of the world's fresh water. Furthermore, despite the crisis, it's still the world's 8th largest economy.

The fact is that the US' recent strategic dominance, fueled by the 2016 coup, was at risk in the face of the possibility of the PT returning to power, which was certain to happen if Lula ran.

Therefore, it is absolutely vital to US geopolitical interests and the interests of the international capital committed to exploiting Brazil's vast natural resources, that Bolsonaro wins the election. Perhaps they preferred a more civilized candidate, but in practice he was the only one capable of defeating Haddad and the PT. Between moderate reformism and fascism, they chose fascism.

Although Bolsonaro is a former Brazilian military man, he has already publicly saluted the US flag, pledged support to Trump, agreed to participate in a military intervention in Venezuela and said he will cede the Alcântara rocket launching base to the United States. In other words, he has made it clear that he will be an unconditional ally in the support of North American geopolitical hegemony. A man like Bolsonaro does not really bother those who supported Pinochet.

This article was translated from Portuguese by Brian Mier and originally appeared in New Socialist.

i Coatsworth, J. (2005, Summer). United States interventions: what for? *Revista: Harvard Review of Latin America*. Retrieved from https://revista.drclas.harvard.edu/book/united-states-interventions

WhatsApp: Bolsonaro's hate machine

By Brian Mier

Brazil has some of the world's most expensive cellular phone airtime. Therefore when Facebook's WhatsApp messaging app came along, which allows users to make free calls over the internet, it caught on fast. Today, over 100 million Brazilians – half the population – use it every day. Brazilians are the largest consumers of WhatsApp in the world.

Twitter was influential in Middle East regime changes in the so-called Arab spring. Facebook helped propel Obama to power in 2008 and 4Chan helped Trump win the US presidency in 2016. The 2018 Brazilian presidential elections appear to be the first anywhere in which WhatsApp will prove to be a deciding factor. Leading candidate Jair Bolsonaro has avoided television appearances in favor of the social media platform, which allows him and his followers to quickly reach millions of people with slanderous misinformation that is not challenged or regulated in any way, and is believed to be factual by a large segment of the population.

Brazil's campaign laws dictate that candidates' television commercials are limited to a certain amount of free airtime which is allocated by the government according to how many congressmen belong to his or her coalition's political parties. This ensures that, whereas all candidates are guaranteed a minimum amount of free air time, the larger parties and coalitions get more. In the 2018 election season, PSDB candidate Geraldo Alckmin, who was initially Wall Street's favorite due to his support of the Temer government's deep austerity cuts and petroleum privatizations, was allocated 5'30" of commercial airtime in each of the two daily 25 minute political commercial blocs. PT candidate Fernando Haddad got 2'22". Fernando Meireles from PMDB got 1'50". For the first time since the end of the dictatorship, however, the leading candidate in a Brazilian Presidential election has been almost invisible on TV. Jair Bolsonaro, from the tiny, neofascist PSL party, has only had 8 seconds of airtime per commercial bloc. Furthermore, he has repeatedly refused to participate in television debates. How has he emerged as electoral front-runner? The first factor was the arrest, with no material evidence, of leading candidate Luiz Inácio Lula da Silva. Unlike 1400 other current candidates in the Brazilian elections who have similar appeals processes underway and were allowed to run for office by the electoral courts, Lula was removed from the election in direct defiance of Brazilian electoral law and a legally binding order from the UN Human Rights Committee. His arrest has clearly led to a rise of fascism in Brazil. The second key factor is Bolsonaro's campaign and supporters use of the WhatsApp messenger platform which is impossible to police for Brazilian crimes such as hate speech, and conspiracy to incite violence and slander, making it a perfect platform for committing character assassination against anyone from ex-lovers to professional and political rivals.

When 4 million women joined the #elenao (#nothim) Facebook group in protest against Bolsonaro and planned one of the largest anti-fascist protests in history, his campaign and his followers (it is nearly impossible to ascertain the difference through WhatsApp) immediately swung into action to discredit the protest. Working through thousands of chat groups of 256 members each, they circulated photos from a recent gay pride parade of topless lesbian activists and said that they were taken at the #elenao protests. They worked to specifically target evangelical Christian women, coupling the photos with messages like, "This is what [PT candidate] Haddad thinks about family values". Around one million people took to the streets on September 30 against Bolsonaro in 300 cities and 21 countries around the world and celebrities like Madonna publicly expressed support for the campaign, but when the poll results started coming in a few days later, woman's support for Bolsonaro had increased, giving him a 5% jump and propelling him into a projected tie with Fernando Haddad in the run off.

TV Producer Janaina Avila recently published a list of 15 lies that the Bolsonaro campaign has specifically targeted evangelical Christians with on WhatsApp. These include the following: 1) If PT candidate Fernando Haddad is elected, children will become property of the state and have their gender declared by government bureaucrats at age 5; 2) While mayor of São Paulo, Haddad distributed penis shaped baby bottles at public preschools; 3) Vice Presidential candidate Manuela D'Ávila, according to a photo-shopped picture, wore a T-shirt that said, " Jesus is a Transvestite"; and 4) One million Bolsonaro supporters took part in a protest on Paulista avenue in São Paulo last week.

Facebook has made efforts to limit the amount of fake news in Brazil, pulling down nearly 200 anonymously run sites connected to the alt-right Movimento Brasil Livre group after it spread the lie that slain Rio city councilwoman Marielle Franco was a former drug trafficker, but the company has not made any effort to slow the spread of lies on WhatsApp. As Ygor Salles, Social Media Editor from the Folha de São Paulo newspaper says, "policing WhatsApp would put Mark Zuckerberg in a catch 22. The success of the app is based on the promise that all communications are encrypted. If they start regulating it, users will believe they were lied to and stop using the platform."

A storm gathers - Chapter Eighteen

We will be together, marching forward

By Gaía Passarelli

I never thought I'd get here.

And sometimes I want to believe that it will not get worse. But then I pinch myself: I did not think Dilma would fall, I did not think Doria would be Mayor of São Paulo, I did not think Trump would be US President. I never thought I would see people wanting to teach the Pope how to read the Bible (literally) or accusing The Economist of being "communist." I also did not think I would see a reporter suffer aggression, or an artist having a family threatened with death.

Last week I read a tweet saying that our generation grew up having democracy as an unshakable right. But this right was not guaranteed for the generation of my parents, who were young during the period of the Military Dictatorship. Nor was it true for my grandparents, who lived through the Vargas years. It may not be true for those who come after us.

But it was true for me, so I had no way of knowing how shaken I would get when I saw the #EleNao protesters gathering in Largo da Batata in São Paulo (and in many cities around the country, I know), a concentration of flags of the most diverse orientations, yet concentrated on one urgent subject: to brake the advance of authoritarianism in Brazil.

In the past weeks we saw a judge preventing an interview, a politician wanting to remove a magazine from the shelves, a military General saying that the Constitution should be rewritten by a "commission of notables", people defending revocation of rights, a candidate saying on television that he will not accept any result other than a victory, which he takes for granted. These are just a few examples that come to mind. I'm sure there are many more. A certain military official linked to a certain candidate said that "books which do not tell the truth about the military regime" should be "taken out of circulation" — which truth, I ask? Certainly there is more to happen these next days, right before the first round of elections that will decide on federal, state, president, governors, senators, and deputies.

I'm 42 and I grew up during the late 70s/early 80s "redemocratization" years in Brazil. When I was a little girl, I saw through the tube TVs (where we could choose from the seven channels available!) that programmes were preceded with a little vignette: a form signed by a censor. To me censorship was this, but of course it was much more. Censorship operated within newsrooms and newspapers, within publishers and record labels, within radios and TVs, selecting in advance what would or would not go public. This text, incidentally, would not. As well as much of the content of today's media in Brazil. This was of course, on behalf of the people of "morals and good manners", as they were called at the time, the equivalent of the "good citizens" and member of the "traditional Brazilian family" of today.

When I was a child, my parents lived surrounded by Latin American expatriates, who sometimes came to live with us from other countries that also lived under dictatorships, such as Chile and Argentina. I did not understand why people talked about missing people, what it meant to shout "Diretas Já", or why there was so much emotion when President Tancredo Neves was elected and so much consternation when he died shortly afterwards. But now I know. Today, I know what happened on Maria Antonia Street fifty years ago, I know why there is a Military Police and the "Voice of Brazil" still airs every evening on every radio in the country. I know because my mother taught me. I know because there are people who remember and tell. People like the old ladies who were protesting last Saturday, ladies like my mother.

I could not imagine that we would march together, up Avenida Rebouças, shouting slogans, arms folded, fists up, helping those who were tired of walking, sharing bottles of mineral water, handing out leaflets to people who screamed in support from buses stranded in the lanes.

I never imagined that we would see Avenida Paulista go silent to hear two girls sing a Brazilian version of the "Bella Ciao" anthem in front of the Conjunto Nacional building.

I never thought we'd get here, but here we are. And for this very reason I am sure that no matter what happens, we will be together and we will be marching forward.

This article first appeared in Hysteria and was translated by Daniel Hunt.

Brazil at the crossroads

By Aline Piva

1968 was a decisive year. It was a year in which the civil rights movements rose with a force never seen before. The world watched as the streets of Paris were taken over by students and workers, causing an intense revision of society and advancing fundamental social rights. But it was also the year in which the Mexican government sent troops in to massacre students in Tlatololco. It was the year in which Brazil was submerged in the bloodiest phase of repression, which eliminated our civil liberties and legalized the unnamable through Institutional Act 5.

Two antagonistic visions of the world clashed – an emancipatory project versus a project of perpetuating the existing order at all costs.

Fifty years later, we find ourselves once again at the forefront of this conflict.

On one side we have the emergence and consolidation of projects which aim to build a more just society, an international system based on reciprocal relations between sovereign nations, as opposed to vassal states. On the other side, we see the resurgence of a kind of Hobbesian State, in both internal and international relations, a State where anything goes to consolidate the real, financial or symbolic power. A state where manipulation of the deep-seated fears and prejudice in our society opens space for the resurgence and empowerment to the worst characteristics of the history of mankind

It is exactly in this context that elections are taking place this Sunday in Brazil. They will have a deep impact not only internally, but also from a geopolitical standpoint.

This election represents the clash of Brazil as a global actor versus a Brazil that is the puppet of transnational interests, willing to give up our sovereignty, our strategic reserves, to open our bases to the gringo military. It is a clash between the rebuilding of our social fabric and republican institutions and the empowerment of the most cruel and dangerous face of the politics of fear and hatred.

What is in play this Sunday is the future of Brazil as a nation.

This article originally appeared in Nocaute and was translated by Brian Mier.

Year of Lead

Part four

Aftermath

Why Bolsonaro won, beyond the clichés

By Brian Mier

Why did the Brazilian people elect a neofascist? If you get your information from the newspapers, you might think that this happened because Brazilians are afraid of rising violence rates or fed up with corruption. These explanations sound great on paper because they function as what sociologist Pierre Bordieu called mind stopping clichés. When hearing something familiar and logical sounding, the brain stops and moves onto another subject.

Violence and corruption. Everyone hates that. What's happening in sports? This is how the Anglo media wants people to process the issue of the arrival of fascism in Brazil, because if the public begins to scratch under the surface it will find uncomfortable truths that implicate their own governments, think tanks, corporations and media institutions. That could lead to some difficult questions, so why not stick to the mind stopping clichés of violence and corruption? The problem is that, although both issues may have been used to manipulate the public, neither of them hold up to scrutiny.

Haddad had more support in the most violent regions

Like all countries that have to deal with the legacy of slavery and the fact that one segment of the population considers another segment to be sub-human, Brazil has always been a violent place. The image of Brazil as a land of violence has been burned into the minds of the Anglo public through films like *Pixote*, *City of God* and *Elite Squad*. Only 6% of Brazilians live in favelas, and many favelas have more middle class residents than poor, but in the minds of many casual northern observers, most Brazilians live in desolate slums full of child soldiers. Could fear of violence have been the deciding factor in electing a military man to the presidency? Brazil certainly sounds scary to many Americans.i

While it is true that violence has risen in Brazil in recent years – especially after the start of the austerity policies that began mildly during the last year of Dilma Rousseff's presidency and were greatly exacerbated by the coup government which took power in 2016 – violence patterns have been marked by a geographical shift which does not strongly correspond with electoral support for Bolsonaro. The case in point is São Paulo state, where Jair Bolsonaro received over ¼ of his total number of votes. Although Brazil witnessed a 14% rise in homicides between 2006 and 2016, São Paulo saw a 46% drop in the same period, with an even greater drop from 2000-2006.ii São Paulo city has seen its homicide rate of 60/100,000 in the year 2000 drop to 7.8/100,000 in 2017, which is significantly lower than most big American cities.iii Likewise, statewide homicide rates have dropped from 26/100,000 to 9.5/100,000 during the same period.iv Although there was a slight increase in the state-wide murder rate during 2017, murders actually dropped by 15% in São Paulo city.v

The case of Rio de Janeiro, where 67% of voters supported Bolsonaro, is also telling. In 2002, Rio de Janeiro had a homicide rate of 60/100,000.vi By 2010 it had dropped to 26/100,000. Murder rates began rising again after the sports mega-events, reaching around 37/100,000 in 2017 – a disturbing statistic, but not one that places Rio de Janeiro among the ten most violent states in Brazil.vii As I have argued before, however, Rio has a unique political and criminal environment.viii For example, a report by Amnesty International shows that 25% of all murders committed in Rio de Janeiro in 2017 were done by police officers.ix Neighboring Minas Gerais has violence issues of its own, but it's police killed around 10 times fewer people per capita in 2017 than the police in Rio de Janeiro.x Furthermore, as Ben Anderson and I discovered while filming the HBO/Vice TV special, *The Pacification of Rio*, there is evidence that the Rio de Janeiro state government cooked the books, and shifted numbers between homicides, violent deaths of undetermined causes and disappearances to make crime rates appear lower during the lead up to the World Cup and Olympics. Therefore, although there is a recent rise in violence in Rio, the real numbers may be lower than they appear due to statistical manipulation by the government to build up support for the military occupation and, even if they are not, these numbers don't compare to the numbers from the early 2000s or rank Rio as one of the most violent places in Brazil.

If the homicide rate in Brazil has fallen so dramatically in the last 15 years in Rio and São Paulo, why did Brazil experience its highest murder toll ever last year? One reason is that the Brazilian northeast has been inundated with crack.xi Last year, 6 of the 10 most violent states in Brazil were located in the Northeast, the region where Fernando Haddad beat Bolsonaro in every state.xii In Ceará, for example, which has a homicide rate 8 times higher than that of São Paulo, Fernando Haddad received 71% of the vote.<u>xiii</u>,<u>xiv</u>

Was fear of violence the reason people in São Paulo elected Bolsonaro, or was fear of violence the reason northeasterners elected Haddad? Let's face it. Everyone is afraid of violence. But if 25% of the votes for an "anti-violence" candidate come from a region of Brazil that has crime rates comparable to places in Europe or Canada, one could come to the conclusion that the either electorate was manipulated or there were other, more important issues at stake.

It's only corruption when communists do it

The other reason commonly cited for supporting Bolsonaro is Brazilians frustration with corruption, which, for the last 5 years has been nearly exclusively associated in the national and international media with the PT. Like the issue of violence, this does not hold up to a minimal level of scrutiny. President Dilma Rousseff was never involved in personal enrichment through corruption. In fact, she herself is a victim of corruption. Impeached for committing a non-impeachable offense, a budgetary infraction that was systematically committed by all leaders of all levels of Brazilian government and legalized two days after she was removed from office, it has subsequently come out that congressmen were bribed to vote in favor of her impeachment.<u>xv</u> ,<u>xvi</u> Luiz Inácio Lula da Silva, who was the one man generally believed powerful enough to block the privatization of Brazil's massive offshore petroleum reserves, was arrested on charges that he committed "indeterminate acts of corruption" related to an apartment the courts were unable to prove he ever owned and thrown in jail before his appeals process played out, in a move which Glen Greenwald says was obviously done to keep him for running for president this year.xvii,xviii,xix Likewise, Fernando Haddad was a victim of corruption when US-backed judge and prosecutor Sergio Moro illegally leaked plea bargain testimony to the press during election season, alleging that it implicates him in a corruption scandal despite the fact that the testimony had already been thrown out by the Public Prosecutor's Office.xx,xxi

Jair Bolsonaro, on the other hand, spent 25 years affiliated with the most corrupt political party in Brazil, the Partido Progressista (PP), led by the most corrupt politician in Brazilian history, Paulo Maluf, who is on Interpol's most wanted list and cannot leave Brazil or will be arrested.xxii ,xxiii Furthermore Bolsonaro is already inviting corrupt politicians to help run his government. These names include:

1) Alberto Fraga, Congressman from the DEM party and gun industry pitchman who was invited to lead his bloc in Congress.xxiv Three weeks before the first round elections, in September, 2018, Fraga was sentenced to 4 years of semi-open imprisonment after being caught on tape charging and receiving bribes from a bus company;xxv

2) Congressman Onyx Lazaroni, who has already confirmed as Bolsonaro's chief of staff, who admitted to taking bribes from the JBS meat packing company to use in an illegal campaign slush fund in 2017;xxvi

3) Congressman Pauderny Avelino from the DEM party,

who was convicted in 2016 of paying cronies millions of dollars above market rate in rents for buildings and used school furniture when he was education minister in Manaus;xxvii and

4) Paulo Guedes, a University of Chicago educated monetarist economist with former ties to the Augusto Pinochet regime in Chile. Bolsonaro has invited him to be his Economic Minister, even though he is currently being investigated by the Public Prosecutor's Office, who want to know how R$1 Billion disappeared from private pension funds he was managing.xxviii

If mind-stopping clichés of violence and corruption do not fully correspond with voting patterns and Bolsonaro's governmental program, why did he win the election? My take is that the election was neither fair nor free. It was the result of a massive fraudulent campaign backed by the US government, Brazilian military and the judiciary to guarantee that the privatizations of the world's largest offshore petroleum reserves implemented by the coup government of Michel Temer are not reversed, and that the US military has access to Brazilian military bases for another possible future petroleum grab in Venezuela. The following events had a much bigger effect on Bolsonaro's victory than violence and corruption:

1) The joint US/Brazil *Lava Jato* investigation imprisoned leading candidate Luiz Inácio Lula da Silva, who promised to reverse petroleum privatizations and re-allocate state oil profits to public health and education. He was jailed before his appeals process was finished on trumped up charges with no material evidence, based on a single plea bargain testimony made by a convicted

criminal in exchange for sentence reduction and partial asset retention;

2) Lula announced he would run for President anyway, as was his right according to Brazilian and international law. The electoral court allowed 1400 candidates with similar legal issues to run, but they made an exception for Lula. Still leading in all election polls from behind bars, with more support than all other candidates combined and double the support of Bolsonaro, the one man easily capable of defeating fascism was barred from running;xxix

3) The UN Human Rights Committee issued a ruling ordering the Brazilian government to allow Lula to run for office. Brazil is a signatory to the UN Protocol on Civil and Political Rights and, according to Brazilian law MP 311/2009, UNHRC rulings are legally binding.xxx The Supreme Electoral Court thus broke Brazilian law and disobeyed the UN when it refused to let Lula run;

4) In a country where TV crews regularly enter prisons to interview drug traffickers and mass murderers, the courts bared Lula from speaking to journalists, illegally prohibiting him for communicating to the public about why they should vote against fascism in the elections;

5) 3.3 million voters, most of whom were poor and Northeastern – essentially the demographic that most supports the PT party – were purged from the voter rolls two weeks before the elections;xxxi

6) After Bolsonaro support surged in the first round election, *Folha de São Paulo* revealed that his campaign was using an illegal slush fund created by hundreds of

businessmen paying up to $4 Million USD each to hire tech firms to illegally acquire personal data from users of the WhatsApp social media app.<u>xxxii</u> According to the article, this was used to create thousands of demographically targeted groups of 256 users each and bombard them with lies and slander against the PT party. These lies were not primarily based on fear mongering about violence and corruption, but on slander that the PT party is run by sexual perverts who want to make everyone's children gay. After Supreme Electoral Court President Rosa Weber received death threats from Bolsonaro supporters and held a meeting with Bolsonaro supporter General Sergio Etchegoyen, she decided to hold off investigations until after the final round of the elections.

International capital and the US government now have exactly what they want in Brazil. All natural resources will be opened to exploitation from foreign capital. The US military will be able to use the Alcantara rocket launching base as a take off point for forays into Venezuela. Brazil's participation in the BRICS is dead in the water and US Petroleum companies will be swimming in Brazilian oil. Regardless of the level of participation by the US and its institutions, these events fit a pattern of US interventions in Latin America over the past 100 years. If we are truly interested in defeating fascism it is important to move beyond clichés and work to identify the real actors at play, so that their power can be countered. In order to do this, we have to move beyond the idea that Brazil operates in a geopolitical vacuum and that the return to neofascism, which was previously installed with ample US government support from 1964-1985, can be explained by oversimplified generalizations about public opinion.

i Favero, D. (2011, December 21). IBGE: 6% da população brasileira mora em favelas. *Terra*. Retrieved from https://www.terra.com.br/noticias/brasil/cidades/ibge-6-da-populacao-brasileira-mora-em-favelas, 4b0d55e5c56fa310VgnCLD200000bbcceb0aRCRD.html

ii SP tem a menor taxa de homicídios do Brasil e redução de 46% nos assassinatos de 2006 a 2016, diz Atlas da Violência. (2018, May 6). *Globo*. Retrieved from https://g1.globo.com/sp/sao-paulo/noticia/sp-tem-a-menor-taxa-de-homicidios-do-brasil-e-reducao-de-46-nos-assassinatos-de-2006-a-2016-diz-atlas-da-violencia.ghtml

iii IPEA.(2017, June 6). *Atlas da Violencia*. Retrieved from http://www.ipea.gov.br/portal/images/170609_atlas_da_violencia_2017.pdf

iv Fontes, G. (2018, February 15). Taxa de um dígito: São Paulo tem melhor resultado do país no combate a homicídios. *Gazeta do Povo*. Retrieved from https://www.gazetadopovo.com.br/politica/republica/taxa-de-um-digito-sao-paulo-tem-melhor-resultado-do-pais-no-combate-a-homicidios-1w6fzj2w7lv204dv6m06xpqsn/

v Ribeiro, A. (2018, January 29). Em 2017, Grande São Paulo registrou 4 homicídios por dia. Retrieved from https://www.destakjornal.com.br/cidades/sao-paulo/detalhe/em-2017-grande-sao-paulo-registrou-4-homicidios-por-dia

vi Waiselfisz, J. (2012). Mapa da Violencia 2012. *Instituto Sangari*. Retrieved from https://www.mapadaviolencia.org.br/pdf2012/mapa2012_rj.pdf

vii Manso, B. (2018, August 28). No Norte e Nordeste, os dez estados mais violentos do Brasil. Retrieved from https://g1.globo.com/monitor-da-violencia/noticia/2018/08/28/no-norte-e-nordeste-os-dez-estados-mais-violentos-do-brasil.ghtml

viii Mier, B. (2015, June 12). Brasil is not Rio. *Brasil Wire*. Retrieved from http://www.brasilwire.com/brasil-is-not-rio/

ix Amnesty International. (2018, January 18). 25% dos assassinatos no município do Rio de Janeiro em 2017 foram cometidos pela polícia. Retrieved from https://anistia.org.br/noticias/25-dos-assassinatos-rio-de-janeiro-em-2017-foram-cometidos-pela-policia/

x Mortos por policiais no Brasil. (2018, May 23). *Globo*. Retrieved from https://especiais.g1.globo.com/monitor-da-violencia/2018/mortos-por-policiais-no-brasil/

xi Nordeste tem 40% dos usuários de crack nas capitais. (2013, September 19). *Gazeta do Povo*. Retrieved from https://www.gazetadopovo.com.br/vida-e-cidadania/nordeste-tem-40-dos-usuarios-de-crack-nas-capitais-cd5lnp77zw3o8hh0nra4mh3ri/

xii Manso, B. (2018, August 28). No Norte e Nordeste, os dez estados mais violentos do Brasil. Retrieved from https://g1.globo.com/monitor-da-violencia/noticia/2018/08/28/no-norte-e-nordeste-os-dez-estados-mais-violentos-do-brasil.ghtml xiii Ceará é o 3º estado com maior taxa de assassinatos no primeiro semestre. (2018, August 29). *O Povo*. Retrieved from https://www.opovo.com.br/jornal/cidades/2018/08/ceara-e-o-3-estado-com-maior-taxa-de-assassinatos-no-primeiro-semestr.html

xiv Veja como os votos por presidente em cada estado. (2018, October 29). *Senado Noticias*. https://www12.senado.leg.br/noticias/videos/2018/10/veja-como-foram-os-votos-para-presidente-em-cada-estado

xv Dois dias após impeachment, Senado aprova lei que permite pedaladas fiscais. (2016, September 2). *IG Brasil Econômico*. Retrieved from https://economia.ig.com.br/2016-09-02/lei-orcamento.html

xvi Funaro diz ter repassado R$ 1 milhão para Cunha comprar votos pelo impeachment de Dilma. (2017, October 15). *O Globo*. Retrieved from https://oglobo.globo.com/brasil/funaro-diz-ter-repassado-1-milhao-para-cunha-comprar-votos-pelo-impeachment-de-dilma-21948977

xvii Lawyer: 'No evidence' that Lula is corrupt. (2018, April 5). BBC. Retrieved from https://www.bbc.co.uk/programmes/p063dcss

xviii Lula não é dono do tríplex, afirmam mais quatro testemunhas. (2016, December 12). *Revista Fórum*. Retrieved from https://www.revistaforum.com.br/lula-nao-e-dono-do-triplex-afirmam-mais-quatro-testemunhas/

xix Amy Goodman and Juan Gonzalez. Interview with Glen Greenwald. (radio interview April 9, 2018). Retrieved from https://www.democracynow.org/2018/4/9/glenn_greenwald_brazils_right_wing_jailed

xx Partido dos Trabalhadores. (2018, October 1). *Nota do PT: Moro vaza mentiras de Palocci para interferir nas eleições* [press release]. Retrieved from http://www.pt.org.br/nota-do-pt-moro-vaza-mentiras-de-palocci-para-interferir-nas-eleicoes/

xxi Delação de Palocci foi recusado pelo Ministério Público por falta de provas. (2018, October 1). *Brasil 247*. Retrieved from https://www.brasil247.com/pt/247/poder/370733/Dela%C3%A7%C3%A3o-de-Palocci-foi-recusada-pelo-Minist%C3%A9rio-P%C3%BAblico-por-falta-de-provas.htm

xxii Macedo, I. (2017, July 21). PP, PMDB, PT e PSDB são os partidos com mais parlamentares sob suspeita. *Congresso em Foco*. Retrieved from https://congressoemfoco.uol.com.br/especial/noticias/pp-pmdb-pt-e-psdb-sao-os-partidos-com-mais-parlamentares-sob-suspeita/

xxiii Carvalho, M. (2016, April 14). Maluf continua na lista de procurados da Interpol, diz procuradoria de NY. *Folha de São Paulo*. Retrieved from https://www1.folha.uol.com.br/poder/2016/04/1760941-ordem-de-prisao-da-interpol-contra-maluf-e-valida-diz-procuradoria-de-ny.shtml

xxiv Caleiro, J. (2018, October 31). Quem é Alberto Fraga, aliado de Bolsonaro, que foi ao topo do Twitter. *Exame*. Retrieved from https://

exame.abril.com.br/brasil/quem-e-alberto-fraga-aliado-de-bolsonaro-que-foi-ao-topo-do-twitter/

xxv Patero, B, Tizzo, L. and Rodriques, M. (Septembro 24, 2018). Justiça condena Alberto Fraga por cobrar propina em contratos de transporte no DF. *Globo*. Retrieved from https://g1.globo.com/df/distrito-federal/noticia/2018/09/24/justica-condena-alberto-fraga-por-cobrar-propina-em-contratos-de-transporte-no-df.ghtml

xxvi Braço direito de Bolsonaro admitiu ter recebido caixa 2 da JBS. (2018, October 31). *Folha de São Paulo*. Retrieved from https://www1.folha.uol.com.br/poder/2018/10/braco-direito-de-bolsonaro-admitiu-ter-recebido-em-caixa-2-da-jbs.shtml

xxvii Linder, J. (2016, March 23). Lider do DEM é condenado de devolver R\$4,6 milhões. *Estado de São Paulo*. Retrieved from https://politica.estadao.com.br/noticias/geral,lider-do-dem-e-condenado-a-devolver-r-4-6-milhoes,10000022770

xxviii Economista de Bolsonaro, Paulo Guedes é alvo de nova investigação do MP. (2018, October 26). *Exame*. Retrieved from https://exame.abril.com.br/brasil/ministerio-publico-abre-nova-investigacao-sobre-paulo-guedes/

xxix Sudré, L. (2018, September 21). Tribunal que barrou Lula aceita outras 1,4 mil candidaturas. *Brasil de Fato*. Retrieved from https://www.brasildefato.com.br/2018/09/21/tribunal-que-barrou-lula-aceita-outras-14-mil-candidaturas-sub-judice/

xxx Câmara dos Deputados da Republica Federativa do Brasil. (2009, June 16). *Legislação Informatizada - DECRETO LEGISLATIVO Nº 311, DE 2009 - Publicação Original*. Retrieved from http://www2.camara.leg.br/legin/fed/decleg/2009/decretolegislativo-311-16-junho-2009-588912-publicacaooriginal-113605-pl.html

xxxi Schreiber, M. (2018, September 25). Eleições 2018: Como os 3,3 milhões de eleitores que não cadastraram a biometria podem influenciar as eleições. *BBC Brasil*. Retrieved from https://www.bbc.com/portuguese/brasil-45635409

xxxii Mello, P. (2018, October 18). Empresários bancam campanha contra o PT pelo WhatsApp. *Folha de São Paulo*. Retrieved from https://www1.folha.uol.com.br/poder/2018/10/empresarios-bancam-campanha-contra-o-pt-pelo-whatsapp.shtml

The not so invisible hand of Uncle Sam

By Bryan Pitts

When you study Latin American history, as I have for well over a decade, you learn to recognize some of the common themes that tie Latin America together. Colonization, indigenous genocide, African slavery, bloody wars for independence, debates over the boundaries of citizenship, and economic dependency are only a few of the commonalities that unite a vast and diverse continent. But there's another theme, and that's the meddling of the United States, whether politically, economically, militarily, or a combination of all three. Few Latin American countries have escaped US invasions, electoral manipulation, or economic pressure. The US seized over half of Mexico's territory in 1848; placed restrictions on Cuban independence after intervening in its war for independence in 1898; sent the Marines to most of Central America in the first third of the 20th century; helped overthrow democratic governments of Guatemala, Brazil, and Chile (among many others) during the Cold War; trained insurgents to fight revolutionary governments in Cuba and Nicaragua; and invaded Panama, Grenada, and Haiti in the last two decades of the 20th century to replace their leaders with US stooges. The famed quote from Mexico's 19th century dictator, Porfirio Díaz, rings true for the entire region. "Poor Mexico. So far from God, so close to the US."

In the wake of the wars in Iraq and Afghanistan, the tried and true method of sending an invasion force is a bit out of style among the American public, leaving the US to find other means of getting its way. This has been especially true after the appearance of the "Pink Tide," when leftist governments were elected in much of the region. These governments charted an independent foreign and economic policy for their countries, most notably when they rejected the U.S. proposal for the Free Trade Area of the Americas. Countries like Brazil helped forge the BRICS area, which sought to bypass US and Northern European economic hegemony. Latin America's leading trade partner became China. Regional integration was on the rise, with the expansion of the Mercosur bloc. At home, economic inequality plummeted anywhere the left came to power in a way that it never had under the US-sponsored neoliberalism of the preceding decades. In response, U.S. government and economic interests (which are becoming ever more indistinguishable anyway) have intervened in more subtle ways, but always with the goal of restoring U.S. political and economic hegemony or, to put it another way, to slap uppity Latin Americans back down where they belong.

Today the US waxes eloquent about its support for democracy in Latin America – and then does everything short of actual military action to undermine it. One of the earliest examples was in Venezuela in 2002, when the George W. Bush administration found itself with pie on its face after prematurely recognizing a coup attempt in Venezuela. In 2009, the Obama administration, led by Secretary of State Hillary Clinton, stood by when the Honduran military and Congress sent leftist President Manuel Zelaya into exile. They turned a blind eye as the new right-wing government repressed social movements and changed the constitution to keep itself in power – the very attempted sin that had been used to justify Zelaya's ouster. In 2012, the US remained silent as Paraguay's Congress hastily impeached Fernando Lugo on flimsy charges. In both cases, the new governments have created friendlier investment climates for US and other foreign corporations, reduced worker and environmental protections, and done pretty much whatever the US tells them when it comes to foreign policy. For a recent example of the latter, Paraguay and Honduras, along with Guatemala, announced plans to move their embassies in Israel to Jerusalem within days of the US announcement.

But Paraguay and Honduras, with combined GDPs just slightly more than that of North Dakota, were never the true prize. The jewel in the Latin American crown all along was Brazil, with its vast lands for agricultural production and timber and mineral extraction and, most importantly, its offshore oil reserves, which the leftist Workers' Party (PT) had stubbornly insisted on keeping under national control, with the profits reserved for education and healthcare. There was money to be made for US corporations and the politicians whose interests are inseparable from theirs, and if there is one thing we have learned from the last century and a half it's that the US will not let something as trivial as democracy get in the way of profits. And this is particularly true when the people who are hurt when right-wing authoritarians take control are black or brown.

In Brazil, the U.S. helped Brazilian prosecutors develop strategies that have been used to target only certain political parties – those most opposed to U.S. hegemony – and the Department of Justice has collaborated with the Brazilian prosecutors to achieve spurious convictions. As early as 2009, the State Department was organizing training sessions in Rio de Janeiro for Brazilian judges, prosecutors, and police, helping them incorporate some of the same strategies that the U.S. has used against organized crime, like coerced plea bargains and prosecution for relatively minor and vaguely-defined financial crimes. One of the keynote speakers at a training session in Rio was Judge Sérgio Moro, who would later take a leading role in corruption investigations against leftist politicians and eventually embark on a tour of the U.S. to tout his accomplishments. Although ostensibly these techniques were to be used to fight terrorism, in Brazil they have been used to selectively prosecute left-wing politicians for alleged corruption, while allowing demonstrably corrupt centrist and right-wing politicians to go free.

At the same time, the Obama administration remained silent as President Dilma Rousseff was removed in 2016 via a parliamentary coup, convicted for budgetary maneuvers that have been used by every other recent president and most governors. Many of the groups that organized street protests in support of her impeachment had ties to US investment firms, or to businesspeople like the Koch brothers.

By July 2017, acting attorney general Kenneth Blanco boasted of the "strong relationship built on trust" between U.S. and Brazilian prosecutors and touted the legally shaky conviction of presidential front-runner Luiz Inácio Lula da Silva for corruption as an example of the fruits of that cooperation. Lula was convicted for receiving uncompleted renovations on an apartment that he had never been proven to set foot in, after he left office, with no discernible *quid quo pro* for the construction firm that was to carry out the renovations. No matter: as far as the Department of Justice was concerned, this was a victory for democratic accountability. How odd that the Department of Justice never seems concerned about corruption when the corrupt politicians in question are from the right. And of course there is the rank hypocrisy of a country that propped up corrupt dictators like Fulgencio Batista and Papa Doc Duvalier lecturing anyone about corruption. Not to mention the utter absurdity of a country that allows unlimited corporate campaign contributions and incarcerates more of its citizens than any other country claiming to have anything useful to teach about democracy.

In Brazil, the result has been a bonanza for U.S. businesses, who have moved in to take advantage of the wave of privatizations enacted by the new president, Michel Temer, particularly in Brazil's massive offshore oil reserves. In president-elect Jair Bolsonaro, the US has an even more obsequious boot-licker to implement its desired economic policies. Bolsonaro has already announced that he will combine the Ministry of the Environment with the Ministry of Agriculture, which sounds a lot like saving space at the zoo by housing hens with foxes. His Minister of the Economy, Paulo Guedes, is perhaps the most grotesque proponent of neoliberal, market-friendly policies who the US has ever had in Latin America (It may be noteworthy that Bolsonaro selected Guedes as an economic advisor shortly after a meeting in New York with corporate think tank Americas Society/ Council of the Americas – AS/COA.)[i] Worst of all, only this week Bolsonaro announced that his Justice Minister will be none other than Sérgio Moro, the judge with numerous and well-documented links to US political interests who did Bolsonaro the favor of removing Lula, his main competitor, from the race.ii,iii

The United States has a shameful record in Latin America and has for over a century. Which is more likely? That the US has suddenly changed its ways and is simply standing aside, allowing Brazil's democratic institutions to work and taking advantage of investment opportunities as they spontaneously appear? Or that the US has had a hand in this process since the beginning, in yet another chapter of unending pursuit of power and money for its own elite? You be the judge.

i A boycott of Americas Quarterly and AS/COA and why it is necessary. (2018, February 22). *Brasil Wire*. Retreived from http://www.brasilwire.com/boycott-americas-quarterly-and-ascoa/

ii Hidden history: the US war on corruption' in Brazil. (2018, January 28). Brasil Wire. Retreived from http://www.brasilwire.com/dont-call-it-brazilgate/

iii Mier, B. (2018, September 1). UN's Sarah Cleveland on Lula and Brasil's international obligations. *Brasil Wire*. Retrieved from http://www.brasilwire.com/sarah-cleveland-on-lula-and-brasils-international-legal-obligations/

Year of Lead

Part five

Anglo media fails Brazil

QUARTERLY

Americas

POLITICS, BUSINESS AND CULTURE IN OUR HEMISPHERE

2017 · VOL. CCLXIX No. 15

VOL. 10 I

RIO

A clos
the Oly

PHO
PA

BEHIND LATIN AMERICA'S HISTORIC CRACKDOWN

CORRUPTION BUSTERS

Iván Velásquez
Colombian prosecutor

Sérgio Moro
Brazilian judge

Thelma Aldana
Guatemalan
attorney general

AS/COA and fake news: how a corporate think tank molds mainstream media narratives on Latin America

By Brian Mier

When Luis Inacio Lula da Silva took office in 2003, one of his first moves was to prioritize open source software for the federal government computer systems in order to reduce costs, increase competition, generate jobs and develop the country's knowledge and intelligence in this area. Although it was never fully adopted by all government ministries, by 2010, this move had saved taxpayers over R$500 million.i,ii Six weeks after taking power, in October, 2016, as he cut funding to support women victims of domestic violence from R$42 million to R$16 million under the excuse that he couldn't afford it, President Michel Temer announced that the government was going to spend R$140 million migrating to Microsoft products for its computer systems.iii,iv Microsoft is not the only corporation that benefited from the 2016 coup against Dilma Rousseff. Boeing is in the process of taking a controlling share over the mixed capital aerospace conglomerate Embraer, the world's third largest airplane manufacturer and a matter of national pride to Brazilians.v,vi After meeting with Monsanto directors in February, 2018, the Temer administration announced plans to legalize use of the Monsanto pesticide Glyphosate, which recently faced a ban in Europe.vii Shortly after auctioning off eight offshore oil fields to international petroleum corporations such as Chevron and Shell in October, 2017, Michel Temer issued a presidential decree providing an estimated R$1 trillion in tax abatement for foreign oil companies working in Brazil.viii,ix Microsoft, Monsanto, Boeing, Chevron and Shell have all benefited financially from regime change in Brazil. What else do they have in common? They are all corporate members of Americas Society/Council of the Americas, the think tank which, under the guise of caring for the Latin American people, has supported austerity policies and right-wing governments in Latin America since its founding by David Rockefeller in the 1960s.x,xi

AS/COA's news magazine *Americas Quarterly* is geared towards an elite public, distributed in airport VIP lounges around the continent, and given out as a membership bonus, with individual membership costs starting at $10,000/year. It's main function, however, seems to be public relations, feeding corporate friendly news stories into media companies across the hemisphere, with commentary from AS/COA staff frequently appearing on CNN, NBC, Bloomberg, NPR, in press agencies like Reuters and AP, and in newspapers spanning the region from *Clarin* in Argentina to the *Los Angeles Times*. Links to these articles, TV and radio appearances are detailed on AS/COA's website and easily available for anyone who wants to quantify bias or look for narrative patterns.xii I chose to look at narrative patterns in AS/COA's media feeds over two periods, for the past year, from February 24, 2017 to February 24, 2018, and during the three month period before Dilma Rousseff's removal from office, on May 13, 2016.

AS/COA's recent priorities

Between February 24, 2017 and February 24, 2018, AS/COA staff either appeared in or were quoted in Anglo media stories 102 times (excluding stories on art, which I am leaving out of this analysis). This includes 39 stories about Venezuela, 13 stories about NAFTA and 7 stories about Brazil.

The stories on Venezuela, the country with the World's largest petroleum reserves, can best be classified as regime change propaganda. There is no attempt to provide balanced coverage in any of the articles to which AS/COA staff contribute to by speaking to anyone from the Venezuelan working class, the majority of which still support the Maduro regime. The language used is similar to that used to describe countries like Libya before US military operations. Venezuela is in a state of catastrophe, democracy has collapsed, and the country is in a state of crisis. As AS/COA's Eric Farnsworth said to CNN, "There are people in Venezuela who are literally starving. This is apocalyptic stuff. I would call Venezuela a failing state."xiii Although hunger is a terrible phenomenon, it is present in all nations in the Americas. According to Department of Agriculture's Economic Research Service, in 2015, 6.3 million American families suffered from extremely low levels of food security.xiv It is highly doubtful that anyone at AS/COA will ever cite this statistic to call the US a failed state.

The 13 stories about NAFTA are exemplary because they illustrate a long term objective of AS/COA and its founder and former director David Rockefeller to bolster neoliberal free trade agreements. Rockefeller was influential in creating both NAFTA and the failed FTAA, and AS/COA has traditionally been ranked among the biggest cheerleaders for these controversial agreements. Although the benefits of NAFTA for the working class have failed to live up to the promises, from the language of the articles AS/COA and its corporate backers support the continuation of NAFTA and are worried that Donald Trump is jeopardizing the agreement.xv

Seven stories on Brazil that appeared in the Anglo media last year include content from AS/COA. Two of these media appearances represent a continuing strategy to treat the controversial and partisan *Lava Jato* prosecution team as superheroes, which started with a 2016 *Americas Quarterly* magazine cover which dressed lead prosecutor Sergio Moro up as a member of the Ghostbusters.

Moro was widely criticized both nationally and internationally for breaking Brazilian law when he released illegally taped phone conversations between Lula and Rousseff to *Globo* television network.xvi,xvii He was criticized for failing to prosecute anyone from the PSDB party, whose top members, like Jose Serra and Aecio Neves, have been involved in a series of multi-million dollar bribery and illegal campaign financing scandals. At the same time he has focused most of his efforts on preventing Ex-president Lula from running for president in 2018. These efforts are based on charges against Lula, with no material evidence, that Lula received illegal reforms on a beach front apartment. The charges are entirely based on one coerced plea bargain testimony by a corrupt businessman who changed his initial story to implicate Lula in exchange for sentence reduction.xviii ,xix,xx,xxi Moro has been accused of conflict of interest, because he wife served as legal advisor to the PSDB Vice-Governor of Parana, Flavio Arns.xxii In December, 2017, Odebrecht lawyer Tacla Duran accused the *Lava Jato* prosecution team of running a sentence reduction industry through Moro's wife's law firm.xxiii Moro has been accused of pressuring businessmen to change their plea bargains to implicate Lula.xxiv Moro has been accused of adulterating financial records from Odebrecht.xxv And Moro was accused of sadistic behavior after he ordered police to arrest former finance minister Guido Mantega during his wife's chemotherapy treatment at Albert Einstein hospital.xxvi Moro was accused of destroying 5 hard drives worth of physical evidence of bribery that had been handed over by Odebrecht, in a move which is widely seen to have been made to protect PSDB politicians. Moro was recently accused of ethical violations when it was uncovered that he is living in a 256 m2 luxury apartment which he owns in Curitiba while collecting a judicial rent subsidy.xxvii He has been accused of legally harassing his critics, as when he ordered the police to raid the house of legal scholar Rafael Valim. Valim had organized a seminar with UN Human Rights Commission lawyer Geoffrey Robertson and had criticized the *Lava Jato* team of using Lawfare.xxviii Most importantly, Moro has been accused of sabotaging the economy by paralyzing Brazil's largest construction companies in 2015. Instead of treating them as too big to fail, his actions caused an immediate 500,000 layoffs in the construction sector and, according a study cited by *BBC*, a 2.5% drop in the GDP.xxix,xxx ,xxxi ,xxxii None of these events have resulted in any question of bias or the ethics of Sergio Moro within AS/COA, however. In a recent article in *Foreign Policy*, AS/COA Vice President Brian Winter lionizes Moro as Brazil's Teddy Roosevelt.xxxiii

2014 presidential election runner up, Aecio Neves, from the PSDB party, was accused on five counts of receiving bribes ranging from R$3 million to R$50 million.<u>xxxiv</u> In short, all counts are a lot more serious than allegedly receiving reforms on an apartment, which has resulted in a 9.5 year prison sentence for ex-President Lula. In one of his last moves before stepping down as Federal Public Prosecutor, Rodrido Janot asked the Supreme Court to drop all charges against Neves. AS/COA ignored this request in a *New York Times* homage to Janot, comparing him to a soldier in a fight to build the rule of law.<u>xxxv</u>

Both Janot and Moro have written for *Americas Quarterly*, and AS/COA regularly flies them up to New York for speaking engagements.<u>xxxvi</u> ,<u>xxxvii</u> Both were honored at an AS/COA event in New York on March 2, 2018.<u>xxxviii</u>

AS/COA during the lead up to the coup

In the book *Merchants of Doubt*, Naomi Oreskes and Erick M. Conway document how, for the last 50 years, corporate funded think tanks and foundations have worked to deliberately confuse the public on the issue of climate change in order to weaken support for air pollution regulation.<u>xxxix</u> A common strategy used by these institutions and their shills is to discredit the science, spread confusion and promote doubt.<u>xl</u> When looking at AS/COA's influence on the media during the three-month period before Dilma Rousseff was first forced out of office, it becomes clear that this was the tactic used to confuse the American public into doubting whether a coup had taken place. Furthermore, this doubt-mongering campaign, waged in AS/COA feeds to the media, in *Americas Quarterly* and by its employees on Twitter, succeeded in molding the dominant Anglo media narrative on the coup, even reproduced in ostensibly liberal publications such as *the Guardian* which only mentions the word coup in quotation marks.xli According to the AS/COA narrative on the impeachment, Dilma Rousseff was not impeached because of the infraction of fiscal peddling which: 1) she was subsequently exonerated from;xlii 2) is common practice in municipal, state and federal branches of government in Brazil;xliii and 3) was legalized a week after she was thrown out of office.xliv According to AS/COA vice president and *Americas Quarterly* editor Brian Winter, who is not an economist, she was thrown out of office because of her handling of the economy. Does it sound confusing to hear someone simultaneously argue that it was not a coup, while stating that the official reason for the impeachment is invalid? It's supposed to. During the three month period before May 13, 2016, when Rousseff was first thrown out of office, AS/COA fed 29 stories into the English language media. 14 of them were about Brazil. AS/COA's three primary messages in these articles are: 1) It's not a coup; 2) Brazil's democratic institutions are working; and 3) The impeachment is a positive thing for Brazil.

On May 3, 2016, Brian Winter emphasized all three of these points in a discussion on National Public Radio with three other neoliberal commentators.xlv The impeachment vote was yet to take place. Impeachment architect Eduardo Cunha was yet to be arrested for receiving $1.5 million in bribes and money laundering.xlvi Information that a prominent stock broker bribed Congressmen to vote in favor of the impeachment had not yet leaked to the media.xlvii Nevertheless, a glib, upbeat Brian Winter was already explaining that it wasn't a coup. " Is it a coup?" he asked, "No, I don't think it's a coup. Is it potentially a flimsy case for which to make an impeachment, especially when you have all this corruption going on in the background? That's arguable."

As the Brazilian Congress, the majority of whom were facing corruption charges of their own, prepared to throw out the first woman president for a technicality which she didn't commit, Winter said, "It's actually progress because it's a product of an independent judiciary and other institutions like the media, like even the maligned Congress, working more or less as they're supposed to."xlviii

As in other media appearances during the lead up to the coup, Winter expressed confidence in the "flimsy" impeachment process, saying, "It's unclear exactly how this is going to end in Brazil. Success is not guaranteed. But as it stands right now, it looks like a positive thing". Two weeks earlier, he spoke even more positively about the impeachment to the *Christian Science Monitor*, saying that Brazil was "on the verge of a tidal change in Brazilian politics".xlix

Part of the job of confusing the public entailed quelling fears that Brazil might be on the verge of a return to dictatorship. As Michel Temer has now turned the Rio de Janeiro State security apparatus over to the Military, who are causing human rights abuses against a primarily black, poor population, and as General Walter Braga Netto says that Rio is a pilot project for the rest of Brazil, one wonders why an AS/COA spokesman would go on National Public Radio and say, "Amid all this chaos and all these incredible things that have happened over the last year, I always tell people the one thing that absolutely will not happen in Brazil is a military coup".[l],[li]

As a comprador class of US-puppets sells off Brazil's natural resources and technological patrimony to international corporations, the companies that finance AS/COA are lining their pockets. Most of these companies are also major advertisers in America's largest media companies. Can they be trusted to provide objective reporting on Brazil?

As Noam Chomsky once said, "If you abandon the political arena somebody is going to be there. Corporations aren't going to go home and join the PTA. They are going to run things."

i Governo Federal irá fazer mega compra de produtos Microsoft. (2016, October 31). *Windows Team Microsoft* [blog]. Retrieved from https://www.windowsteam.com.br/governo-federal-ira-fazer-mega-compra-de-produtos-da-microsoft/

ii Rodrigues, D. (2016, October 28). Temer trocará software livre por programas da Microsoft em todo o governo. Vice. Retrieved from https://motherboard.vice.com/pt_br/article/ypnmwg/temer-vai-trocar-software-livre-por-programas-da-microsoft-em-todo-o-governo-federal

iii Temer reduz em mais da metade verbas para políticas públicas às mulheres. (2017, April 2). *Rede Brasil Atual*. Retrieved from https://www.redebrasilatual.com.br/cidadania/2017/04/temer-reduz-em-mais-da-metade-verbas-para-politicas-publicas-as-mulheres

iv Bergamo, M. (2016, December 18). Governo faz compra gigante na Microsoft. *Folha de São Paulo*. Retrieved from https://www1.folha.uol.com.br/colunas/monicabergamo/2016/12/1841194-governo-faz-compra-gigante-na-microsoft-e-grupos-veem-risco-para-software-livre.shtml

v Boadle, A. (2018, February 25). Boeing terá fatia de 51% em nova empresa com Embraer, diz jornal. *Èpoc.* Retrieved from https://epocanegocios.globo.com/Empresa/noticia/2018/02/epoca-negocios-boeing-tera-fatia-de-51-em-nova-empresa-com-embraer-diz-jornal.html

vi D'Avila, M. (2017, December 28). Boeing and Embraer: don't sell Santos Dumont's dream. *Brasil Wire*. Retrieved from http://www.brasilwire.com/boeing-v-embraer-manuela-davila/

vii Oliveira, C. (2018, February 8). Agenda da Agricultura com Monsanto sugere aprovação do 'Pacote do Veneno'. Rede Brasil Atual. Retrieved from https://www.redebrasilatual.com.br/ambiente/2018/02/agenda-da-agricultura-com-a-Monsanto-sugere-aprovacao-do-pacote-do-veneno

viii Governo eleva para R$600 bi previsão de arrecadação com leilões de pre-sal. (2017, October 10). *Folha de São Paulo*. Retrieved from http://www1.folha.uol.com.br/mercado/2017/10/1931454-governo-eleva-para-r-600-bi-previsao-de-arrecadacao-com-leiloes-de-pre-sal.shtml

ix Angelo, C. (2017, December 2). Câmara aprova MP do Trilhão para o setor de petróleo. *Terra*. Retrieved from https://www.terra.com.br/noticias/climatempo/camara-aprova-mp-do-trilhao-para-o-setor-de-petroleo,b916076970027e0f906d09ba873478f90w2bzgtc.html

x AS/COA. (last modified at time of publication: 2019, January 25). *COA Corporate Member*s [web page]. Retrieved from https://www.as-coa.org/content/coa-corporate-members

xi For example: Apoyo en el Consejo de las Américas a Mauricio Macri: "Los cambios estructurales llevan tiempo. (2018, August 30). *El Clarin*. Retreived from https://www.as-coa.org/articles/apoyo-en-el-consejo-de-las-am%C3%A9ricas-mauricio-macri-los-cambios-estructurales-llevan-tiempo xii AS/COA. (last modified at time of publication: 2019, January 25). *In the news* [web page]. Retrieved from https://www.as-coa.org/about/our-publications/in-the-news

xiii Gillespie, P, Brochetto, M. and Newton, P. (2017, July 30). Venezuela: How a rich country collapsed. *CNN Business*. Retrieved from https://money.cnn.com/2017/07/26/news/economy/venezuela-economic-crisis/index.html

xiv Howard, J. (2016, September 9). Fewer go hungry, but 'this is no time to celebrate'. *CNN*. Retrieved from https://edition.cnn.com/2016/09/09/health/hunger-families-food-security-america/index.html

xv Weisbrot, M., Lefebvre, S., and Sammut, J. (2014, February). Did Nafta help Mexico? An assesment after 20 years. *Center for Economic and Policy Research*. Retrieved from http://cepr.net/documents/nafta-20-years-2014-02.pdf

xvi Richter, A. (2016, March 29). Moro pede desculpas ao STF por divulgar conversa de Lula e Dilma. *Agencia Brasil*. Retrieved from http://agenciabrasil.ebc.com.br/politica/noticia/2016-03/moro-admite-ao-stf-equivoco-ao-divulgar-conversa-de-lula-e-dilma

xvii Robertson, Geoffrey. (2017, April 19). The Case for Lula. *Foreign Affairs*. Retrieved from https://www.foreignaffairs.com/articles/brazil/2017-04-19/case-lula

xviii Reverbel, P. (2017, March 17). O que há contra o PSDB na Lava Jato? Você perguntou e a BBC Brasil responde. *BBC Brasil*. Retrieved from https://www.bbc.com/portuguese/brasil-39299007

xix Delações mostram investigado de esquema em Furnas como articulador de Aécio Neves. (2017, April 20). *Carta Capital*. Retrieved from https://www.cartacapital.com.br/politica/delacoes-mostram-investigado-de-esquema-em-furnas-como-articulador-de-aecio-neves

xx Delator revela 'milhões em espécie' para José Serra. (2018, January 1). *Istoé*. Retrieved from https://istoe.com.br/delator-revela-milhoes-em-especie-para-serra/

xxi Weisbrot, M. (2018, January 23). Brazil's democracy pushed into the abyss. New York Times. Retrieved from https://www.nytimes.com/2018/01/23/opinion/brazil-lula-democracy-corruption.html

xxii Portilho, F. (2014, December 6). Esposa de juiz Sergio Moro assesorou vice-governador do PSDB. *Pragmatismo Politica*. Retrieved from https://www.pragmatismopolitico.com.br/2014/12/esposa-juiz-sergio-moro-e-assessora-psdb.html

xxiii Mier,B. (2017, December 4). Corrupt: Lava Jato and Sergio Moro's sentence reduction industry. *Brasil Wire*. Retrieved from http://www.brasilwire.com/corrupt-lava-jato-sergio-moros-sentence-reduction-industry/

xxiv Lava Jato só aceita delação com mentiras sobre Lula e família, diz defesa. (2017, November 26). *Folha de São Paulo*. Retrieved from https://www1.folha.uol.com.br/poder/2017/11/1938392-lava-jato-cria-versoes-para-tentar-prejudicar-lula-e-familia-diz-defesa.shtml

xxv Cavalcante, H. (2017, November 30). Documentos em delação de executivos da Odebrecht foram adulterados, diz Duran. *Rede Brasil Atual*. Retrieved from https://www.redebrasilatual.com.br/politica/2017/11/documentos-em-delacao-de-executivos-da-odebrecht-foram-adulterados-diz-tacla-duran

xxvi Acayaba, C. and Justi, A. (2016, September 22). Mantega é preso em nova fase da Operação Lava Jato. *Globo*. Retrieved from http://g1.globo.com/sao-paulo/noticia/2016/09/mantega-e-preso-em-nova-fase-da-operacao-lava-jato.html

xxvii Albuqueque, A. (2018, February 2). Moro tem imóvel em Curitiba, mas recebe auxílio-moradia. *Folha de São Paulo*. Retrieved from https://www1.folha.uol.com.br/poder/2018/02/moro-tem-imovel-em-curitiba-mas-recebe-auxilio-moradia.shtml

xxviii Mier, B. (2018, February 25). As Rio military takeover intensifies, Lava Jato investigators harass prominent critic. Brasil Wire. Retrieved from http://www.brasilwire.com/as-rio-military-takeover-intensifies-lava-jato-investigators-harass-prominent-critic/

xxix Mier, B. (2017, September 25). How manufactured economic crisis in Brazil paved the way for a soft coup. *Upside Down World*. Retrieved from http://upsidedownworld.org/archives/brazil/manufactured-economic-crisis-brazil-paved-way-soft-coup/

xxx Jeronimo, J. (2015, January 30). Obras paradas: o outro lado de Lava Jato. *Istoé*. Retrieved from https://istoe.com.br/402288_OBRAS+PARADAS+O+OUTRO+LADO+DA+OPERACAO+LAVA+JATO/

xxxi Neder, V. (2017, June 21). Efeito Lava Jato fez construção cortar 500 mil vagas em 2015, diz IBGE. Estado de São Paulo. Retrieved from https://economia.estadao.com.br/noticias/geral,efeito-lava-jato-fez-construcao-cortar-500-mil-vagas-em-2015-diz-ibge,70001853492

xxxii Costas, R. (2015, December 2). Escândalo da Petrobras 'engoliu 2,5% da economia em 2015'. *BBC Brasil*. Retrieved from https://www.bbc.com/portuguese/noticias/2015/12/151201_lavajato_ru

xxxiii Winter, Brian. (2017). Profile of Sergio Moro. *Foreign policy global rethinkers*. Retrieved from https://2017globalthinkers.foreignpolicy.com/2017/profile/sergio-moro?43a6f5eea1=&c0244ec121=

xxxiv Delações mostram investigado de esquema em Furnas como articulador de Aécio Neves. (2017, April 20). *Carta Capital*. Retrieved from https://www.cartacapital.com.br/politica/delacoes-mostram-investigado-de-esquema-em-furnas-como-articulador-de-aecio-neves

xxxv Darlington, S. and Londono, E. (2017, September 6). For Brazil's

269

Departing Top Prosecutor, 'One Last Cannon Barrage'. New York Times. Retrieved from https://www.nytimes.com/2017/09/06/world/americas/brazil-corruption-lula-dilma-rousseff-prosecutor-rodrigo-janot.html

xxxvi Janot, R. (2018, June 1). The lessons of car wash. *Americas Quarterly*. Retrieved from https://www.americasquarterly.org/content/lessons-car-wash

xxxvii Moro, S. (2016, May 23). Systematic corruption can become a sad memory of Brazil's past. Americas Quarterly. Retrieved from https://www.americasquarterly.org/content/judge-moro-systemic-corruption-can-become-sad-memory-brazils-past

xxxviii AS/COA. (2018, March 2). Latin americas battle against corruption: what comes next? [web page]. Retrieved from https://www.as-coa.org/events/latin-americas-battle-against-corruption-what-comes-next

xxxix Oreskes, N. and Conway, E. (2010). *Merchants of Doubt*. London: Bloomsbury Press.

xl McKie, R. (2010, August 8). Merchants of Doubt by Naomi Oreskes and Erick Conway. *The Guardian*. Retrieved from https://www.theguardian.com/books/2010/aug/08/merchants-of-doubt-oreskes-conway

xli For example: Phillips, D. (2018, January 24). Brazilian court upholds corruption conviction for ex-President Lula. *The Guardian*. Retrieved from https://www.theguardian.com/world/2018/jan/24/brazilian-court-upholds-corruption-conviction-for-ex-president-lula

xlii Perícia conclui que Dilma não participou de pedaladas fiscais. (2016, June 27). *Globo*. Retrieved from http://g1.globo.com/jornal-nacional/noticia/2016/06/pericia-conclui-que-dilma-nao-participou-de-pedaladas-fiscais.html

xliii Adelaide, J. (2015, October 7). Para entender as "pedaladas fiscais". *Revista GGN*. Retrieved from https://jornalggn.com.br/noticia/para-entender-as-pedaladas-fiscais

xliv Dois dias após impeachment, Senado aprova lei que permite pedaladas fiscais. (2016, September 2). IG Brasil Economico. Retrieved from https://economia.ig.com.br/2016-09-02/lei-orcamento.html

xlv Desjardins, L. (2016, May 3). Understanding the political crisis in Brazil [transcript]. National Public Radio. Retrieved from https://dianerehm.org/shows/2016-05-03/understanding-the-political-crisis-in-brazil

xlvi Articulador do impeachment de Dilma, Cunha completa um ano de prisão. (2017, October 19). *Folha de São Paulo*. https://www1.folha.uol.com.br/poder/2017/10/1928364-articulador-do-impeachment-de-dilma-cunha-completa-um-ano-de-prisao.shtml

xlvii Funaro diz ter repassado R$ 1 milhão para Cunha comprar votos pelo impeachment de Dilma. (2017, October 15). *Globo*. Retrieved from https://oglobo.globo.com/brasil/funaro-diz-ter-repassado-1-milhao-para-cunha-comprar-votos-pelo-impeachment-de-dilma-21948977 xlviii Políticos que votam impeachment são acusados de mais corrupção que Dilma, diz jornal americano. (2016, March 29). BBC Brasil. Retrieved from https://www.bbc.com/portuguese/noticias/2016/03/160329_latimes_impeachment_rm

xlix Thomson, J. (2016, April 15). Could generational change ease Brasil's politics of corruption? *Christian Science Monitor*. Retrieved from https://www.csmonitor.com/World/Americas/2016/0415/Could-generational-change-ease-Brazil-s-politics-of-corruption?cmpid=push004s

l Frazão, F. and Pennafort, R. (2018, February 27). 'Rio é um laboratório para Brasil', diz interventor. *Estado de São Paulo*. Retrieved from

li Desjardins, L. (2016, May 3). Understanding the political crisis in Brazil [transcript]. National Public Radio. Retrieved from https://dianerehm.org/shows/2016-05-03/understanding-the-political-crisis-in-brazil

The strange case of *The Guardian* & Brazil

The Guardian is the closest thing that the UK has to a mainstream progressive newspaper, and it had, until relatively recently, a rich history of quality investigative reporting. In the 1970s its coverage of Latin America, with writers the calibre of Richard Gott, was responsible for fixing stories like that of Chile's in the public consciousness, and with that fuelling solidarity movements for the region's oppressed peoples, suffering under sub-fascist imperial rule. It continues to host important and talented writers, and publish valuable material, particularly in its *Comment is Free* section.

But in 2018 *The Guardian* is in trouble, financially and editorially. A far cry from the 1970s, it just published a sycophantic eulogy to former US President George HW Bush, whose own CIA oversaw the horrors of Operation Condor.i

To get a sense of the mindset now running *The Guardian*, contrast that of Bush Senior with its sour, dismissive obituary of lifetime champion of human rights, long serving Cabinet Minister and Labour MP Tony Benn, who wrote of the newspaper in 2008:

"*The Guardian* represents a whole batch of journalists, from moderate right to moderate left – i.e. centre journalists – who, broadly speaking, like the status quo. They like the two-party system, with no real change. They're quite happy to live under the aegis of the Americans and NATO. They are just the Establishment. It is a society that suits them well."ii

Earlier in 2018 *The Guardian* faced criticism for running propagandist advertisements for the Saudi Arabian regime, and is now facing intense scrutiny over an apparently false article claiming that Trump ally Paul Manafort visited Wikileaks publisher Julian Assange in the Ecuadorian Embassy.iii ,iv The story was quickly debunked, and the paper is now refusing to answer questions as to how they came to publish such claims without evidence. No other media outlet corroborated the report.

Ex-*Guardian* writer Jonathan Cook said:

"*The Guardian's* coverage of Latin America, especially of populist leftwing governments that have rebelled against traditional and oppressive US hegemony in the region, has long grated with analysts and experts.v Its special venom has been reserved for leftwing figures like Venezuela's Hugo Chavez, democratically elected but official enemies of the US, rather than the region's rightwing authoritarians beloved of Washington."

It appears that *The Guardian* operates under editorial influences that go beyond assumed norms; from meetings with HSBC lawyers to decide what information can and cannot be published, so as to protect its advertising revenue, to the raid on its premises which resulted in destruction of GCHQ/NSA surveillance documents leaked by Edward Snowden in 2013.vi,vii In light of this, how much of what *The Guardian* reports, especially internationally, can we be confident is being published in good faith?

The newspaper's historical reputation means it is trusted amongst progressives in Latin America, but nuance is very often lost in translation. Few anti-imperialist Brazilians will realise, for example, that *The Guardian* has supported practically all western military interventions for three decades, and based on that, almost certainly would again, should the situation worsen with Venezuela. With an already undistinguished record in the country, *The Guardian* was caught in 2017 publishing regime-change propaganda on Brazil's northern neighbour, with some of their Brazil-based writers defending it on social media.viii,ix Double standards on Venezuela, Honduras, and Brazil are some of the most obvious telltale signs.

Why then, should anyone assume that an exception to their usual blanket support of US/UK foreign policy would be in Brazil? It is uncontroversial that the North Atlantic allies preferred that the Workers Party (PT) was removed from power, for a range of highly obvious strategic and economic reasons, and when viewed as a whole, *The Guardian's* coverage of Latin America is in line with foreign policy, even if often discreetly so. NATO have now accepted Colombia as an associate member and are poised to do the same with Brazil.x This is not coincidence.

The Guardian and the Coup

As movement towards the 2016 coup progressed, disturbing patterns and anomalies in *The Guardian's* reporting emerged. Concerns about repeated and misleading "just the facts" reporting of Dilma Rousseff's impeachment and Lula da Silva's conviction were amplified by the emergence of serious and damning firsthand accounts of their censoring of key information, and chillingly, material published in the newspaper from unknown persons or entities.

Our own account dates to March 2015, the week of the first organised mass protest calling for the impeachment of Dilma Rousseff, following her re-election five months prior. We received an email from a *Guardian* reporter to complain about our critique of international media coverage during the 2014 election.xi He encouraged us to instead focus on cultural stories, effectively to leave politics to the professionals. This was clearly not a possibility given what was already afoot in the country, and *The Guardian's* failure to report it.

With Rousseff facing impeachment, *The Guardian* ran a succession of articles over the subsequent year which helped reinforce perception that the Kafkaesque process to remove her was fair and just. "Millions of Brazilians protest 'horror' government" the newspaper proclaimed.xii A profile of Koch-funded far-right Libertarian group MBL -one of the organisers of those protests – allowed its members to claim, unchallenged, that their organisation was sustained financially by the sale of T-Shirts and stickers.xiii MBL's funding and the Atlas Network to which it belongs, was exposed in a June 2015 investigative report by *Agencia Publica*, yet Brazil's *Guardian* writers were not interested.xiv George Monbiot's exposure of dark money from the Koch brothers funding Far-Right/"Libertarian" groups in the UK is the kind of journalism the world needs.xv Yet in 2015 *Guardian* writers in Brazil knew full well that the same thing was happening here, and they didn't say a word.

This 2015 profile of Rousseff condescendingly related her

personal history of resistance and torture to a political "stubbornness" which was being blamed for Brazil's situation:

> "In the 1970s, Rousseff was imprisoned and tortured during the military dictatorship without giving up the names of her comrades in the Marxist underground. Today, however, her unwillingness to engage in debate and build alliances is widely seen as a key factor in a political crisis that has seen her become the most unpopular president since the return of democracy in 1985."xvi

This was at best window dressing of the pro-coup narrative in Brazil for a sympathetic foreign audience, and of course there was no suggestion whatsoever of ulterior motive, vested economic interests, lawfare or outside influence; the impression was that *impeachment was deserved, and inevitable.*

In March 2016, with the first congressional vote on her fate imminent, *Guardian's* sister paper *The Observer* published an editorial which insisted that "Rousseff's duty is plain: if she cannot restore calm, she must call new elections – or step aside", and alluded to the threat of military intervention. At this key moment, with international alarm growing at her farcical impeachment, *The Guardian/Observer* effectively called for Dilma to resign, and endorsed the putschists effort to decapitate the Workers Party leadership. They have never atoned for this historic error, if indeed that's what it was.xvii

This editorial was followed shortly thereafter by the now infamous headline "The Man Who Could Fix Brazil: country see hope for salvation in Vice President" lauding

Rousseff's usurper, Michel Temer.<u>xviii</u> This piece, written by Latin America editor Jonathan Watts, caused an immediate storm. Even the fiercest critics of Rousseff rarely had any actual faith in her conservative VP as anything more than a means to an end. Hours later the headline was gone, with Watts claiming to have been unaware of it, and to be fair to him, the text was radically different to what the headline and standfirst suggested.

At this point a Brazil-based writer for the paper made contact privately and explained that neither he, nor Jonathan Watts knew who was writing these anti-Rousseff articles and headlines. If those responsible for coverage of Brazil didn't know, then we must ask who was behind them. This question has never been answered, or even acknowledged.

Coverage of every Anti-Dilma protest contrasted with *The Guardian's* rare mention of regular demonstrations and resistance against the coup, a pattern of censorship by omission which continued after Temer took power.<u>xix</u> ,<u>xx</u> ,<u>xxi</u> This reflected a long term failure, not just on *The Guardian's* part, to represent, consult or give regular voice to Brazil's progressives, unions and social movements, without exoticisation and depoliticisation. In a rare instance when it did acknowledge the resistance movement against the coup, during the impeachment itself, it did so with a caveat that "many of those protesting didn't support Dilma or her party".<u>xxii</u> Even the word coup, when it appeared at all, was used in scare quotes.

Only once Rousseff was as good as gone did the tone toward her change.

Documented US Department of Justice involvement in the *Lava Jato* anti-corruption probe is a media taboo, and so effective is self-censorship of it that even the public admission by US Attorney General Kenneth Blanco in 2017, boasting of its collaboration on the operation, and lauding the prosecution of former President Lula, is absent from any coverage of his case in *The Guardian*.xxiii When challenged in a personal conversation on why the US DOJ's role in the case had not been reported, one of its writers claimed that "our readers wouldn't be interested in that information".

Throughout Lula's prosecution, his defence team repeatedly held press conferences in which they explained the case itself, for example, how the original Petrobras graft charges had been removed from it.xxiv *The Guardian* did not seem interested, and rarely if ever attended these events, erroneously including the Petrobras scheme in it's description of Lula's imprisonment when the actual charge was "undetermined acts", related to "corruption" via reforms which never took place, on a beachfront apartment that there was no evidence he ever owned. For this he was jailed for 9 years, vindictively increased to 12 after appeal, and denied *habeas corpus* only after intervention by a top military general.xxv,xxvi

How odd, even in terms of basic journalistic curiosity, to be so stubbornly uninterested in new information, not least facts that completely alter perception of the country's biggest political rupture for decades.

In June 2018, Dilma Rousseff visited the UK, on a tour of universities, trade unions and media outlets. The ousted

President gave a two-hour interview to *The Guardian's* Jonathan Watts, with an editor and others present, in which she described how Lula's prosecution was "phase two" of the *coup d'etat* which removed her, and that it would open the door for the ascension of Neofascist Jair Bolsonaro. For some reason *The Guardian* did not publish the exclusive interview with the first female leader of Latin America's largest nation, nor quote Rousseff's prescient warning.

In contrast, during 2016/17, *The Guardian* published three letters from the Brazilian Ambassador to the UK, on an international PR drive launched by Temer's Post-Coup Government, insisting that all was well with democracy in his country.xxvii

Background noise

The Guardian and its writers were amongst the first to infer that the protests which swept Brazil in 2013 were in any way "Anti-Dilma", before they had actually shifted rightward in their character.xxviii,xxix By failing to properly explain, it also gave the impression that Rousseff herself was culpable for the Military Police violence meted out against the demonstrations. In reality her then likely future adversary, PSDB Governor of São Paulo, Geraldo Alckmin, controlled the *Policia Militar*. Then Mayor of São Paulo, Fernando Haddad said earlier this year that "we will never know if Alckmin gave the order" for an attack on protesters and journalists, outrage at which turned tens to hundreds of thousands on the streets over the subsequent days.

In 2014 it was the era of ubiquitous "doubts upon the

preparedness of Brazil to host the World Cup", with gruesome tales of violence and anticipated mass protests like those that had happened a year prior.xxx ,xxxi Such predictions of societal collapse during the election year World Cup proved to be an embarrassing failure of foreign media in the country.

In the election that followed, *The Guardian* threw its weight behind Marina Silva, depicted as the *genuinely* progressive candidate to beat Workers Party's incumbent Dilma Rousseff.xxxii This was a fairytale version of the evangelical Christian and former environmental campaigner, who was bringing with her a similar Neoliberal platform to that of the candidate she went on to endorse, the "pro-business" Aécio Neves.xxxiii Neves would refuse to concede defeat, call his supporters to the streets, and vow to make Rousseff's second mandate ungovernable, with his PSDB party launching the petition for her impeachment, which Marina Silva would support, having lost to her at two successive elections.

Carnaval always provides a picturesque backdrop for any Brazil story. Following Rousseff's re-election, in 2015 *The Guardian* had "Brazil scales back Carnaval festivities as drought and weak economy persist".xxxiv Again, feeding the failed state narrative, the paper was doubling down on coverage of the São Paulo water crisis, despite the previous three months having record-breaking rainfall in the affected region. In reality, the 2015 São Paulo Carnaval was the then biggest yet. In pre-coup 2016, feeding the pro-impeachment narrative, *The Guardian* went with "Brazil's Carnaval lovers face sobering moment as country braces for recession".xxxv In 2017 *The Guardian* headline on the politicisation of Carnaval suggested that it contained messages of protest towards Dilma Rousseff despite her having been removed from office the previous year.

In 2018, in its sentence-long summary on Rio's zeitgeist-grabbing Tuiuti, *The Guardian* removed the word Neoliberal from the samba school's vampiric depiction of President Michel Temer – something even *Globo* didn't censor. Whilst paying lip-service to the struggle against neoliberal orthodoxy in the North, this is not so in Latin America, and the failed state-friendly "Brazil as monster" was a better fit.<u>xxxvi</u> A photo of the enormous Bloco Maluco Beleza was used to illustrate a story about a tiny and unrelated extreme-right event celebrating dictatorship-era torturers, and in an earlier Carnaval preview focussed on crime and corruption, they stated simply that "President Dilma Rousseff was impeached in 2016 for breaking budget rules in a corruption scandal".<u>xxxvii</u> *Just the facts.* Repeated emphasis of the "legality & constitutionality" of Rousseff's removal was the coup's very own alibi.

Latin America editor Jonathan Watts was replaced in 2017 by his predecessor Tom Phillips, the two having traded BRICS partners China for Brazil and vice versa. Phillips covered Brazil from 2005-2013, including the first election of Dilma Rousseff.

In 2011, with Rousseff now in office, Tom Phillips published an article on a supposed wave of "anti-establishment" comedians, featuring notorious alt-right comic Danilo Gentili. In it, he quotes the Italian-Brazilian:

"Vote for Dilma because she was tortured?" he

quipped. "Fuck that. Did I ask her to be? Seriously," he went on, drawing nervous giggles from the packed audience. "A president has to be smart. If she was caught and tortured, it's because she was an idiot." It was the edgiest moment in an 80-minute monologue – attempting to poke fun at a woman who had been brutally tortured by the dictatorship. But Gentili, 32, a highly controversial but also wildly popular comedian who is blazing a trail for stand-up comedy in South America's largest nation, is a man who enjoys living on the edge." xxxviii

Accused of criminal acts of misogyny, homophobia, and investigated for racism, Gentili went on to be a vocal advocate of Dilma's ouster, and one of neofascist Jair Bolsonaro's most high profile supporters.xxxix In the years prior to his election, Gentili invited him regularly onto his TV chat show "The Night", whose other guests included a serving UK Ambassador.xl Colonel Brilhante Ustra, the secret police chief responsible for Rousseff's two year long torture which included electric shocks to her vagina, was later eulogised by Jair Bolsonaro during his vote for her impeachment. Living on the edge, indeed.

2018 Election

The Guardian's election coverage began badly, with the headline "Trump of the Tropics", an inadequate and misleading US-centric comparison, which did more to endorse and popularise Jair Bolsonaro in Brazil than it did discourage potential voters.xli

There are of course far worse places to read about Bolsonaro. On the pages of *The Guardian*, there's no doubt what he is, and it isn't trying, at least not yet, to make him sound rational, reasonable or competent, as the *Wall Street Journal* and *Bloomberg* have attempted - the promise of extreme neoliberalism at the point of a gun in the most resource rich nation on earth is too valuable for them to waste worrying about human rights.

When Brazilian women brought to the streets one of the biggest anti-fascist mobilisations in history against Bolsonaro, with the so called #*EleNão* (Not him) protest, despite the candidate's racism, misogyny, rape apologism, homopobia and calls for genocide, *The Guardian's* Tom Phillips felt the need to "both sides" the story.xlii The paper then followed with a focus on the "legitimate concerns" of Bolsonaro's female supporters and opponents of feminism.xliii

Election coverage in *The Guardian* hammered the grim inevitability of a Bolsonaro victory, at one point Phillips claiming on Twitter that he "could not find a single Haddad voter", despite being on a tour of North and North Eastern regions where Haddad won convincingly. The paper also drew complaints for a dismissive portrayal of Bolsonaro's progressive adversary. The ostensibly "left liberal" *Guardian's* lack of intellectual curiosity or enthusiasm for Brazil's actual left is strange, and the dismissal of Haddad reinforced the notion that failure and inviability of the left's choice was the issue – not that the leading candidate had been removed from the race via politically motivated abuse of the law.

As Lula was forced out of the race, *Guardian* writers were criticised for their attitude towards his replacement Fernando Haddad.

During the election, *The Guardian* repeatedly used Brian Winter, of Wall Street think tank and lobby, Council of the Americas (AS/COA), as an election pundit.xliv A ghostwriter of autobiographies for conservative leaders across Latin America, until mid 2015 Winter was head of Reuters Brasil, leaving after a scandal where he was accused of censoring an admission that the Petrobras corruption scandal's roots pre-dated the Workers Party Governments being blamed for it (a narrative used at that time as a justification for Rousseff's removal).xlv Winter has since acted as an international cheerleader for Operation *Lava Jato*, and its superstar inquisitor-judge Sérgio Moro, who after jailing Lula and thus preventing him from running in an election he was near guaranteed to win, accepted the position of Justice Minister in the extreme-right Jair Bolsonaro Government.xlvi Since its inception in 2014, *The Guardia*n published several lengthy pieces on Sérgio Moro, Operation *Lava Jato* and his task force in the right wing stronghold of Curitiba, articles which were of very little interest to anyone outside Brazil.xlvii

Winter and Phillips echoed each other's insistence that Bolsonaro's election was inevitable, with neither adequately describing how that position came to be, for example the simplification that the key to his popularity was driven by fear of crime, which ignored statistics that showed he was most popular in the safest areas and least popular in the most dangerous.xlviii

The Guardian also called on ex-IMF economist Monica De Bolle, who repeatedly drew false equivalence between Neofascist Bolsonaro and Centre-Left Fernando Haddad during the first round of the election. One of the crowning, yet unheralded achievements of the Workers Party's time in office was that they repaid the IMF in full, against the lending body's own wishes, and became a creditor, having accumulated enormous foreign reserves – that were conspicuously never mentioned in any media discussion related to the country's economic health, at least while Rousseff was in office.

By inviting institutional neoliberals as if impartial pundits, one of whom's organisation is bankrolled by Chevron, ExxonMobil and a who's who of Wall Street and was actually involved in the 1973 coup in Chile, what are we to conclude about the Guardian?xlix

Pierre Omidyar-financed media platform *The Intercept* was created as *The Guardian* refused to publish leaked Snowden documents in a manner that was to founding editor Glenn Greenwald's satisfaction. Many of the first batch released concerned Brazil, his country of residence, and showed how deeply surveilled Dilma Rousseff's Government was.l How many of those documents remain unpublished that are relevant to Brazil's current situation, and the US/UK role in it, is anyone's guess, but *The Intercept's* recruitment of *Guardian* writers during the 2018 election was a disappointing backwards step by a platform which was set up to provide the kind of investigation and analysis that they do not.

Coverage of Brazil in continental Europe did not seem to suffer the same issues as *The Guardian* and Anglophone media, and *Guardian* reporters have urged against critique of the media. This, right when it is needed the most. Media criticism provides a membrane through which the public can observe workings of power they may otherwise not perceive. By requesting freedom from scrutiny, they're asking for the paper trail to be ignored. Progressive media critics are harder on *The Guardian* because they're one of the few platforms from which anyone has any expectation at all.

There are clearly questions for *The Guardian* on Brazil and Latin America as a whole that they ought to answer if they are to preserve any of the dwindling trust shown by a readership which has historically counted on them to inform their view of world affairs. A platform with enormous reach, we hope for the sake of social progress, and the need to confront fascism, that is it is not too late for *The Guardian* to put its house in order, rebuild its reputation, and give itself honourable purpose. If not, independent progressive media will continue to replace it.

i Knightly, K. (2018, December 3). The Guardian's Bush obituary plumbs new depths of sycophantic hypocrisy. Off-Guardian. Retrieved from https://off-guardian.org/2018/12/03/the-guardians-bush-obituary-plumbs-new-depths-of-sycophantic-hypocrisy/

ii Taylor, I. (2014, April). The politics of Tony Benn. *Socialist Review.* Retrieved from http://socialistreview.org.uk/390/politics-tony-benn

iii Mayhew, F. (2018, March 9). Guardian defends Saudi Prince adds despite criticism of regime in paper, saying ads 'in no way affect our editorial position. Press Gazette. Retrieved from https://www.pressgazette.co.uk/guardian-defends-saudi-prince-ads-despite-criticism-of-regime-in-paper-saying-ads-in-no-way-affect-our-editorial-position/

iv Harding, L. and Collyns, D. (2018, November 17). Manafort held secret talks with Assange in Ecuadorian embassy, sources say. The Guardian. Retrieved from https://www.theguardian.com/us-news/2018/nov/27/manafort-held-secret-talks-with-assange-in-ecuadorian-embassy

v Cook, J. (2018, November 28). Guardian ups its vilification of Julian Assange [blog post]. Retrieved from https://www.jonathan-cook.net/blog/2018-11-28/guardian-vilification-julian-assange/

vi 'A conspiracy of silence – the HSBC, the Guardian and the defrauded British public. (2015, March 5). *Media Lens.* Retrieved from http://www.medialens.org/index.php/alerts/alert-archive/2015/788-a-conspiracy-of-silence-hsbc-the-guardian-and-the-defrauded-british-public.html

vii Borger, J. (2013, August 20). NSA files: why the Guardian in London destroyed hard drives of leaked files. *The Guardian.* Retrieved from https://www.theguardian.com/world/2013/aug/20/nsa-snowden-files-drives-destroyed-london

viii Emersberger, J. (2010, December 21). Note to Rory Caroll re Venezuela [blog]. *Z Blogs.* Retrieved from https://zcomm.org/zblogs/note-to-rory-carroll-re-venezuela-by-joe-emersberger/

ix Emersberger, J. (2017, May 5). The Guardian takes aim at Venezuela's democracy. *Off-Guardian.* Retrieved from https://off-guardian.org/2017/05/05/the-guardian-takes-aim-at-venezuelas-democracy/

x The Atlantic Council and Latin American Regime Change. (2017, December 28). *Brasil Wire.* Retrieved from http://www.brasilwire.com/the-atlantic-council-latin-american-regime-change/

xi Echoes in the echo chamber. (2015, March 11). *Brasil Wire.* Retrieved from http://www.brasilwire.com/echoes-in-the-echo-chamber-ghosts-of-64/

xii Watts, J. (2016, March 14). More than a million Brazilians protest against 'horror government'. *The Guardian.* Retreived from https://www.theguardian.com/world/2016/mar/13/brazil-anti-government-protests-dilma-rousseff-rio-de-janeiro xiii Douglas, Bruce. (2015, April 24). Brazil activists to walk 600 miles for 'free markets, lower taxes and privatisation'. *The Guardian*. Retrieved from https://www.theguardian.com/world/2015/apr/24/brazil-activists-march-free-markets-margaret-thatcher-rand-paul

xiv The right's new cloths. (2015, September 29). *Brasil Wire*. http://www.brasilwire.com/the-rights-new-clothes/

xv Monbiot, G. (2018, December 7). How billionaires are fueling the hard right cause in Britain. *The Guardian*. Retrieved from https://www.theguardian.com/commentisfree/2018/dec/07/us-billionaires-hard-right-britain-spiked-magazine-charles-david-koch-foundation

xvi *Watts, J. and Douglas, B. (2015, August 23). Dilma Rousseff: can Brazil's fighter survive the turmoil. The Guardian.* Retrieved from https://www.theguardian.com/world/2015/aug/23/dilma-rousseff-brazil-president-impeach-scandal

xvii The Observer view on Brazil. (2016, March 20). The Guardian. Retrieved from https://www.theguardian.com/commentisfree/2016/mar/20/observer-view-on-brazil-olympic-games-corruption

xviii Watts, J. (2016, April 3). The man who could fix Brazil: country sees hope for salvation in Vice President. *The Guardian*. Retrieved from http://web.archive.org/web/20160403101327/https://www.theguardian.com/world/2016/apr/03/brazil-michel-temer-dilma-rousseff-impeachment

xix Douglas, B. (2015, August 17). Brazilian president under fire as tens of thousands protest in 200 cities. *The Guardian*. Retrieved from https://www.theguardian.com/world/2015/aug/16/brazil-protests-dilma-rousseff

xx Brazil's prescribed revolt: a tale of two protests in São Paulo. (2016, March 16). Brasil Wire. Retrieved from http://www.brasilwire.com/brasils-prescribed-revolt-a-story-of-two-protests-in-sao-paulo/

xxi 15m: the big hush. (2017, March 16). *Brasil Wire*. Retrieved from http://www.brasilwire.com/15m-the-big-hush/

xxii Watts, J. and Douglas, B. (2016, April 3). 'We won't accept a coup': groups unite to save beleaguered Dilma Rousseff. *The Guardian*. https://www.theguardian.com/world/2016/apr/03/brazil-beleaguered-rousseff-anthems-protests-fill-streets-impeachment

xxiii The Atlantic Council. (2017, July 19). *Lessons From Brazil: Fighting Corruption Amid Political Turmoil*[video file]. Retreived from https://youtu.be/rR5Yiz84b5c

xxiv Mier, B. (2018, July 14). Lula's Kafkaesque Imprisonment: Defense Lawyer Valeska Martins Speaks. *Brasil Wire*. https://www.youtube.com/watch?v=eaUBmWrILrI&list=PL94gOvpr5yt2uBUe7dgAQJ-eAszqenVKd&index=4

xxv No evidence that Lula is corrupt (2018, April 5). *BBC World Service* [radio interview]. Retrieved by https://www.bbc.co.uk/programmes/p063dcss

xxvi Mier, Brian. (2018, November 12). Army chief admits threatening the Supreme Court to jail Lula. *Brasil Wire*. Retrieved from http://www.brasilwire.com/army-chief-admits-threatening-supreme-court-to-jail-lula/

xxvii For example: Santos, E. (2017, August 16). Brazil's problems are nothing like as bad as Venezuela's [letter to the editor]. *The Guardian*. Retrieved from https://www.theguardian.com/world/2017/aug/16/brazils-problems-are-nothing-like-as-bad-as-venezuelas

xxviii Watts, J. (2013, June 18). Brazil protests erupt over public services and World Cup costs. *The Guardian*. Retrieved from https://www.theguardian.com/world/2013/jun/18/brazil-protests-erupt-huge-scale

xxix Watts, J. (2013, June 28). Brazil's left and right struggle for ownership of protests. *The Guardian*. Retrieved from https://www.theguardian.com/world/2013/jun/26/brazil-protests

xxx Former Brazilian footballer decapitated by drug traffikcers. (2013, October 30). *The Guardian*. Retrieved from https://www.theguardian.com/football/2013/oct/30/brazilian-footballer-decapitated-world-cup-rio

xxxi Watts, J. (2014, June 12). Anti-World Cup protests in Brazilian cities mark countdown to kick-off. *The Guardian*. Retrieved from https://www.theguardian.com/football/2014/jun/12/anti-world-cup-protests-brazilian-cities-sao-paulo-rio-de-janeiro

xxxii O'Toole, G. (2014, October 3). Brazil's Marina Silva: a triumph for underdogs and a lesson for civil society. *The Guardian*. Retrieved from https://www.theguardian.com/global-development-professionals-network/2014/oct/03/marina-silva-brazil-election-green-civil-society

xxxiii Watts, J. (2014, October 12). Brazil election blow for Rousseff after Silva backs rival for presidency. *The Guardian*. Retrieved from https://www.theguardian.com/world/2014/oct/12/brazil-election-blows-rousseff-silva-backs-rival

xxxiv Douglas, B. (2015, February 11). Brazil scales back Carnival festivities as drought and weak economy persist. *The Guardian*. Retrieved from https://www.theguardian.com/world/2015/feb/11/brazilian-cities-scale-back-carnival-drought-economy

xxxv Watts, J. (2016, January 12). Brazil's Carnival lovers face sobering moment as country braces for recession. *The Guardian*. Retrieved from https://www.theguardian.com/world/2016/jan/12/brazil-carnival-economic-crisis-recession

xxxvi Phillips, D. (2018, February 13). Samba-school carnival parade depicts troubled Brazil as 'monster'. *The Guardian*. Retrieved from https://www.theguardian.com/world/2018/feb/13/samba-school-carnival-parade-depicts-brazil-as-monster xxxvii Phillips, D. (2018, February 10). Brazilians turn to carnival as an escape from crime and corruption. *The Guardian*. Retrieved from https://www.theguardian.com/world/2018/feb/10/brazil-carnival-escape-crime-corruption

xxxviii *Phillips, T. (2011, October 2).* Brazil's stand-up comics lead social revolution against powerful elites. *The Guardian*. Retrieved from https://www.theguardian.com/world/2011/oct/02/brazil-comedy-standup-danilo-gentili

xxxix Danilo Gentili, sempre controverso, adora soltar o verbo, mas derrapa entre o engraçado e a ofensa. Veja os principais momentos em que ele causou polêmica. (2017, April 18). *IG*. Retrieved from https://gente.ig.com.br/fofocas-famosos/2017-04-18/danilo-gentili-polemicas.html

xl Gentili, D. (2017, March 20). Interview with Jair Bolsonaro [Video]. Retrieved from https://www.youtube.com/watch?v=o8ECr0eDEGo

xli Phillips, T. (2018, April 19). Trump of the tropics: the 'dangerous' candidate leading Brazil's presidential race. The Guardian. Retrieved from https://www.theguardian.com/world/2018/apr/19/jair-bolsonaro-brazil-presidential-candidate-trump-parallels

xlii Phillips, T. (2018, September 21). 'Stop this disaster': Brazilian women mobilise against 'misogynist' far-right Bolsonaro. *The Guardian*. Retrieved from https://www.theguardian.com/world/2018/sep/21/brazilian-women-against-jair-bolosonaro-misogynist-far-right-candidate

xliii Kaiser, A. (2018, October 14). 'I don't see any reason for feminism': the women backing Brazil's Bolsonaro. *The Guardian*. Retrieved from https://www.theguardian.com/world/2018/oct/14/bolsonaro-brazil-presidential-candidate-women-voters-anti-feminism

xliv For example: Phillips, T. (2018, October 8). In Brazil, only the grandest of coalitions can now defeat Bolsonaro. *The Guardian*. Retrieved from https://www.theguardian.com/world/2018/oct/08/in-brazil-only-the-grandest-of-coalitions-can-now-defeat-bolsonaro

xlv "Podemos tirar se acha melhor". (2015, March 24). *Carta Capital*

xlvi AS/COA (2016, February 1). *Corruption busters change the course of Latin American history- Americas Quarterly* [video]. Retrieved from https://www.youtube.com/watch?v=vhXbUb83SFM&feature=youtu.be&t=29

xlvii For example: Watts, J. (2015) Brazil's anti-corruption prosecutor: graft is 'endemic. It has spread like cancer'. *The Guardian*. Retrieved from https://www.theguardian.com/world/2015/dec/30/brazil-anti-corruption-prosecutor-deltan-dallagnol-lava-jato-investigation

xlviii Mier, B. (2018, October 31). Why Bolsonaro won: beyond the cliches. *Brasil Wire*. Retrieved from http://www.brasilwire.com/why-bolsonaro-won-beyond-the-cliches/

xlix A boycott of Americas Quarterly and AS/COA, and why it is needed. (2018, February 22). *Brasil Wire*. Retrieved from http://www.brasilwire.com/boycott-americas-quarterly-and-ascoa/

l Borger, J. (2013, September 24). Brazilian president: US surveillance a 'breach of international law'. *Guardian*. Retrieved from http://ww.theguardian.com/world/2013/sep/24/brazil-president-un-speech-nsa-surveillance

How the US left failed Brazil

By Brian Mier, Sean T. Mitchell, and Bryan Pitts

On November 29, 2018, the socialist magazine and news site *Jacobin* co-sponsored a public interview with Fernando Haddad, the 2018 presidential candidate of Brazil's Workers' Party (PT). The former São Paulo mayor and federal education minister was introduced at Manhattan's People's Forum by *Jacobin's* founding editor, Bhaskar Sunkara. To a packed house, Sunkara praised Haddad and the governments he was part of for designing programs that lifted "millions of people out of poverty... [and gave] millions the chance to have basic access to education and access to higher education. [...] The impact of these governments," he noted, "should not be understated." Sunkara left no doubt about the significance of the PT governments that held Brazil's presidency from 2003 to 2016. Despite the congressional coup (carried out in concert with the media) that unceremoniously removed the party from power and Brazil's subsequent lurch to the far right, he argued that the achievements of the PT in power allow us to "take comfort in the fact that left politics can achieve change and this change can impact millions of people."

For its over 13 years in the presidency, the PT was successful at "uplifting millions of Brazilians out poverty, seriously expanding social citizenship, and making Brazil a significant international actor," as was noted in *Jacobin* in 2018–recognizing the PT's success at massive reform in one of the world's most brutally unequal countries.i Over the last year, *Jacobin* and other major outlets of the US left have been clear about the dangers of Brazil's now president-elect, neo-fascist Jair Bolsonaro, and in their admiration for the PT's historic accomplishments. Shortly after Haddad's electoral loss, *Jacobin* even published some of his political writings from "1998 — the peak of neoliberalism," Haddad noted.ii

After an electoral defeat to Bolsonaro fueled largely by fake news and blatantly partisan judicial measures against the PT, Brazil's largest leftist party is now often extolled on the US left for its democratic socialist successes.iii,iv Yet it is easy to forget what a transformation this was for North American leftist outlets. Reading critiques of the PT in major US left outlets when the party was in power might have led one to believe that 2014, not 1998, was Brazil's "peak of neoliberalism." It might have created the impression that the compromises of democratic socialism that frequently win support from those publications when proposed for the Global North are unacceptable capitulations to capital when successfully implemented in the Global South.

During much of the PT's time in power, most major publications of the US left were presenting a different narrative about the party than the positive one finally embraced in 2018. In this telling, the PT was ineffectual, hopelessly neoliberal, and had demobilized and co-opted the unions and movements of a bitterly divided left. There was some truth in each of those critiques, but they were applied with such wild caricature that the praise the PT is now receiving from those same publications in the wake of its defeat by an ominous neo-fascism is stupefying.

We focus mostly on *Jacobin* in this essay because it is the publication perhaps most associated with the rise of electorally competitive democratic socialism in the United States and because it so clearly exemplifies the broader trend we identify. Astoundingly, of 38 articles published on Brazilian politics we were able to find in *Jacobin* from 2014-2017, all 38 presented a negative view of the PT. We write this essay in the hope that the next time powerful sectors of the Global North left are offered the opportunity to show solidarity with democratic socialist success and struggles in the Global South, they will not fail so tragically.

The myth of the neoliberal PT

Critique of the PT as neoliberal was particularly hyperbolic during the period from 2014 (as right-wing mobilization gained force in Brazil) through 2017 (well after the parliamentary coup against PT president Dilma Rousseff). For example, in his widely read 2014 book on the politics of Brazil's World Cup and Olympics, Dave Zirin, sports editor of *The Nation*, lamented a "popular impression that Lula genuinely cared about the poor— even as he was turning Brazil into a neoliberal paradise."v As impeachment proceedings raged in 2016, a frequent *Jacobin* author argued that the right was kicking "wide open the doors of neoliberalism opened by the PT itself over the last decade," while, an article by another frequent contributor stated that "the PT, after all, guided Brazil through neoliberalization."vi,vii

To be sure, the PT engaged in numerous compromises and questionable alliances during its time in power, most significantly the maintenance of the so-called macroeconomic policy, "tripod" of inflation targeting, floating exchange rates, and meeting yearly primary fiscal surplus targets.viii However, the "tripod" was originally instituted not by the PT, but, in 1999, under the indubitably neoliberal government of PSDB president Fernando Henrique Cardoso. One can find other elements of neoliberal policy during the PT governments —all valid targets of left critique. However, the idea that the PT was straightforwardly neoliberal or, more jarringly, that the party "guided Brazil through neoliberalization" long after neoliberalism's "peak" in 1998, is a smear that beggars belief. Despite its numerous compromises with neoliberalism, during the PT's time in power the party pursued policies of wage and benefit increases that helped lift some 40 million people out of poverty, vastly expanded university access for working class and Afro-Brazilian students, extended labor rights to Brazil's miserably exploited domestic servants and stimulated internal production and consumption of nationally manufactured goods.ix,x,xi ,xii All this after a prolonged period of neoliberalism and austerity that preceded Lula's election in 2002.

Why, as the forces behind a parliamentary coup sought to undo these crucial and hard-fought gains, would left wing publications argue that the PT "did nothing to challenge class power or threaten the elite," that it failed to "make good on its promises of 'social ascension,'" or that the party was engaged in "ongoing attacks on workers and democratic rights"'—to take a sampling of representative 2014-2017 assertions in Jacobin?xiii,xiv ,xv Why, as the coup was being consolidated with the transparently political corruption conviction of Lula, and as a 20-year freeze on social spending was written into Brazil's constitution, would a left wing publication print spuriously that it is "unclear whether a PT government would diverge from the path set by [post-coup president Michel] Temer... neither the party nor Lula has committed to overturning the despicable array of austerity measures and labor reforms implemented by Temer and his cronies"?xvi

A fetish for the vanguard

These critiques of the PT put foreign left journalists in a bind. If the party that nearly eliminated hunger, lifted up to 40 million people from poverty, and dramatically expanded higher education for the poor and Afro-Brazilians was made up of neoliberal posers, what happened to the real left?xvii

Fortunately for those who prefer ideological purity to winning elections, Brazil has no shortage of far-left parties with a dizzying array of acronyms – PCB, PSTU, PCO, MAIS, MRT, and more. All of them are very small parties, mostly Trotskyist, and, to a significant degree, middle-class. Alongside their commitment to extreme factionalism, the main characteristic that unites these parties is electoral inviability. In 2018 they managed to elect not one candidate to any office.xviii The only presidential candidate between them, the PSTU's Vera Lucia, received 55,762 votes (0.05%), or 11th out of 13 candidates.

To read foreign left media, one would never know how irrelevant these parties are. As *Jacobin* authors were writing off PT as it was besieged from the right, they also extolled these parties for critiquing "the PT's transformation into a party of order and neoliberal policies" and ascribed them a leading role in an imagined "mass student movement in solidarity with workers [that] could catalyze a wider radicalization and mobilization against [...] [PT-led] austerity."xix,xx

Still, despite their enthusiasm for these parties, Anglophone left media writers are aware that they are electorally irrelevant. But there is one party to the PT's left with a moderately successful record – the Socialism and Liberty Party (PSOL), which broke from the PT in 2004. In 2018, PSOL elected 10 federal deputies, its best showing ever, leaving it tied for the 14th-largest party in Congress.xxi It is home to some of Brazil's best-known leftists, including the country's only openly gay congressperson, Jean Wyllys; Marcelo Freixo, a Rio de Janeiro state deputy who was nearly elected Rio mayor in 2016; and the globally-revered Rio city councillor, Marielle Franco, assassinated in 2018. Still, outside Rio, where the historic weakness of the PT left an electoral vacuum, the PSOL amounts to a party that performs what Gramsci called a moralist or educational role, with no viable plan to take power. The party is strong among the student movement and academics but is rife with divisions over issues like support for Palestine and Venezuela. Yet it is to the comparatively bourgeois PSOL that Anglophone writers look for the Brazilian left's salvation. As one writer for *Jacobin*, a member of the Democratic Socialists of America (DSA), matter-of-factly explained in 2017, the party was "the most electorally significant left party in Brazil," a laughable claim, but par for the course.xxii

Amid the resistance to the neoliberal policy onslaught

brought by post-coup de-facto President Temer, *Jacobin's* writers supported the "socialist left" PSOL as the best alternative to an "ex-left" PT "mired in corruption and embracing of the neoliberal agenda." In this telling, it was the PSOL and its allied social movements that would spark "a direct confrontation with capital by workers mobilized in their unions and social movements."xxiii,xxiv Although street mobilizations and general strikes are important tactics for the left, it is unclear why progressive journalists writing in English believed that the PSOL, which has no union federations and only one major social movement – the Homeless Workers' Movement (MTST) – allied with it, might be more capable of accomplishing this than the PT, which has close relationships with the country's largest labor union federation and its largest social movements. Imagine if *Jacobin* had covered the 2016 US presidential election solely from the perspective of supporters of Jill Stein, ignoring Bernie Sanders and Hillary Clinton supporters alike; for all intents and purposes, this is what *Jacobin* did in Brazil from 2014-2017, with its uncritical endorsement of the PSOL.

Despite simplistic analyses of the PT in US-left media, the PSOL itself has a much more nuanced relationship to the party. While PSOL offered principled opposition to the PT's more conciliatory tendencies while it was in power, the party is in general a faithful ally of the PT in Congress, forcefully opposed the 2016 coup and the imprisonment of Lula, and offered its support to Haddad in the second round of October's presidential election.xxv,xxvi ,xxvii To the extent that US left Brazil writers acknowledged this shift in their favorite party, it was primarily to criticize it, through arguing, for example, that, although the PSOL "must do more base-building work to be less of a middle class party," drawing closer to the PT is not the right way to accomplish that, since "the PT itself has long since abandoned base-building efforts outside of election time."<u>xxviii</u>

The missing voice of the working class

US left media's dismissal of the PT in favor of the PSOL and other smaller far-left parties is not an isolated issue. It is emblematic of a systematic rejection of the most important parties and movements on the Brazilian left in favor of smaller groups with far more limited impact but far more expansive claims of ideological purity. Nearly without exception, the parties, unions, and social movements that authors in outlets like *Jacobin* spurn are the groups with the most organic links to the Brazilian popular classes, while the smaller groups they embrace are characterized by their ties to middle-class academics.

Between 2014 and 2017, most leftist US press misrepresented or ignored Brazil's largest labor union federation, the Unified Workers' Central (CUT), and its largest social movement, the Landless Workers' Movement (MST). The unions and movements like CUT and MST that make up Brazil's working-class, organized left have a complex relationship with the PT: at times, antagonistic, but generally supportive. They were a key mobilizing factor in four consecutive PT presidential victories and the 47 million votes for Haddad in 2018. Despite this, nobody in *Jacobin* talked to them. Why?

In 2017 the CUT led three huge protests against the coup and Temer's labor and pension reforms: 1) the April 28 general strike, Brazil's largest ever; 2) the largest protest even held in Brasília, on May 24, which led to a declaration of martial law in the capital; and 3) and the June 30 general strike, which, though smaller than the first, shut down large swathes of over 100 cities.xxix,xxx Even as the AFL-CIO displayed solidarity with CUT, *Jacobin* ran an article that, without citing any source, blamed the CUT for trying to block the April 28 strike that it organized.xxxi,xxxii Then it ignored the May 24 protest and claimed that the June strike "was seen as a complete failure."xxxiii

The faulty assumption here is that that CUT was co-opted by the "neoliberal" PT. These claims were ubiquitous in US left media during the crucial period when the right began to undo the gains of prolonged left governance and mobilization. For example, just before Dilma's impeachment, an article in *Jacobin* claimed that CUT "maintains a relationship of strong collaboration with the government."xxxiv After the coup, another asserted that the PT still "maintains a fierce hold on the unions."xxxv Reading this, one would get the false impression that the CUT's aim is not fighting for higher wages but defending the PT and allying with whomever is in power. After the coup, in May 2017, one *Jacobin* author asserted, "Even now [...] CUT hesitates to call its base to struggle, always subordinating these mobilizations to the electoral aims of Lula and the PT."xxxvi Never mind the millions of workers who had just participated in the April 2017 CUT-organized general strike. When Temer proposed draconian pension reforms, a frequent *Jacobin* author dismissed CUT's potential for resistance because it had always been part of a "governista base [...] accustomed to negotiating with the devil."xxxvii

In 2017, when CUT São Paulo President Douglas Izzo was asked if his union had been co-opted by the PT, he laughed and asked why there are so many CUT led strikes against PT governments.xxxviii The fact is, despite historical ties with the PT, there is no legal connection between the two entities. Former CUT members continue to make up the largest group within the PT in Congress, but they are required to leave CUT before entering the PT. The position of CUT (legally controlled by its 7 million members through elections and assemblies) as a force behind the PT, not a puppet of the party, is reflected in the Lula administration's prioritization of job generation and strong wages over neoliberal tenets of wage suppression and labor flexibility. Moreover, despite the claim in *Jacobin* that "Brazilian unions have been demobilized during the PT's reign," strikes steadily increased during the PT years, culminating with 2,050 in 2013.xxxix ,xl

The Landless Workers' Movement (MST) is another key actor of the Brazilian organized left. It was influential in the legalization of homesteading on unproductive or stolen land and, despite constant media opposition and agribusiness violence, has obtained deeds for around 400,000 small farms since the 80s.

In contrast to their disdain for CUT, *Jacobin* authors seldom directly criticize what David Harvey, in a personal conversation with one of the authors, called "the most perfect social movement in the world." Rather, they generally ignore the MST. In the one article between 2014 and 2017 that dealt with the MST in any depth, *Jacobin* ran a previously unpublished seven-year-old interview with Gilmar Mauro, one of the MST's 52 national directors.<u>xli</u> Why skip over 7 years of interviews and public statements by Mauro? In the first round of that year's presidential election, most MST leaders supported PSOL candidate Plínio de Arruda Sampaio. In the *Jacobin* interview, when Mauro said, "The PT is a party of the established order. [...]. It's actually the best manager of and for capital in the country," it was reflective of the frustration that many in the organized left felt at the compromises the PT had made. More importantly, this criticism, made during a period when the PT was in power, was in perfect keeping with the message *Jacobin*'s Brazil contributors were sending about the PT after the coup in 2017.

Running a 2010 interview in 2017, however, obscured shifts in the MST's relationship with the PT. After Arruda failed to get 1% of the vote in the first round of the presidential election, the MST supported Dilma Rousseff. After her victory, they concluded that PSOL didn't have a feasible plan for taking the presidency and strengthened their critical engagement with the PT. If *Jacobin* writers had spoken to anyone from the MST during the coup or its aftermath, they would have encountered a nuanced explanation of its support for the PT. In a 2017 interview, Mauro said, "We are facing a coup in Brazil [...] that aims to take political power and apply a set of regressive measures to cancel what the working class achieved during recent years, [...] This is why we are supporting Lula."<u>xlii</u>

Although MST land occupations dropped during the PT years, the Lula administration created dozens of policies that significantly improved living conditions for family farmers. One example was the Food Acquisition Program

(PAA), which mandated that public schools and hospitals in rural areas buy all their food from family farmers.<u>xliii</u> This and other policies help explain why small farmers still produce 70% of food consumed by Brazilians and why, despite many well documented PT compromises with agribusiness, the MST continues to support the PT.<u>xliv</u>,<u>xlv</u> Neither CUT nor MST support the PT unconditionally. When they do support the party, it is because of the concrete ways their members' lives improved under the PT.

The only social movement frequently mentioned in *Jacobin* during the coup period was the Homeless Workers Movement (MTST), led by 2018 PSOL presidential candidate Guilherme Boulos who, as the son of wealthy São Paulo doctors, is the only prominent Brazilian popular social movement leader who does not come from working class origins. This provided disproportionate coverage for the social movement most closely allied to *Jacobin's* Brazil writers' favorite political party, while dismissing Brazil's largest, most popular social movement and union federation as PT stooges.

Why all the hate?

Jacobin and other US left outlets presented a one-sided narrative about the PT over many years. In light of that coverage, and in the wake of the PT's brutal defeat to neo-fascism, it is perplexing to see the party canonized as demonstrating that "left politics can achieve change," to return to Sunkara's introduction of Haddad.

There are many important left critiques of the PT, and they are frequently made in Brazil–though usually with more nuance and a greater range of perspectives than have been represented on the US left. Why did US left media eschew listening to different left actors and advancing a more careful analysis? Why did they present such a cartoonishly negative portrait of a left party in power, just as it faced dire threats to achievements in promoting equality that many on the US left can only dream of? We offer a few possible reasons.

First, it seems that ideological perfection, the obligation to push for socialism without consideration of institutional constraints, is a requirement only of Global South governments and political parties. One is tempted to suggest an unconscious colonial exoticism here: If political progress in the Global North must be made through ugly compromise and incrementalism, the tropics are frequently made the site of Global North fantasies of utopia, as Haitian anthropologist Michel-Rolph Trouillot has suggested.xlvi

Second, it is possible that editors or authors simply misread Brazil in light of the United States. For editors at *Jacobin*, the de-facto mouthpiece for the "Bernie wing" of the Democratic Party, the DSA, and other factions deemed "far left" in the US context, the narrative of a corrupt, neoliberal institutional party challenged by upstart socialists must have been immediately recognizable. The PT must be the Democratic Party, while the PSOL would have looked like the DSA and Bernie Sanders. But this analogy doesn't stand up to scrutiny: the PT instituted or expanded policies like race- and class-based quotas in university admissions, public university expansion, conditional cash transfers, wage increases, universal health care, job-creating infrastructure projects, and more. Their policies and priorities are much closer to those of Sanders and the DSA than to the Clintonite Democrats. Indeed, Haddad recently went to Vermont to work on a Progressive International with Sanders; he is not known to have received any invitations from the Clinton Foundation.xlvii

Third, perhaps the US left was led astray by positive coverage of Lula in the global financial press. In his critique of the PT, Dave Zirin writes, "Lula, the fire-breathing radical had become a darling of the *Economist* and *Financial Times* crowd, who regularly contrasted his leadership with that of the "irresponsible" Chávez."xlviii Just as the existence of the Soviet Union forced capital to accept the rise of social democracy in the Global North, so Hugo Chávez's Bolivarian leftist project caused many non-leftists to support Lula as a safer alternative, including Zirin's "*Economist* and *Financial Times* crowd."xlix,l "If the neoliberals at the *Economist*, *Financial Times*, *Wall Street Journal*, and World Bank love Lula, he must be terrible," we can imagine the thought process proceeding—as logical as it was tragically incorrect.

Fourth, although US left publications could have avoided this pitfall if their editors had listened to a broader cross-section of the Brazilian left, one party, the PSOL, was given the dominant voice. In *Jacobin*, articles were written almost entirely by authors affiliated with the PSOL, including their two most frequent Brazil contributors. There's nothing wrong with a journalist preferring any particular left party. But if most of an outlet's authors who write about one party are affiliated with its biggest leftist rival, might this not slant the coverage? Until 2018, when *Jacobin* began to make overtures to Haddad as the PT presidential candidate, this key outlet for the US left ignored perspectives on Brazil that deviated from the PSOL platform.

In 2014, right-wing candidate Aécio Neves refused to accept his loss to Rousseff in the presidential election. In 2015, the right organized mass demonstrations, while mainstream Brazilian and foreign media parroted narratives of PT corruption and economic mismanagement. In 2016, Congress impeached Rousseff in a congressional coup, and the judicial system ramped up corruption investigations that disproportionately targeted the PT. In 2017, Brazil's unions and social movement engineered mass protests against Temer's reforms.

All this time, *Jacobin* and other US left media outlets repeated the refrains that the PT was neoliberal, that it had abandoned or co-opted labor unions and social movements, and that a far smaller leftist party, the PSOL, was the authentic voice of Brazil's left. Less important than the degree of truth or falsehood of these accusations was their timing, as the right executed a plan to accomplish judicially what it could not at the ballot box – defeat the PT. The eventual result of the right's plan was the election of a neo-fascist who has promised to carry out a "cleansing" the likes of which Brazil has never seen, a campaign that has the organized left, the poor, Afro-Brazilians, and indigenous and LGBT people square in its sights.li

To their credit, US left media have unequivocally condemned Bolsonaro, and *Jacobin* is helping lead a solidarity campaign for the PT and Brazilian left. But what if the US left had moderated its criticism earlier to defend the PT against the developing coup? Would there have been greater solidarity with Rousseff? Greater resistance to the Temer government's attacks on the working class? An earlier recognition of the threat of Bolsonaro? There's no way to know. But perhaps it's time for the US left to turn its critical gaze back on itself.

i Sunkhara, B. (2018, September 27). Brazil's next President: an interview with Fernando Haddad. *Jacobin*. Retrieved from https://www.jacobinmag.com/2018/09/fernando-haddad-pt-brazil-lula-elections

ii Haddad, F. (2018, November 10). Fernando Haddad reflects. *Jacobin*. Retrieved from https://jacobinmag.com/2018/11/fernando-haddad-workers-party-brazil-marxism

iii Mier, B. (2018, October 5). WhatsApp: Bolsonaro's hate machine. *Brasil Wire*. Retrieved from http://www.brasilwire.com/whats-up-fascism-phone-app-delivers-probable-bolsonaro-victory/

iv Weisbrot, M. (2018, January 23). Brazil's democracy pushed into the abyss. *New York Times*. Retrieved from https://www.nytimes.com/2018/01/23/opinion/brazil-lula-democracy-corruption.html

v Zirin, D. (2014). *Brazil's Dance with the Devil*. Chicago: Haymarket Books.

vi Purdy, S. (2016, April 18). Hypocricy wins the day. *Jacobin*. Retrieved from https://jacobinmag.com/2016/04/dilma-rousseff-impeachment-coup-temer-bolsonaro

vii Fernandes, S. (May 25, 2016). The right marches on Brazil. *Jacobin*. Retrieved from https://jacobinmag.com/2016/04/dilma-rousseff-impeachment-coup-temer-bolsonaro

viii Bresser-Pereira, C. (2013). O governo Dilma frente ao "tripé macroeconômico" e à direita liberal e dependente. *Novos Estudos CEBRAP*. 95 (March). Retrieved from http://www.scielo.br/scielo.php?script=sci_arttext&pid=S0101-33002013000100001

ix D'Ércole, D. (2011, June 11). Cerca de 40 milhões de pessoas ingressaram na Classe C, aponta pesquisa da FGV. *O Globo*. Retrieved from https://oglobo.globo.com/economia/cerca-de-40-milhoes-de-pessoas-ingressaram-na-classe-aponta-pesquisa-da-fgv-2756988

x Carvalho, I. (2013). Dez nos de cotas nas universidades: o que mudou? *Revista Fórum*. Retrieved from https://www.revistaforum.com.br/digital/138/sistema-de-cotas-completa-dez-anos-nas-universidades-brasileiras/

xi Matoso, F. (2015, June 1). Dilma assina regulamentação dos direitos das domésticas, diz Planalto. *Globo*. http://g1.globo.com/politica/noticia/2015/06/dilma-assina-regulamentacao-dos-direitos-das-domesticas-diz-planalto.html

xii IPEA.(2009, August). *Nota Tecnica: Impactos da Redução do Imposto sobre Produtos Industrializados (IPI) de Automóveis*. Retrieved from http://ipea.gov.br/agencia/images/stories/PDFs/2009_nt015_agosto_dimac.pdf

xiii Fernandes, S. (2017, May 19). Assessing the Brazilian Workers Party. *Jacobin*. https://jacobinmag.com/2017/05/assessing-the-brazilian-workers-party

xiv Steinman, I. (2015, July 10). Rio's Student Resistance. *Jacobin*. https://www.jacobinmag.com/2015/07/youth-protests-dilma-rousseff-pt/

xv Purdy, S. (2016, March 18). Brazil on edge. *Jacobin*. Retrieved from https://jacobinmag.com/2016/03/rousseff-lula-pt-petrobras-coup-brazil

xvi Hochuli, A. (2017, July 15). The meaning of Lula's conviction. *Jacobin*. https://jacobinmag.com/2017/07/lula-conviction-corruption-temer-neves-lava-jato

xvii Brazil removed from World Hunger Map. (2014, September 16). *AP*. Retrieved from https://www.apnews.com/5c74f94eadaf47c28995416d5e9fae85

xviii Quantidade de deputados estaduais eleitos por partido. (2018). *UOL*. Retrieved from https://noticias.uol.com.br/politica/eleicoes/2018/raio-x/assembleias/numero-de-deputados-estaduais-eleitos-por-partido/?uf=ac

xix Fernandes, S. (2014, October 2). Post Politics in Brazil. *Jacobin*. Retrieved from https://www.jacobinmag.com/2014/10/post-politics-in-brazil/

xx Steinman, I. (2015, July 10). Rio's Student Resistance. *Jacobin*. https://www.jacobinmag.com/2015/07/youth-protests-dilma-rousseff-pt/

xxi César, G. (2018, October 8). Saiba como eram e como ficaram as bancadas na Câmara dos Deputados, partido a partido. *Globo*. Retrieved from https://g1.globo.com/politica/eleicoes/2018/eleicao-em-numeros/noticia/2018/10/08/pt-perde-deputados-mas-ainda-tem-maior-bancada-da-camara-psl-de-bolsonaro-ganha-52-representantes.ghtml

xxii Mahoney, E. (2017, April 26). Why Brazil is striking on Friday. *Jacobin*. Retrieved from https://www.jacobinmag.com/2017/04/brazil-temer-general-strike-pension-reform-lula-corruption

xxiii Purdy, S. (2016, October 6). Honeymoon for the Brazilian right. *Jacobin*. Retrieved from https://jacobinmag.com/2016/10/honeymoon-for-the-brazilian-right

xxiv Purdy, S. (2016, September 6). Fora Temer. Jacobin. Retrieved from https://jacobinmag.com/2016/09/brazil-impeachment-rousseff-temer-pt-psol-coup

xxv Calgaro, F. (2016, April 16). Contrário ao impeachment, PSOL diz que processo é 'farsa' e 'engodo'. *Globo*. Retrieved from http://g1.globo.com/politica/processo-de-impeachment-de-dilma/noticia/2016/04/contrario-ao-impeachment-psol-diz-que-processo-e-farsa-e-engodo.html

xxvi Madeiros, J. (2018, June 6). Prisão de Lula: nota da Presidência do PSOL. *Esquerda Online*. Retrieved from https://esquerdaonline.com.br/2018/04/06/prisao-de-lula-nota-da-presidencia-do-psol/

xxvii Calgaro, F. (2018, October 9). PSOL declara apoio a Haddad no segundo turno das eleições presidenciais. *Globo*. Retrieved from https://g1.globo.com/politica/eleicoes/2018/noticia/2018/10/09/psol-declara-apoio-a-haddad-no-segundo-turno-das-eleicoes-presidenciais.ghtml

xxviii Fernandes, S. (2018, January 28). The Lula Question. Jacobin. Retrieved from https://www.jacobinmag.com/2018/01/lula-appeal-case-workers-party-brazil-left

<u>xxix</u> Rossi, M. (2017, June 30). Com protestos e bloqueios pontuais em grandes cidades, paralisações são menores que última greve geral. *El Pais*.

<u>xxx</u> Cavalcanti, H. (2017, June 30). Com setor de transportes mobilizado, Brasília tem grande adesão à greve. Rede Brasil Atual. Retrieved from https://www.redebrasilatual.com.br/politica/2017/06/brasilia-tem-menos-mobilizacao-nas-ruas-mas-grande-adesao-a-greve-por-varios-setores

<u>xxxi</u> Connel, T. (2017, May 12). In Grim Times, Brazil's Young Workers Take Charge of Future. AFL-CIO [blog]. Retrieved from https://aflcio.org/2017/5/12/grim-times-brazils-young-workers-take-charge-future

<u>xxxii</u> Badaró, M. (2017, May 23). The Continental Strikes. *Jacobin*. Retrieved from https://jacobinmag.com/2017/05/brazil-general-strikes-russian-revolution-dictatorship-temer-labor-reform

<u>xxxiii</u> Hochuli, A. (2017, July 15). The meaning of Lula's conviction. *Jacobin*. Retrieved from https://jacobinmag.com/2017/07/lula-conviction-corruption-temer-neves-lava-jato

<u>xxxiv</u> Arcary, V. (2016, February 11). The alternative to Lulism. Jacobin. Retrieved from https://www.jacobinmag.com/2016/02/lulism-lula-rousseff-impeachment-petrobras-cunha-corruption-brazil/

<u>xxxv</u> Mahoney, E. (2017, April 26). Why Brazil is striking on Friday. *Jacobin*. Retrieved from https://www.jacobinmag.com/2017/04/brazil-temer-general-strike-pension-reform-lula-corruption

<u>xxxvi</u> Badaró, M. (2017, May 23). The Continental Strikes. *Jacobin*. Retrieved from https://jacobinmag.com/2017/05/brazil-general-strikes-russian-revolution-dictatorship-temer-labor-reform

<u>xxxvii</u> Fernandes, S. (May 25, 2016). The right marches on Brazil. *Jacobin*. Retrieved from https://jacobinmag.com/2016/04/dilma-rousseff-impeachment-coup-temer-bolsonaro

<u>xxxviii</u> Mier, B. (2016, March 17). There is no negotiation whatsoever: an interview with Douglas Izzo. *Council on Hemispheric Affairs*. Retrieved from http://www.coha.org/there-is-no-negotiation-whatsoever-union-leader-douglas-izzo-talks-about-labor-rights-in-post-coup-brazil/

<u>xxxix</u> Fogel, B. (2015, December 17). South Africa does not need a 'Lula moment'. *Jacobin*. https://jacobinmag.com/2015/12/south-africa-zuma-anc-mandela-sacp-cosatu-numsa

<u>xl</u> Marcelino, P. (2017, February 8). Sindicalismo e neodesenvolvimentismo Analisando as greves entre 2003 e 2013 no Brasil. *Tempo Social: a revista da sociologia da USP*. V. 29 (3). pp 201-227

<u>xli</u> Fernandes, S. and Levy, C. (2017, February 1). The coalition that couldn't: an interview with Gilmar Mauro. *Jacobin*. Retrieved from https://www.jacobinmag.com/2017/02/brazil-pt-mst-social-movements-temer-rousseff

<u>xlii</u> Mier, B. (2017, September 6). The MST and the fight to change the Brazlian power structure: and interview with Gilmar Mauro. *Council on*

Hemispheric Affairs. Retrieved from http://www.coha.org/mst-and-the-fight-to-change-the-brazilian-power-structure-an-interview-with-gilmar-mauro/

xliii International Policy Center for Inclusive Growth (2013). *Structured demand and smallholder farmers in Brazil: the case of PAA and PNAE*. Retrieved from https://includeplatform.net/knowledge-portal/structured-demand-and-smallholder-farmers-in-brazil-the-case-of-paa-and-pnae/

xliv Agricultura familiar: 70% da sua comida é produzida assim. (2018, November 27). *Terra*. Retrieved from https://www.terra.com.br/noticias/agricultura-familiar-70-da-sua-comida-e-produzida-assim,02d344528dde2fe8c34c492cb91dc142kmht6irr.html

Trouillot MR. (2003) Anthropology and the Savage Slot: The Poetics and Politics of Otherness. In: Global Transformations. Palgrave Macmillan, New York

xlv Ewing, R. (2005, March 1). End of Brazil GMO ban to curb rampant black market. *USA Today*. Retrieved from https://usatoday30.usatoday.com/tech/news/biotech/2005-03-01-brazil-gmo-ban_x.htm

xlvi Trouillot, MR. (2003). Antropology and the Savage Slot: The Poetics and Politics of Otherness. *Global Transformations*. New York: Palgrave Macmillan.

xlvii Weigel, D. (2018, December 1). Bernie Sanders turns focus to the White House and the World. *Washington Post*. Retrieved from https://www.washingtonpost.com/powerpost/bernie-sanders-turns-focus-to-the-white-house-and-the-world/2018/12/01/dc01f7ae-f4f1-11e8-80d0-f7e1948d55f4_story.html?utm_term=.516f3cd13589

xlviii Zirin, D. (2014). *Brazil's Dance with the Devil*. Chicago: Haymarket Books.

xlix Graeber, D. (2014, May 30). Savage capitalism is back, and it will not tame itself. *The Guardian*. Retrieved from https://www.theguardian.com/commentisfree/2014/may/30/savage-capitalism-back-radical-challenge

l Castaneda, J. (2006, May/June). Latin America's left turn. *Foreign Affairs*. Retrieved from https://www.foreignaffairs.com/articles/south-america/2006-05-01/latin-americas-left-turn

li Bolsonaro ameaça: "Vamos varrer do mapa esses bandidos vermelhos" (2018, October 21). *Carta Capital*. https://www.cartacapital.com.br/politica/bolsonaro-ameaca-201cvamos-varrer-do-mapa-esses-bandidos-vermelhos201d

Year of Lead

Part six

The Sandcastle

Chile-Brazil: a new laboratory for the far-right

By Joana Salém Vasconcelos
and Rejane Carolina Hoeveler

Still shocked by the electoral results in Brazil, many Brazilians are asking how an avalanche of votes for Jair Bolsonaro and General Hamilton Mourão took place and what exactly will happen when a right wing extremist government takes over. We are still a long way off from answering this, but the connections between Bolsonaro's main economic guru, Paulo Guedes, and the Augusto Pinochet dictatorship in Chile (1973-1990), give us important leads about the underlying plans.

Until recently, Paulo Roberto Nunes Guedes, 69, was relatively unknown to the Brazilian public. Although he was a columnist for *Epoca* magazine and *O Globo* newspaper and founder of the Millenium Institute, the economist spent decades isolated from the mainstream, rejecting all of Brazil's economic plans for the last 35 years, from those of President José Sarney to Dilma Rousseff. Reading some of his articles it becomes clear why.[i] Guedes shows an aversion to the social contract guaranteed in the 1988 Constitution, which he interprets as an obstacle to his political project. For him, Brazil suffered from an "interventionist curse" which has blocked the "irreversible evolutionary process (...) towards a great open society."[ii]

On May Day, 2017, Guedes wrote, "the right wing hegemony governed for two decades and the left wing hegemony governed for three, both with a disastrous, interventionist economic model."iii In his mind, the 30 years of democratic Brazil, from Fernando Collor to Itamar Franco, Fernando Henrique Cardoso, Lula and Dlima all comprised part of the same hegemonic left. Looking at this *tabula rasa*, it's not hard to understand his political preferences. The social rights system guaranteed in the 1988 Constitution may have survived to the present day, at least on paper, but Guedes is part of the group that wants to exterminate it by capitalizing on the authoritarian wave of Jair Bolsonaro. This implies a radicalization and destruction of the democratic contract. But how will he try to do it?

From Chicago to Chile

Guedes got his PhD in Economics from University of Chicago, a center of Austrian-American neoliberalism dominated by figures like Milton Friedman, in 1978. As Friedman says in his book *Freedom of Choice*, it was a time in which his "apostles" were "wandering in the desert". Forged in Chicago, Guedes economically-extremist vision has not caught on in Brazil until now. But the contrary happened in Chile. The first laboratory of the Shock Doctrine, as Naomi Klein designated the process, resulted from the Freidman-Pinochet alliance.iv It was there that the brothers in faith from Chicago found perfect partners for their economic plans after September 11, 1973: Chilean militarism and fascism promised, at the same time, repression and "innovation".

The inspiration for Guedes' recent proposals for pension and education reform come from the Pinochet dictatorship, tied to the idea of a "subsidiary state."

Antithetical in many ways to the Brazilian Constitution of 1988, the Chilean Constitution of 1980 was imposed by the dictatorship and preserved to this day. Contrary to the idea of State as guarantor of rights, the subsidiary Chilean State was relieved of the responsibility for promoting welfare to its citizens and converted into a financier for market expansion. This has taken place through massive transfers of public resources to the private sector while generating a perverse public debt.

In Chicago, Guedes earned his doctorate with a 63 page, typewritten dissertation.v His work, according to *Folha de São Paulo* newspaper, "was never published and had no repercussions in Brazil," which caused him to resent his more successful colleagues.vi This bitterness became public recently, when he called his ex-student, economist Elena Landau, "mediocre", alleging that he had flunked her during her Master's degree work at PUC University in Rio.vii Elena Landau, 9 years younger than Guedes, was one of the most important economists in Fernando Henrique Cardoso's privatizations, coordinating the sale of Electrobras state energy company for the National Destatization Council during the 1990s. With her transcripts in hand, Landau disproved his claim, saying, "It's Paulo who was a poor professor.viii He missed classes and didn't correct papers."

Professor Paulo Guedes entered the University of Chile in a suspicious manner during the 1980s, during the height of the dictatorship, after a broad purge of critical intellectuals. As Federico Fullgraf writes, the Chilean dictatorship viewed the universities as one of the main "theaters of war", a territory to be retaken from the "Marxist enemy".ix In the place of critics, professors were hired who were aligned with the only school of thought that the military supported in academia. Milton Friedman and his allies had been attracting Chilean economists to Chicago since the 1950s, working to reinsert them into academic positions in the country's main universities. However it was only with Pinochet that the Chicago Boys political experiment consolidated. Guedes was part of this movement, along with his colleague, the Chilean businessman Jorge Constantino Demetrio Selume Zaror. In returning from Chicago, where he first met Guedes, Selume also joined the economic cathedral of the University of Chile. In a few years he became Pinochet's director of budgets and oversaw privatizations of state companies such as Chliectra and Entel. At the same time, he built a financial empire which included banks and real estate. Among them, Rupanco, a 47,000 hectare farm which had been redistributed to the workers during the Salvador Allende government, but that was appropriated by the military in 1979 and given to the El Cabildo S.A. Company, which was later taken over by the Selume family.x According to Fullgraf, " Selume is a kind of unofficial spokesman of the hard line Pinochet supporters in the private sector.xi

It was in this manner, taking over the position of a professor who was arbitrarily fired by the dictators, that Guedes left his part-time teaching jobs at PUC-Rio, IMPA and FGV-Rio, in exchange for, according to him, a "too good to refuse" salary of $10,000/month. When asked about his ties to the Chilean dictatorship, however, he changes the subject to his supposed academic qualifications and tells a story of how he was once inspected by Pinochet's political police.xii

Private retirement pensions and the shock of poverty

During the years in which Guedes lived in Chile, José Pinera, the most powerful Chicago Boy and brother of current Chilean President Sebastian Pinera, completely privatized the retirement system through a decree issued by Dictator Pinochet on November 13, 1980. In this system, formed today by an oligopoly of six private pension funds, wage earners are required to deliver 10% of their salaries for capitalist speculation with no counterpart from the employer. Currently, after 30 years of contribution, 90% of Chilean retirees receive pension checks worth less than half of the national minimum wage of 154,000 Pesos (approximately $220).xiii Symptomatically, the pension system privatization does not apply to members of the military.

Driven by the same kind of pro-capitalization rhetoric that paved the way for Michel Temer's failed pension reform efforts in 2017, the Chilean pension system represents the appropriation of more than 10 million worker's retirement funds. Today, five of the six existing pension funds manage 69.6% of the country's GDP and 94.6% of its social security contributions, having accumulated profits of $ 1.5 million a day in 2017, according to the Sol Foundation.xiv
The collection system is based on individualism, not solidarity, because each worker depends exclusively on himself to increase the value of his pension. Furthermore, pensioners are susceptible to market volatility, trapped in the pension fund managers' mathematical models. During recent years, the retirement pension crisis has led to dramatic increases in suicides of Chilean seniors: nearly 1000 in 5 years. Since 2016, popular anger against the

privatized retirement system has caused gigantic street protests, led by the #No+AFP movement.

In Brazil, the project that would accelerate the deterioration of public welfare was rejected by the population in 2017. But popular resistance was only one of the factors that blocked the Temer government from approving the project, as it was also bogged down in the costly bribery dynamics of a system of corrupt political parties. It is worth noting here that Paulo Guedes is under investigation on the federal police's Operation Greenfields, which is investigating fraud in management of private pension funds that generated R$6 billion in profit between 2009 -2013. There is also evidence of money laundering by the HSM Educational SA Company, which paid Guedes millions of reais in speaking fees.xv

Guedes privatization crusade finds itself confronted by resistance on the streets on the one hand, and on the other, by a governmental machine which wants a piece of the spoils. This is why he seems be thinking of the Pinochet era when he calls for a shock of capitalism that can only be imposed through militaristic force, all for his own benefit.xvi

Pinochetista clans and big data

The Millennium Institute has an ideological sister organization in Santiago with much more influence over its nation's politics: The Liberty and Development Institute, a private organization run as a company which was founded in 1990 in the luxurious neighborhood of Las Condes.xvii Organized by business leaders and high level cabinet ministers from the Pinochet administration like Hernán Buchi, Carlos F. Cáceres, Cristián Larroulet and Luis Larrain Arroyo, the Institute is recognized for working as a revolving door for business executives from major corporations to enter the government and consolidate their company's market positions from inside the state apparatus.

This organization provided ten important members of the government of President Sebastian Pineira, who recently said, "On the economic front, Bolsonaro is heading in the right direction."xviii It is not only the Pineira family, however, who view the emergence of Bolsonaro positively. His right wing extremist competitor from the 2017 Chilean presidential elections, José Antonio Kast, is the Chilean politician most invested in a partnership. The businessman of German descent was the fourth most popular presidential candidate last year, with 523,000 votes. On October 18th, Kast traveled to Rio de Janeiro to meet with Bolsonaro. Afterwards, he published a photo smiling next to the captain in his social media accounts. "Today we met with Jair Messias Bolsonaro and wished him luck in the election. We gave him a Chile jersey so that we can continue strengthening the relationship between both countries and, together, build an alliance that can definitively defeat the left in Latin America," he said.xix

In addition to both being admirers of Pinochet, Kast and Bolsonaro rely on a political strategy based on clans. Senator Felipe Kast, nephew of José Antonio Kast, ran for office as part of the coalition which elected Pinera, and was his planning minister in his previous government. During the primaries, Felipe Kas was supported by Jorge

Selume Aguirre, the son of the businessman who studied with Guedes – a 37 year old psychologist who was recently nominated as Pinera's Communications Secretary. Selume Jr.'s resume features a diploma from Adrés Bello University (part of the Laureate, for profit university multinational, directed by his father), and years of work at Cambridge Analytica. Not less important is the fact that young Selume is the owner of Artool, the largest Chilean big data company.

If there are signs that the Jair Bolsonaro campaign in Brazil could have been strengthened – as was the case of Donald Trump in the US – with the theft of millions of people's personal data from the social media networks, among them WhatsApp, and the dissemination of fake news on a previously unseen scale, the Chilean far-right has all of the tools to do it.

A revolving door with private education

The narrow circle of Brazilian and Chilean right wing extremists closes with the Arab businessman Jorge Selume, father of Pinera's recently nominated communications secretary. As previously mentioned, Selume was Guedes' classmate in Chicago during the 1970s. During the 1980s, he built an economic empire from the largest financial operation ever to take place in Chile at the time. Together with Laz Diez Mesquitas, a consortium of Arab-owned companies, he bought Banco Osorno and sold it to Santander in 1985 for 495 million dollars. At the same time he served as Pinochet's Budget Director.

Today it is more and more clear that education and

culture are priority frontiers for the expansion of neo-pinochetista business negotiations. Jorge Selume Jr. created a powerful communications and political marketing machine with Artool and spurred the election of 46 mayors from the Partido Renovacion Nacional in 2016, using Cambridge Analytica techniques. Furthermore, Banco de Chile and Banco Santander, which together hold at least half of the national population's bank accounts, are among Artool's top clients.xx

Meanwhile, Jorge Selume, the father, has been investing in education for years and is now one of the most influential executives in the for-profit education multinational Laureate, which is being investigated for fraud in the private university accreditation system.xxi In Brazil, Laureate has prioritized distance learning. It is no coincidence that Paulo Guedes defends a "shock of digital inclusion in grammar school," Bolsonaro has been talking about distance learning for children and the name of Stravos Xanthopoylos, international relations director for the Brazilian Association of Distance Learning, has been cited for Education Minister in the future right wing extremist government- if the ministry will even continue to exist.xxii

What is in store for us?

During his first interview with the international press after his connection with Jair Bolsonaro became public in November, 2017, Guedes said, "The last 30 years have been a disaster – we corrupted democracy and stagnated the economy (...) We should have done what the Chicago Boys defended."xxiii

When asked why he would associate with known defender of the Brazilian military dictatorship, during an event organized by the Credit Suisse bank in São Paulo, Guedes classified this type of question as "patrolling". In talking about his long conversations with Bolsonaro, he repeated one of his favorite catchphrases, playing on the words on the Brazilian flag: "Who knows if order isn't speaking with progress?"

It is not hard to decipher the message between the lines. The first time that Latin America witnessed an organic union between the military and the Chicago Boys in a government was in 1973 in Chile, a chapter of history written in buckets of blood. All that is left for Brazilians is to find out what kind of situation this dangerous association will lead to.

This article originally appeared in LeMonde Diplomatique Brasil, and was translated by Brian Mier.

i Gaspar, M. (2018, September). O Fiador. *Revista Piauí*. Ed. 144. Retrieved from https://piaui.folha.uol.com.br/materia/o-fiador/

ii Guedes, P. (2018, April 4). Maldição dirigista. *O Globo*. Retrieved from https://oglobo.globo.com/opiniao/maldicao-dirigista-22571004

iii Guedes, P. (2017, May 1). Atolados no Pantano. *O Globo*. Retrieved from https://oglobo.globo.com/opiniao/atolados-no-pantano-21279887

iv Klein, N. (2010, March 10). Milton Friedman did not save Chile. Retrieved from https://www.theguardian.com/commentisfree/cifamerica/2010/mar/03/chile-earthquake

v Guedes, P. (1978). *Fiscal policy, public debt and external indebtedness in non monetary two sector open growth models* [unpublished doctoral disssertation]. University of Chicago, Chicago, IL, USA.

vi Mena, F. (2018, October 9). Economista de Bolsonaro, Paulo Guedes viveu mudança radical em Chicago. *Folha de São Paulo*. Retrieved from https://www1.folha.uol.com.br/mercado/2018/10/economista-de-bolsonaro-paulo-guedes-viveu-mudanca-radical-em-chicago.shtml

vii Gaspar, M. (2018, September). O Fiador. *Revista Piauí*. Ed. 144. Retrieved from https://piaui.folha.uol.com.br/materia/o-fiador/

viii Bergamo, M. (2018, September 6). Economista de Bolsonaro e sua ex-aluna Elena Landau trocam farpas na internet. *Folha de São Paulo*. Retrieved from https://www1.folha.uol.com.br/colunas/monicabergamo/2018/09/economista-de-bolsonaro-e-sua-ex-aluna-elena-landau-trocam-farpas-na-internet.shtml

ix Fullgraf. F. (2018, September 27). Paulo Guedes, o "Chicago Boy" de Bolsonaro e seus vínculos com a ditadura Pinochet. *Revista Fórum*. Retrieved from https://www.revistaforum.com.br/paulo-guedes-o-chicago-boy-de-bolsonaro-e-seus-vinculos-com-a-ditadura-pinochet/

x Monckeberg, M. (2009). *Los magnates de la prensa*. Santiago: Debate

xi Fullgraf. F. (2018, September 27). Paulo Guedes, o "Chicago Boy" de Bolsonaro e seus vínculos com a ditadura Pinochet. *Revista Fórum*. Retrieved from https://www.revistaforum.com.br/paulo-guedes-o-chicago-boy-de-bolsonaro-e-seus-vinculos-com-a-ditadura-pinochet/

xii Oliveira, J. (2018, October 9). Plano econômico de Paulo Guedes, guru de Bolsonaro, depende de uma 'bala de prata' para funcionar. *El País*. Retrieved from https://brasil.elpais.com/brasil/2018/10/02/politica/1538508720_526769.html

xiii Marchas en Chile contra la sistema privado de pensiones. (2018, April 22). *El Mercurio*. Retrieved from https://ww2.elmercurio.com.ec/2018/04/22/marchas-en-chile-contra-sistema-privado-de-pensiones/

xiv Reverbal, P. (2017, May 16). Como é se aposentar no Chile, o 1º país a privatizar sua Previdência. BBC Brasil. Retrieved from https://www.bbc.com/portuguese/internacional-39931826

xv MPF abre investigação contra Paulo Guedes por suposta fraude em fundos de pensão. (2018, October 26). *Ultimo Segundo*. Retrieved from https://ultimosegundo.ig.com.br/politica/2018-10-26/investigacao-contra-paulo-guedes-operacao-greenfield.html

xvi Guedes, P. (2018, February 19). Choque de Capitalismo. *O Globo*. Retrieved from http://avaranda.blogspot.com/2018/02/choque-de-capitalismo-paulo-guedes.html

xvii Liberdad Y Deserollo. (2018). *Que es LYD?* [webpage]. Retrieved from https://lyd.org/quienes-somos/

xviii Cebrian, B. (2018, October 9). Presidente chileno elogia plano econômico de Bolsonaro, premiê espanhol o vê com preocupação. *El Pais*. Retrieved from https://brasil.elpais.com/brasil/2018/10/09/internacional/1539068989_316141.html

xix Kast, J. (2018, October 18). [Facebook post]. Retreived from https://www.facebook.com/joseantoniokast/photos/a.890414411050386/1939830292775454/

xx Saleh, F. (2018, March 27). Jorge Selume: el señor big data a cargo de la Secom. *El Mostrador*. Retrieved from https://www.elmostrador.cl/noticias/pais/2018/03/27/jorge-selume-el-senor-big-data-a-cargo-de-la-secom/

xxi Jimenez, B. (2014, May 9). Laureate: todos los caminos conducen a Selume. *El Mostrador*. Retrieved from https://www.elmostrador.cl/noticias/pais/2014/05/09/laureate-todos-los-caminos-conducen-a-selume/

xxii Soares, J. (2018, August 30). Posto Ipiranga no educação. *O Globo*. Retrieved from https://epoca.globo.com/posto-ipiranga-da-educacao-de-bolsonaro-presta-consultoria-para-presidenciavel-via-whatsapp-23025460

xxiii Caleiro, J. (2018, August 31). Paulo Guedes critica "patrulhamento" por conversar com Bolsonaro. *Exame*. Retrieved from https://exame.abril.com.br/economia/bolsonaro-me-chamou-para-conversar-diz-paulo-guedes/

The Sandcastle - Epilogue

Send in the clowns

On December 10, 2018, the 70th anniversary of the Universal Declaration of Human Rights, Brazilian President elect Jair Bolsonaro and his Vice Presidential running mate, General Mourão, received their diplomas from the Supreme Electoral Court (TSE).

They were presented with the inaugural certificates after a lecture on democracy by Rosa Weber, the Supreme Court judge who, in April, declared she was voting counter-intuitively, under military threat, in denying habeas corpus to then certain winner of the 2018 election, former President Lula da Silva. This was one link in a chain of events which saw a neofascist elected and altered the course of Brazilian history.

There was already dark irony to it occurring on this anniversary, as Bolsonaro is on record saying that he does not believe in human rights. He thinks they are a communist thing or as his more articulate neofascist pin-up Augusto Pinochet put it, a very wise invention of Marxists.

In three weeks he will assume the Presidency of a forever promising, incomplete, wealthy and chronically unequal country of almost 220 million souls, many of whom will live in fear of his prejudices, hatred, irrationality, profound stupidity, and that of his dim-witted offspring, opportunist allies and far-right supporters.

Violent, incompetent, and corrupt; the wager is now how long Bolsonaro's imbecilic spectacle can last. Self-

destruction ahead of schedule is the best hope Brazil's progressives, minorities – even majorities, have.

As Italians did with Berlusconi before him, Brazilians will discover that satire does not function with a Bolsonaro; no joke will raise a smile, no dose of schadenfreude will suffice. Even as his sandcastle of asinine, toxic rhetoric disintegrates, grimly and inevitably, into the South Atlantic, the only relief will be that Brazil itself is not taken with it.

Avoiding mention of his name is etiquette, evading his grinning mask of a face, a strategy.

People are understandably saving themselves for the struggles ahead.

We all float down here

"Vai acabar com essa palhaçada" (he's going to end this clown show) was an election slogan used by Bolsonaro campaign and his supporters. His ministerial appointments suggest precisely the opposite.

Perhaps unsurprisingly given the nature of his election, many of his voters already have buyers' remorse, not least due to the prevalence of corrupt politicians in a government which came to power with specious rhetoric of anti-corruption. A cursory glance over the history of fascism could have tipped them off.

'Brazil: Love it or leave it' - a notorious slogan of the dictatorship in the early 1970s - chillingly re-emerged following the election, yet the torpor amongst progressives

has partially cleared for the return of Brazil's famed gallows humour. There is now an eerie calm to the final month before Bolsonaro's inauguration. The next four years will be marked by violent oppression and resistance, but many are sensing that the new extreme-right government will collapse ahead of schedule.

The coming era will be dangerous, regardless of how intellectually stunted and pathetic Bolsonaro's cabinet is. But just three weeks before taking office, the most incompetent looking administration for thirty years is already imploding, with some predicting that his Presidency may be even more short lived than that of Fernando Collor, who survived two years from 1990-92.

It must be reiterated that Bolsonaro is no "Trump of the Tropics" as The Guardian and others tried to depict, and the anticipation of him in power shouldn't be equated either, nor should parallels be made between campaigns against them. In Brazil's case, it faces actual overt, documented, genocidal threats –a situation which came about with the connivance of the United States, and involving both Republican and Democrat administrations.

With the first significant number of military figures in the Government since redemocratisation in 1989, there is a surreal quality to watching the transition unfold. Bolsonaro's first cabinet will contain over 30% Military personnel for the first time since the reign of Dictator Ernesto Geisel from 1974-79.

Joining the GSI, the cabinet of Institutional Security, is General Augusto Heleno. Invited by Bolsonaro as potential VP, then as Defence Minister, Heleno was the first commander of the UN's MINUSTAH stabilisation mission in Haiti. During his time in Haiti he notoriously led an armed assault on Cité Soleil, against members of the Lavalas Pro-Democracy Movement. The action killed dozens of people including community leader Dread Wilme (Emmanuel Wilmer). Some consider the Federal Military intervention in the State of Rio de Janeiro to have been inspired by the operations in Haiti, while those in Haiti consider the opposite. Days after the election, Heleno claimed that Brazilian intelligence agency ABIN and the Federal Police, which had evidently failed to protect the Rousseff administration from subversion, had discovered a terrorist plot against President-elect Bolsonaro.

Ernesto Araújo is the new Foreign Minister, Chanceler in Brazilian nomenclature, or "4chan-celer" as he has been nicknamed. Araújo advocates a range of recycled conspiracy theories, such as Cultural Marxism, UFO contact with the United Nations, and also believes that climate change is a hoax. Like Bolsonaro himself, Araújo wants to align Brazil unreservedly with the strategic and economic interests of the United States – to the delight of Washington. Former Foreign and Defence minister Celso Amorim, one of the world's most respected diplomats, who helped elevate Brazil's Itamaraty Foreign Ministry to its pre-coup reputation, has called Araújo's appointment a return to the middle ages.

Araújo is one of several ministers picked by the philosopher king of Brazil's extreme-right, Olavo do Carvalho. Olavo is a former astrologer, charlatan mystic, mediocre journalist, and self-imposed exile in Richmond, Virginia, where he ran until recently an obscure think tank called the "Inter-American institute for Philosophy,

Government and Social Thought", whose website mysteriously vanished following the election. In recent times he has headed the deeply odd "Brasil Paralelo" project, which was a years-long live-action roleplay for what looks very much like Bolsonaro's incoming Government.

Brazil's new Education minister, Ricardo Vélez Rodríguez, was also suggested by Olavo do Carvalho. A self-defined "Anti-Marxist" he is a devout supporter of the "School without Party" initiative which claims to eradicate "communist indoctrination" from Brazil's education system, while at the same time proposing that teachers are versed in the philosophies of Margaret Thatcher. Emphasis of policy under the new government is cost cutting through distance learning in basic education, privatisation and a voucher system for privatised schools inspired by policy implemented in Pinochet's Chile.

Another climate change skeptic is new environment minister, the "Liberal" Partido Novo's (Banco Itaú) Ricardo Salles. A darling of ruralists, his election campaign material defended their right to shoot MST Landless Workers Movement members and leftists, and he has his own environmental fraud case pending against him. He claimed not to have adequate data to evaluate deforestation. Bolsonaro wants to sell off and open the Amazon for exploitation to foreign corporations, this is why he has been called a threat not just to Brazil, but to the world. Salles is his choice to implement that.

On the day that the Neofascist President elect named Salles his new Environment Minister, two MST coordinators – Rodrigo Celestino and José "Orlando"

Bernardo da Silva – were assassinated on their camp in Paraiba.

Science and Technology will be headed by Brazil's first Astronaut, Marcos Pontes. Budgets have halved since 2013, and there has been a major brain drain to Europe and North America as research programmes were regularly shuttered since Michel Temer took office. There is no indication that policy will change with this kind of ceremonial appointment.

Heading the newly combined Ministry of "Women, Family and Human Rights" is ultraconservative Evangelical pastor, Damares Alves. FUNAI, the National Foundation for Indigenous Peoples, will also be folded into the new body, and the appointment of Alves to head to such a frankenstein's monster of a ministry is pure vandalism. Alves seeks to outlaw abortion in the case of rape, one of the few circumstances in which it is currently legal in the country. She has proposed what has been deemed Bolsa Estupro, a small cash allowance for victims of rape in exchange for not having the pregnancy terminated.

Alves also claims to have seen Jesus Christ climb a Guava tree. "He was so beautiful," said the future minister, during an evangelical service, in which she described how she had tried to stop an erratic Mr. Christ from climbing the tree, as she feared that he would get hurt. "He has already suffered so much on the cross", she said.

Pastor Alves has proposed a "cultural counter-revolution in schools", despite having no specific remit for Education.

Even the supposedly credible member of his cabinet, Chicago Boy Paulo Guedes, has been called a "maniac", even by Neoliberal standards, and Brazil is his new laboratory. Bolsonaro's Finance Minister is key to the project and to Wall Street's support for it. In 2005 Guedes founded Instituto Millenium, a think tank drawing together Neoliberals from Brazil and outside, including journalists, economists and politicians, seen as a successor to IBAD, the foreign funded NGO which disseminated anti-government propaganda ahead of the 1964 military coup. Over the next decade its alumni would come to dominate the economic media narrative in Brazil.

After linking up with Guedes, allegedly on Wall Street advice, what followed was Bolsonaro's 'road to Damascus' conversion to the rhetoric of free markets and the minimal state. Guedes, a founder of what became BTG Pactual Bank, also worked in Chile during the Pinochet era. He describes that genocidal dictatorship as "an intellectual point of view". As for free trade, Angela Merkel has warned that the election of Bolsonaro jeopardises completion of trade deals that have been forged for years, such as that between Mercosul and the European Union. The proposed move of Brazil's embassy to Jerusalem, and withdrawal of Palestinian recognition will affect significant trade of meat and poultry to Arab countries, whilst he and his allies' rhetoric on China risks the crucial economic relationship with Brazil's biggest trading partner.

Guedes'programme is effectively to privatise/de-nationalise everything.

"Poison Muse" Tereza Cristina is the new Agriculture

Minister. She is so named for her enthusiasm to further deregulate toxic pesticides on behalf of the industry and Big Agro, in a country which an average person already consumes over seven litres of agrotoxins per year, with all the serious health problems that such legalised, programmed poisoning brings.

Health Minister Luiz Henrique Mandetta, a former Military doctor, has been investigation for corruption since 2015. Like Cristina, from the hard right Dictatorship-heir party, "Democratas", Mandetta formerly at private healthcare giant Unimed, is expected to oversee a privatisation programme of the SUS public health system. The Bolsonaro effect hit SUS before he even took office, with Cuba withdrawing over 8000 doctors following his xenophobic comments, many of whom were serving in remote or dangerous areas where Brazilian doctors refused to work, that are now left without healthcare provision.

4 Star General Fernando Azevedo will be Minister of Defence. Supreme Court President Dias Toffoli, after a succession of decisions from whom were instrumental in Bolsonaro's election, said he was consulted in a phone call from the President-elect and quickly approved the appointment of Azevedo, who had worked with the judge as an advisor.

Operation Lava Jato Inquisitor-Judge Sérgio Moro is the most controversial appointment of the lot. Having insisted he would not enter politics, his acceptance to head the new Justice and Security super ministry sent his most vocal supporters into spirals of denial and cognitive dissonance. Having jailed the election's likely winner, on a ridiculous charge, leaving the way open for Bolsonaro's victory, then joining his government, it is the final sorry end to the fairytale of Operation Lava Jato, lauded internationally as a crucial step in Brazil's development, when it was always a political instrument. General Heleno remarked, "It will be an honor to be sitting at the table with Dr. Sérgio Moro. He is a great value of the country, a man respected here and abroad". Moro, after illegally wiretapping President Rousseff while in office, and releasing the recordings to the media, again illegally, contributing to both the mediatic campaign for her impeachment, and for the prosecution of former President Lula, will now have effectively carte blanche over surveillance.

Chief of Staff will be Onyx Lorenzoni, overseeing transition and facing corruption charges of his own. Onyx has admitted that Moro hatched the plan to jail Lula back in 2005, while Moro has defended Onyx's reputation publicly, and now intends to pursue "corruption in the Trade Union movement".

Pega fogo, cabaré

With his inauguration three weeks away, and the euphoria of his victory subsided, Bolsonaro is now engulfed in BolsoGate, a corruption scandal that is both serious and farcical. It will be a test of how much Brazilian conservatives actually care about corruption cases when the Workers Party are not implicated. We already know the answer.

After the exposure of so-called ghost employees on the payroll, it was revealed last year that his son, Federal Congressman Eduardo Bolsonaro, also charged with making threats against a female journalist, managed to increase his personal fortune by 432% since 2014. His brother Flavio, now elected as Senator, is the focus of this latest scandal to hit the family.

The Department of Control of Financial Activities (COAF) released a report of unusual financial activity in the bank accounts of a former aide to Flavio Bolsonaro. In the COAF statement the former driver of Flavio Bolsonaro, Fabricio Jose Carlos de Queiroz, is alleged to have moved R$1.2m illegally between January 2016 and January 2017. Seven aides to Bolsonaro have so far been found to be involved, with future first lady Michelle Bolsonaro, also implicated.

A feature of the suspicious activity was a long succession of bank withdrawals and deposits just below the figure that automatically triggers an audit for money laundering in Brazil's banking system – a common way to disguise illegal financial activity. Jair Bolsonaro tried to explain away the accusations during a press conference at a Brazilian Navy ceremony in Rio de Janeiro, which only generated new doubts about the story. So, a long game to create a political dynasty has left them looking like a would-be mafia family. The driver in question has was being paid R$20k a month by the Bolsonaros, with whom he has an apparently close friendship, photographed with them at their barbecues and fishing trips. Suspicion is that the driver is what Brazilians call a laranja, (orange) – Brazilian slang for a bagman.

The sums involved already exceed those alleged but unproven in the case which saw Lula jailed and prevented from running in an election that would have seen him face, and most likely beat, Jair Bolsonaro. Had details of the new case against the Bolsonaros emerged publicly when first known – 15th October – it could have affected the election, with the candidate then already reeling from a corruption scandal, the discovery of illegal campaign slush fund which was bankrolling a vast disinformation campaign on Facebook's WhatsApp messaging platform. With that case brushed under the carpet, along with his charge for inciting racial hatred, he continued to victory without facing the legal obstacles that had taken likely winner Lula from the race.

With the election over, and Bolsonaro elected on spurious anti-corruption rhetoric, the new case is getting more attention, and not confined to ideological adversaries, with a group of political aides, and his sons, Federal Congressman Eduardo, Senator Flavio, and Rio State Congressman Carlos, all implicated in one way or another.

Coincidentally or not, in 1992 the testimony of his driver brought about the impeachment of Fernando Collor, but given the role of a compromised judiciary in Brazil's coup and lurch to authoritarianism, it would be naive to expect salvation to arrive wearing a toga, despite it representing hope for those communities and social groups most at risk. Both Justice and Security Minister Sérgio Moro, and Prosecutor Deltan Dallagnol, his wingman in the Curitiban Lava Jato taskforce, have so far brushed aside corruption scandals facing the President elect.

There has also been a wave of infantile feuding within the PSL party which rose from almost nothing to be the second biggest in Congress on Bolsonaro's wave - a motley bunch, many of whom with little or no political experience. Leaked messages showed PSL Congresswoman

Joyce Hasselmann attacking Bolsonaro's sons, and her blog post from 2014 has been unearthed in which she called the idea of his Presidential candidacy "a joke". She released a video urging her supporters not to clink to the link, claiming it was a "virus". Hasselmann recently became the most voted female congresswoman in history, solely down to her positioning and vociferous support for Bolsonaro.

The state of Bolsonaro's cabinet will put all the propaganda about Rousseff's Government between 2013-2016 in perspective. A group of centre left technocrats were depicted as incompetent fraudsters and a recession caused primarily by the global slowdown in commodities, and exacerbated by the Coup's own sabotage, was wildly framed as the "worst economic crisis in Brazilian history", when, just 25 years prior, Brazil had 4000% inflation.

How long this government will survive is anyone's guess, but any investor who believed insistances in the Wall Street Journal and Bloomberg that a Bolsonaro Government would bring stability to the country were comically misled. If by some miracle Brazil thrives it will be despite, not because of Bolsonaro, and it is a question of when, not if, the crash comes. At the very best we expect a return to pre-recession, pre-Lava Jato GDP, at best perhaps augmented by a short term boost in foreign direct investment.

Meanwhile, in terms of human rights, equality and social cohesion, development, health, education and culture, it will be a political catastrophe that will face fierce and organised resistance.

Some are betting that sooner or later the Military will simply take over, either via VP Mourão, who already outranks the President elect, or by more senior figures such as the wildly powerful head of institutional security Sergio Westphalen Etchegoyen, and/or head of the Army General Villas Boas. After coming this far, Jair Bolsonaro could well find himself thrown under the bus.

"Pega fogo, cabaré", or let the cabaret burn, as they say in Brazil.

Images

p.13 Houses of Parliament (Public Domain)

p.27 Sergio Moro (Louis Kim)

p.39 Nelson Rockefeller visit to Brazil 1969 Sao Paulo
(Keystone Press/Alamy)

p.59 Celso Amorim (Marcello Casal Jr./Agência Brasil)

p.75 Hillary Clinton at COA May 2009 (State Dept/Public Domain)

p.91 Quem Matou Marielle? Graffiti (Daniel Hunt)

p.97 Valeska Martins (Teixeira Martins Advogados)

p.113 Lula da Silva (Federal Government of Brazil)

p.137 Wall Street a new era (Henry Han/CC)

p.151 Electronic Voting Machine (José Cruz/CC)

p.171 BOPE Metro (Clarice Castro/Portal do Governo do Rio de Janeiro)

p.179 Paulo Freire (Instituto Paulo Freire)

p. 191 FHC and Aecio Neves (Wellington Pedro/Imprensa MG)

p.199. Maria do Rosario & Jair Bolsonaro (Marcelo Camargo/Agência Brasil)

p. 211 WhatsApp (Public Domain)

p.217 Protesters Against Censorship 1968 (Reprodução)

p.221 1747 Bowen Map of North America and South America
(Public Domain)

p.225 Bolsonaro election leaflet on pavement (Daniel Hunt)

p.237 Augusto Pinochet with Henry Kissinger 1976
(Ministerio de Relaciones Exteriores de Chile)

p.245 AQ Public Advertisement/Media Montage (Louis Kim)

p.301 Flags of Chile, Brazil and Mercosur (Clauber Cleber Caetano/CC)

p.315 Clowns (Louis Kim)

CPSIA information can be obtained
at www.ICGtesting.com
Printed in the USA
FSHW011826130519
58106FS